Case Studies in Child Counseling

Nov 9 6, 13.

Nov 16 3, 8

Nov 23 2, 12

Nov 30 9, 15

Case Studies in Child Counseling

Larry B. Golden
Associate Professor
The University of Texas at San Antonio

Meredith L. Norwood
Associate School Psychologist
North East Independent School District—San Antonio, Texas

Merrill, an imprint of
Macmillan Publishing Company
New York

Maxwell Macmillan Canada
Toronto

Maxwell Macmillan International
New York Oxford Singapore Sydney

Cover art: © Chris O'Leary
Editor: Linda A. Sullivan
Production Editor: Jonathan Lawrence
Art Coordinator: Peter A. Robison
Artist: Jane Lopez
Cover Designer: Cathleen Norz
Production Buyer: Pamela D. Bennett
Electronic Text Management: Ben Ko, Marilyn Wilson Phelps

This book was set in Zapf Calligraphic by Macmillan Publishing Company and was printed and bound by Arcata Graphics/Martinsburg. The cover was printed by New England Book Components.

Printed in the United States of America

Macmillan Publishing Company
866 Third Avenue
New York, NY 10022

Macmillan Publishing Company is part of the
Maxwell Communication Group of Companies.

Maxwell Macmillan Canada, Inc.
1200 Eglinton Avenue East, Suite 200
Don Mills, Ontario M3C 3N1

Library of Congress Cataloging-in Publication Data
Golden, Larry B.
Case studies in child counseling / by Larry B. Golden and Meredith Norwood.
p. cm.
Includes bibliographical references and index.
ISBN 0-02-344421-5
1. Child psychotherapy—Case studies. 2. Children—Counseling of—Case studies. I. Norwood, Meredith. II. Title.
RJ504.G64 1993
618.92'891409—dc20 92-10994
CIP

Printing: 1 2 3 4 5 6 7 8 9 Year: 3 4 5 6 7

Foreword

One of my favorite tests from the history of counseling is the Cornish Test of Insanity. The test included "a tap of running water, a bucket, and a ladle. The bucket was placed under the tap of running water, and the subject was asked to bail the water out of the bucket with the ladle. If the subject continued to bail without paying some attention to reducing or preventing the flow of water into the pail, he or she was judged to be mentally incompetent."*

I relate this illustration because my primary aim in counseling is prevention. If all we do in counseling with children, for example, is put out psychological fires, our profession is probably lost. So why is a counselor like me, who believes so strongly in prevention, writing the foreword to a book that is primarily aimed at doing therapy with children who have been diagnosed as having problems? The answer is easy. Despite our best efforts in prevention, there are many children who are deeply troubled, who have fallen through the safety net of our school and family systems. They need individual attention and intense one-to-one counseling.

In my work as a child counselor in Pennsylvania some years ago, I recall doing a counseling group with 10- and 11-year-old children. There were only about eight or nine in the group. The group had a typical preventive, developmental focus; that is, to get the kids to open up about themselves and their feelings. We had a lot of fun in the group. Sometimes we played games where children identified common feelings and experiences by using the letters of their first names. Sam, for example, might say something like "*S* stands for sad, *A* stands for alone, and *M* stands for mad."

One day while playing this game we began talking about past experiences that made us sad. Like all such discussions, some common themes emerged—losing a pet, having a friend move away, breaking a favorite toy, and so on. This particular day, however, was not to be ordinary. The dialogue went something like this:

Counselor:	Rita, you have your hand up. What makes you sad?
Rita:	I'm sad on Christmas night when all the presents are opened and there aren't any surprises left.
Janice:	I'm unhappy when I don't get what I asked for.
Counselor:	You feel pretty bad, Janice, when that happens to you.
Janice:	Well, not that bad, I guess. But, you know . . .

* Morgan, C., & Jackson, W. (1980). Guidance as a curriculum. *Elementary School Guidance and Counseling, 15*, 99.

Randy: Yeah! I know. I hardly ever get what I really want. I'm not even sad about it any more.
Nick: I am!
Randy: What didn't you get?
Nick: A shotgun.
Randy: I don't blame your parents for not giving you a shotgun! I wouldn't trust you with one either. (pause) Just joking.
Counselor: Anyone else feeling sad about anything?
Janice: I guess I'm not sad very much of the time. Things usually go okay with me.
Randy: I wouldn't be sad either if I had parents with as much money as yours.
Counselor: Randy, you seem to be in a mood for making jokes today. Janice, how did you feel about what Randy just said?
Janice: Nothing. I didn't feel bad because I expect him to be funny. That's the way he is all the time. (pause) He doesn't know what it feels like to be really sad.
Randy: Yes I do!
Janice: No you don't!
Nick: You never feel sad, Randy. All you do is make jokes about what everybody says.
Counselor: Hold on a second. We seem to be ganging up on Randy.
Nick: Why shouldn't we? All Randy does is make fun of people.
Janice: Yeah! That's all he does.
Counselor: Randy, what would you like to say?
Randy: You know why I wouldn't give Nick a shotgun?
Nick: Cause you're too cheap!
Janice: Yeah!
Counselor: Why wouldn't you give Nick a shotgun, Randy?
Randy: Because I found my grandpa dead, in our barn, beside his shotgun.

After a long silence and some repentant comments from Janice and Nick, this group of children proceeded to have one of the most insightful and moving discussions I've ever had the privilege to join. The discussion was preventive in nature, and it helped Randy get into the open what he had held in for such along time. But Randy needed more attention than this group could provide, and fortunately he was able to receive good therapy from an experienced counselor.

So, we who work with children need this book, *Case Studies in Child Counseling*. We need it for a variety of reasons. We need it because of boys like Larry Golden's Joshua, "the boy who trashed his final," and the boy who told his English teacher, "Let my family see me dead!" We need it because of Barbara Herlihy's "Mandy: out in the world," an 11-year-old who told about her world in a simple drawing: "When she drew a picture of her family as her *parents* would like it to be, she drew the five of them sitting on a sofa in front of a TV. When she drew the family as *she* wanted it, she drew her mother in the kitchen, her father in front of the TV, her brother behind the wheel of a car, her baby sister asleep, and herself alone in her room playing the flute."

As editors Larry Golden and Meredith Norwood note, we need this book because "it is filled with real-life therapy experience." It gives richness to the therapies we learned in the classroom—person-centered, Adlerian, cognitive-behavioral, and family therapy. It takes the mystery out of difficult terminology—dysthymia, attention-deficit hyperactivity disorder, post-traumatic stress disorder, separation anxiety. One of the problems in a profession like counseling is that we create language to set ourselves apart, language that makes us seem important. Unfortunately, the language we use often alienates those we are trying to reach and to help, and can be confusing even to our own colleagues. For example, while reading a book on behavior therapy years ago, I came across a sentence that read something like this: "When a neutral stimulus, that is, one previously not capable of eliciting this particular response, is repeatedly paired with the innate elicitor, that stimulus acquires the capacity to elicit the response even in the absence of the original, innate stimulus." If we are to become better counselors and therapists, we need books like *Case Studies in Child Counseling* that help to make the language of therapy understandable and full of life.

Finally, we need this book because of the therapists who bring their case studies to us. All have impressive credentials not only because of their research and writing but also because of their long history of day-to-day, face-to-face work with clients. I don't know them all personally and professionally, but some I do. Barbara Peeks, a family therapist and school consultant from Lincoln, Nebraska, is an outstanding practitioner. In addition to handling her caseload and other writing, she has guest-edited a special issue on "Parents and Education" for a journal I edit, *Elementary School Guidance and Counseling*. Barbara Herlihy is another fine counselor, and her book (with Larry Golden) on ethics published by the American Association for Counseling and Development has been widely praised. Terry Kottman, a clinician at the University of North Texas and an editorial board member for *The School Counselor,* is able to articulate, about as well as anybody I know, ways to help children manage their often troubled lives. Jeff McWhirter, of Arizona State University, is a mentor for many graduate students and a highly regarded scholar in the field of child counseling. These are representative of the quality professionals who have been brought together by Larry and Meredith to help us better understand what it takes to counsel successfully with troubled children.

Several decades ago in his classic book, *The Counselor in a Changing World,* G. Gilbert Wrenn wrote:

> We must understand the new social forces that are influencing young people, as well as the rest of us—and we must learn to apply new psychological insights into the nature of the individual. . . . Counselors must anticipate social

> change, not necessarily its rate and magnitude, but at least its direction. It is difficult to appreciate how swiftly things are changing. Perhaps the estimate that the sum total of human knowledge doubles every ten or fifteen years may provide some idea of what is going on. We must move fast merely to keep up.

What Wrenn said then applies as well today.

Case Studies in Child Counseling provides us with ideas about applying psychological principles to help children who are faced with the demands of a rapidly changing society marked by dysfunctional families, substance abuse, cultural conflicts, and political upheaval. The practices discussed in this book hold the promise that children in a chaotic world can be guided toward manageable lives through the care of sensitive, creative, and informed counselors. I hope, along with Larry and Meredith, that those who read it "will grow to love this little book."

Edward R. Gerler, Jr.
North Carolina State University

Preface

This book is intended as a contribution to the experiential literature in the field of psychotherapy. We hope it will be of use to two audiences: (1) counselors in training and (2) mental health practitioners who specialize in work with children. For both audiences we offer 16 unique and outstanding cases.

Our first step was to examine a number of other casebooks. Typically, these books are designed to illustrate specific interventions or diagnostic categories. For example, a particular case might demonstrate the methods of Carl Rogers or the etiology of dysthymia. While this approach has advantages, we saw it as unrealistic. How many therapists select one strategy and then apply it exclusively? How many clients present an organized set of symptoms that fit a neat niche in the *DSM-III-R*?

We decided on a different approach. We sought seasoned practitioners and challenged them to capture what therapy was *really* like. We asked them to select a case that was near and dear because we wanted readers to encounter the heart of psychotherapy. We encouraged our authors to write in the first-person *I*, include actual dialogue, and reflect on the meaning of the case from a personal perspective. We invite you, the reader, to meet 16 practitioners face to face.

We realized, however, that the very idiosyncrasy that would be this book's attraction could thwart attempts to compare and contrast one case with another. We have addressed this problem in several ways. First, we've prepared a simple chart (following the table of contents) that allows an at-a-glance comparison of the 16 cases. For example, the reader will see that Donna Turley, a school psychologist, employs existential play therapy with a 5-year-old female with autisticlike symptoms who has a *DSM-III-R* diagnosis of Pervasive Developmental Disorder. Our second strategy was to write a brief introduction to summarize and point out the highlights of each case. Finally, we required our authors to organize their cases under the following subheads:

Introduction. The initial paragraphs of each case lay out the presenting problem and background information about the client. (This section is not titled.)

Conceptualization. Here the author discusses therapeutic goals and strategies. The author may also discuss theoretical orientation, such as psychodynamic, systems, cognitive, behavioral, and so on.

Process. Actual client contacts are described. What happened in the sessions? How did the therapist's relationship with the client change over time?

Outcome. The author describes the results, for better or worse. It is important to note that we did not ask our authors to give us their most successful case but, rather, their most interesting, a case that touched the therapist.

Discussion. With the benefit of hindsight, the author explains what he or she might have done differently. In addition, the author describes his or her personal and professional growth that resulted from this encounter with a troubled youngster.

We hope that the reader will grow to love this little book. It is filled with real-life therapy experience and is intended as a supplement to theoretical works on the topic of childhood emotional disorders and their treatment.

We thought it significant that several of our contributors chose case studies from their early days of training and supervision. This should encourage those of us who train counselors. Practica and internships offer experiences that are all too rare in day-to-day practice. The debriefing of sessions with a supportive mentor, the recognition of personal issues, and even the requirement to transcribe dialogue and account for therapeutic results have a powerful net effect on the emerging therapist.

We wish to acknowledge the help we received with data entry from Isabel Garcia, proofreading and indexing from Stef Harris, and expert assistance from Production Editor Jonathan Lawrence, copyeditor Martha Morss, and Editor Linda Sullivan of Macmillan.

Larry B. Golden
Meredith L. Norwood

To Sarah Norwood Golden, dearest daughter

Contents

Summary of Cases

Therapist	Discipline	Child
David B. Baker	Psychologist, private practice	Girl, 9
Arthur J. Clark	School psychologist	Boy, 11
Larry B. Golden	Psychologist, private practice	Boy, 12
Lauren J. Golden	Social worker, private practice	Girl, 8
Sharon Gordetsky Joan J. Zilbach	Psychologist, agency Psychiatrist, private practice	Boy, 9
Barbara Herlihy	Counselor, private practice	Girl, 11
Terry Kottman	Counselor, university clinic	Boy, 4
J. Jeffries McWhirter	Psychologist, private practice	Boy, 12
Barbara Peeks Ray L. Levy	Family therapist, school consultant Psychologist, private practice	Girl, 12
Vimala Pillari	Social worker, agency	Boy, 12
Linda Provus-McElroy	Counselor, private practice	Girl, 6
Dick T. Sampson Toshiaki Sato Kamiko Miyashita	Family counselor Professor of Psychology Health visitor, Supervisor	Girl, 6
Jose T. Sepulveda, Jr.	School counselor	Boy, 6
Jules Spotts Jane Brooks	Psychologist, private practice School psychologist	Boy, 7
Bruce St. Thomas	Psychotherapist, private practice	Girl, 7
Donna Lee Turley	School psychologist	Girl, 5

Ann: A Case of Mistaken Anxiety

David B. Baker

David Baker presents the case of 9-year-old Ann who complains of stomachaches. On the surface this case looks like Adjustment Disorder with Anxious Mood (DSM-III-R 309.24). Ann has somatic complaints and fearful thoughts about robbers which began following a police officer's visit to her class. Baker responds to the parents' sense of urgency and treats Ann's anxiety in a straightforward manner with a combination of supportive counseling and behavior modification. Nothing changes.

Baker goes back to the drawing board. He examines the case from a family systems perspective but fails to unearth dysfunctional patterns. Likewise, a psychodynamic interpretation proves unsatisfactory; there is no evidence of an underlying trauma or conflict.

The parents become agitated following a conference with Ann's teacher. Ann is not completing her assignments and is disruptive. As the class work becomes more and more demanding, Ann is less able to keep up with her peers. Finally, Baker arrives at a diagnosis of Attention-Deficit Hyperactivity Disorder (DSM-III-R 314.01). Dramatic results are obtained with Ritalin. There is, after all, a time and place for the medical model.

Nine-year-old Ann Muir had been complaining of stomachaches for almost a week. She would frequently come into her parents' room during the night complaining that her stomach hurt. In the mornings Ann was often tired and wanted to stay home from school. Her mother gave her an over-the-counter medication for her stomachaches, but it did not help. Concerned about a medical problem, Ann's parents made an appointment with their pediatrician to have Ann examined.

A routine physical examination was completed, but no physical basis for the stomachaches was found. The pediatrician suggested that they see a psychologist to determine if there were any behavioral or emotional factors that would explain Ann's stomachaches. The Muirs had never seen a psychologist before and asked the pediatrician for a referral, which is how I came to work with them. I was relatively new to private practice but was working closely with a number of pediatricians in the area. My predoctoral internship was at a children's hospital, and I had finished postdoctoral training in a private pediatric practice under the supervision of a licensed psychologist. The years spent in those settings allowed me to gain a better understanding of the interface between medicine and psychology and provided numerous opportunities to consult with pediatricians regarding the psychosomatic complaints of their young patients.

When the Muirs called my office to schedule an appointment, there was an urgency in Betty Muir's voice. Betty reported that she and her husband Tom wanted to see me as soon as possible. It didn't matter when the appointment was scheduled, she said, just as long as they could come in soon. When asked what her most pressing concern was, Betty replied that Ann was continuing to have difficulty sleeping and was irritable and moody all the time. She explained that this was causing a great deal of tension in their home. Betty also stated that she felt helpless standing by while her daughter was clearly upset and in distress.

In response to Betty's request I arranged for an initial meeting the next afternoon. Since I had limited information, I felt it would be best not to include Ann in the first visit. I also felt that seeing the parents alone might be helpful in lowering their anxiety (which I thought might be a contributing factor in Ann's symptoms).

Tom and Betty presented themselves as a typical middle-class family. Tom is 38 years old and Betty is 37. They grew up in the same town and had been high school sweethearts who married shortly after Betty's graduation. Tom left high school early to attend vocational school. He earned a GED as well as a trade degree in electronics. Although neither parent attended college, they have high hopes that their daughter will.

Tom works for the local utility company, a job he has had for the past 12 years. Betty is employed as a secretary at an insurance company. Ann is their only child and it took a number of years for her to be conceived. Tom and Betty reported that they had almost given up hope of ever having children and felt fortunate to have had Ann. They reported that their family means everything to them and is their first priority in life.

Tom's father was an alcoholic who seldom spent time at home. As a result, Tom felt a strong need to be involved and available to Ann and Betty. He spoke fondly and affectionately of his wife and child. The more he spoke, the more upset he appeared. While he recognized that I could not perform miracles, he was openly hoping that I would. On numerous occasions Tom said, "I just want her [Ann] to be her happy self."

A review of Ann's developmental history did not reveal any significant difficulties or delays. The most persistent problem had been recurrent ear infections. Tom's report about his father was the only indication of any family problems. Ann's school achievement had been satisfactory, but Tom and Betty felt she could apply herself more. They questioned whether they had spoiled Ann too much since she was an only child. They wondered if they didn't expect enough of her. They also believed that being an only child accounted for Ann's seeming lack of friends. She had participated in gymnastics and soccer but didn't seem to have a lot of interest in developing relationships with other children.

According to Tom and Betty, Ann had become increasingly terrified of sleeping in the dark and had a persistent fear that robbers would come into the house and steal Tom and Betty. They described Ann as changing from a child who was normally active and energetic to one who was more withdrawn, anxious, and depressed. Ann was showing little interest in her homework, and Betty claimed it was difficult to motivate Ann to complete it. In the past Ann would sleep with her door closed. Now she had to have it open at night, and she would frequently come into Tom and Betty's room to make sure that robbers had not gotten them.

Tom and Betty were eager for me to see Ann, so an appointment was scheduled for the following afternoon. Tom was unsure of how to best explain the office visit to Ann. I suggested that they both tell Ann of their concern about her fears and stomachaches and that they had met someone who helped kids and their families. They could describe me as a "talk doctor," someone who talked to kids and families about things that they were worried or upset about and who tried to figure out ways to solve problems. I told them that I would visit with Ann for awhile and then ask them to join us.

When they returned the following day, Ann separated easily from her parents and appeared eager to visit with me. Ann seemed a happy and energetic child. She is of average height and weight for her age and has strawberry-blond hair and freckles. Upon seeing the toy box, Ann looked to me as if to ask permission to search through the toys. I told her that she was free to explore. She browsed through the toy chest quickly and then sat on the couch and faced me. I asked if she knew why she had come. She smiled and said that her mom and dad said I would talk to her about being scared at night. I was surprised and pleased that Ann was willing to be so forthcoming about her fears. She stated that these fears began shortly after she attended a home safety program at school. Apparently, a police officer had come to the school and talked to the children about precautions they should take to protect themselves if they were home alone after school. Ann claimed that there were a lot of ways a robber could get into a house, and she worried that if she closed her door at night robbers could get in without her knowing it and hurt or kidnap her parents. She said these worries were keeping her up at night and causing her stomach to hurt so much that she needed to go to her parents' room and get in their bed. Other than these worries, Ann said that everything else was fine, although she admitted that she did not like school much and would prefer to stay home. After school she attends a day-care program which she said was OK except that the other kids were not friendly and did not include her in games or like her very much. I asked Ann of all the things she mentioned what would be the most important thing to take care of right now. Without hesitation she said, "The scary stuff about the robbers."

CONCEPTUALIZATION

Ann's case was puzzling to me. I felt that her expressed fears and her behavior raised numerous issues, and I did not feel any certainty in one particular diagnosis. It seemed that any number of perspectives could be invoked to develop a rationale for intervention.

A family systems perspective would suggest that Ann's symptoms were somehow serving to create a distraction from difficulties within the parental subsystem. Ann was literally coming between her parents while they were in bed together, or at least she had to have her bedroom door open so that she could see her mother and father in bed.

A more traditional and psychodynamic interpretation might suggest that Ann's symptoms were the expression of some conflict with one or both of her parents. Instead of openly expressing anger or rage, she may have projected it onto the robbers and then experienced guilt in the form of fear for her parents' well-being.

Themes of vulnerability, fear, and threat, particularly in relation to sleeping alone in bed at night, were suggestive of possible sexual trauma. Perhaps Ann was unable to express this directly and was developing fears and exhibiting psychosomatic behaviors instead.

Whatever the underlying mechanism, it was clear that Ann was experiencing significant distress in the form of anxiety and somatic complaints which were quite disturbing to her parents. To assess the numerous explanations for Ann's situation would take time, and I found myself wanting to respond to the parents' urgent request for help. Perhaps the anxiety was infectious. In any case, I found myself feeling pressured to do something quickly.

Since I was unsure of the underlying dynamics, I chose to focus on a particular symptom, namely, Ann's anxiety. For the time being, I accepted that Ann's fear of robbers coming into the house at night was based on an unrealistic fear caused by the safety presentation at school. I also believed this fear had been conditioned by the attention and comfort she received from her parents. This seemed like a parsimonious explanation and one for which a concrete behavioral intervention could be developed, implemented, and evaluated. In addition, I would have time to get to know Ann and her parents and hopefully be able to respond to the information I gathered rather than to the family's anxiety. I proceeded to schedule a session with Ann and her parents for the purpose of developing a home-based anxiety reduction program.

■ PROCESS

In our first joint session I worked with Ann and her parents to outline the sequence of events in Ann's bedtime routine including the onset of anxious thoughts and behaviors. Ann was most frightened that robbers would come into the house through the windows or the sliding patio doors. Even though her parents explained that they locked everything before going to bed, Ann was not convinced. She claimed that if they were tired they might forget to check. We decided that Ann would assist her parents in closing up the house before bedtime. Ann said that she would feel much less anxious if she saw that everything was properly closed and locked, and it would be easier for her to go to bed. A checklist was made of the doors and windows that Ann and her parents would secure before going to bed. We then discussed strategies for helping Ann keep her door closed. Tom and Betty encouraged Ann to try to sleep with the door closed but to no avail. I suggested that each night after they had all checked that the house was locked up, Tom and Betty tuck Ann in bed and close her door as far as possible until Ann began to feel anxious. This seemed agreeable to Ann. It was also decided that if Ann were able to stay in her room for the night (except of course if there were an emergency) Betty would make Ann her favorite breakfast of pancakes.

During the first week the plan worked with mild success. It appeared that to some extent everyone was enjoying the routine as a new bedtime ritual. The family showed me a checklist they had constructed to use in checking the doors and windows each evening. For the first three nights Ann tolerated having her door closed a little more each evening. According to Tom, these increments added up to about a foot. While this was an improvement, he was still impatient.

During the second session I spent most of my time with Ann. I was interested in determining if any other traumas or stressors were contributing to Ann's fears. She denied that anything worried her other than the school safety presentation. She was active during our session, and her attention was easily distracted by extraneous stimuli such as objects on my desk and noise from the outer office. Ann commented that she would like to play with some of the toys I had in the closet, and I told her that we would do that at our next session. I told Tom and Betty that I would see Ann by herself next week, and the week after I would meet with them to discuss progress.

We began the third session by playing with the toys in the closet, as Ann had requested. She played with the dollhouse and the hand puppets. Her play was age appropriate, and she seemed to enjoy the activity. She set up a house where she was the mother and took care of the baby and cooked food. She used the hand puppets to dramatize two people meeting each other and going off to play. Ann played with the materials briefly and was not responsive to any inquiry or elaboration on her play themes. She asked if we could use the colored markers, and I provided her with drawing paper. She commented that she enjoyed drawing more than anything else and was a good art student. Ann did not want to talk as she drew and worked with some effort to draw and color a rainbow and a pony. I would have liked Ann to be more verbally expressive about her activities with the materials, but I did not push the point and chose to follow her lead. I did not notice anything that would suggest an underlying trauma or conflict.

Toward the end of the session I reminded Ann that I was going to meet with her parents next week. I asked how she felt about the meeting and if there were anything that I might need to talk about with her parents. She could not think of anything, and I asked if there were things that perhaps she would not want me to talk about with her parents. Again, she could not think of anything. It was my sense that she was being sincere. When I asked how things were going with the door-closing plan, she replied that she was still scared of having the door closed at night. At the end of the third session I saw Betty briefly to confirm our meeting the following week.

When I saw Tom and Betty, they were agitated and upset. Tom was particularly vocal about his dismay with the way things were going. According to him nothing had really changed, and he did not have much faith that it would get better anytime soon. Ann could only close her door a few inches and was again coming into their bedroom every night. Tom was angry with me for not being effective and angry with Ann for not managing her behavior. I felt uncomfortable and unsure of what to do next. Again, I felt a strong pull to do something and to do it immediately. Since Tom had a lot to say I decided to stay with his frustration and use the session to determine if there were any issues between Tom and Betty that they had not mentioned earlier. I explored with them the effect Ann's behavior was having on their relationship and how they were coping with the situation. Again, I did not get the sense that they had any hidden agendas, deviant patterns of parenting, or pathological interactions with Ann. Their concerns were valid, and their frustrations understandable.

Betty broke into Tom's monologue to emphasize that their frustration was prompted by a conference they had with Ann's teacher earlier in the week. Apparently, Ann was frequently getting into trouble for talking in class and not completing her assignments. Betty did not see this as a major problem but believed that it must be significant since the teacher had called them to discuss it. The teacher felt that Tom and Betty should be aware of Ann's behavior since her reprimands were not having much impact on Ann. Betty said she was glad in some ways that Ann was being more outgoing since she had a history of not getting along with other children and was often left out of activities. Tom was quiet. When I asked for his opinion, he said that he felt Ann's teacher was being too strict and rigid. He related that he had never liked school and often got into trouble. Academic tasks were always a struggle, and Tom never felt capable. In class he would often act the part of the clown, and as a result he had strained relationships with many of his teachers. In fact, trouble at school had caused him to drop out in the tenth grade and attend trade school. However, he took the teacher's concern as another example of how disturbing Ann's behavior was. I obtained permission to speak with Ann's teacher and scheduled an appointment with Ann for the next week.

At this point I was getting a sense that Ann was having more difficulties outside of the home than I realized. In my haste to deal quickly with her nighttime anxiety I had not been paying sufficient attention to her day-to-day activities. I had accepted both what Ann and her parents had told me about her difficulty with peers and her dislike of school and concluded that these things were not a source of great concern. It was becoming clear these issues needed to be addressed.

Ann's teacher, Mrs. Spring, appreciated my call and was glad that Ann and her family were working with me. She reported that Ann was inattentive in class, appeared distractible, and did not get along well with other children. When I asked about the safety presentation, Mrs. Spring reported that the presentation was specifically geared to children and the children enjoyed it. In fact, the same officer had been coming to her class for the past three years because parents and children found the program to be beneficial. Mrs. Spring also said that she had assured Tom and Betty that Ann's disruptive and inattentive behaviors had been going on long before the presentation. Mrs. Spring felt confident in her observations since she had known Ann since the first grade. She believed that Ann's current difficulties were due to the demands of the curriculum. According to Mrs. Spring the class work was becoming more demanding and Ann was having trouble keeping up. It seemed that Ann was capable of doing the work, but her off-task behavior was interfering with her ability to understand directions and complete assignments.

This new information about Ann's symptoms—inattention, distractibility, impaired social relations—seemed to indicate an Attention-Deficit Hyperactivity Disorder (ADHD). I decided to gather more information. I called Tom and Betty and asked them to complete two behavior rating scales, and I sent teacher versions of the same rating scales to Mrs. Spring. Results of the parent measures indicated significant depressive symptoms, social withdrawal, and somatic complaints. The teacher reports indicated that Ann was inattentive, aggressive, and unpopular. Thus, Ann appeared to have external behavior problems at school and problems of an internal nature at home.

During the fifth visit with Ann I administered a measure to assess problem-solving style. Ann's performance indicated a rather impulsive style. Ann was curious to know why we were doing these things and said that her parents were also "taking some tests" about her. I explained that I was trying to get more information about her so we could figure out ways for her to worry less and be more happy at school. She acknowledged that she was not happy at school and had gotten her name written on the board. This upset her greatly, and the more we talked about the incident the more upset she became. Ann started to cry and told me that she hated school, that she was always picked on, that no one liked her, and that she was always getting her name on the board.

I felt fairly confident that Ann did indeed have ADHD and that this should be the primary emphasis in treatment. Her fear and anxiety seemed to be secondary. The information from Ann's teacher was very revealing in that it provided a picture of Ann's day-to-day functioning in a structured and task-oriented environment. As task demands increased, Ann was less able to keep up with her peers. I speculated that the pressure to keep up as well as Ann's difficulty with regulating her attention and behavior were significant stressors which were being expressed through off-task behaviors at school and anxiety at home.

I talked to Ann about my thoughts. I told her that I often talked to kids who had trouble with their schoolwork. I explained that sometimes these children want to do well at school but they have difficulty understanding directions and paying attention to all the things they have to do. I went on to tell her that there were a lot of different things we could do to help her with her problems at school. Despite my attempts to give Ann information and reassurance, she continued to feel upset and focused on what a difficult and unhappy place school was for her. I accepted her need to talk about this and offered reflections of her feelings and support which seemed comforting and appropriate. At the end of the session I called Betty in and talked to her and Ann about my impressions. I suggested that Betty make an appointment with a pediatrician who I knew specialized in ADHD. With Betty's signed consent form, I said I would personally speak to him and share my observations once the appointment was made. We decided to meet again after they had seen the pediatrician. The next day Betty called to say that they would be seeing the pediatrician in a few days. I called to discuss the case with the pediatrician and shared my concerns and observations.

OUTCOME

Ann's parents called me a week later and asked to schedule an appointment to talk about Ann and ADHD. They explained that they had seen the pediatrician who, after meeting with the family, had Mrs. Spring complete some forms. On reviewing all the data, the doctor confirmed the diagnosis of ADHD. Ann was started on 5 milligrams of Ritalin twice a day, and her progress would be monitored through weekly parental and teacher reports to the pediatrician's office. The pediatrician had given Tom and Betty some information to read, and they were eager to talk with me further about ADHD. By the time I saw the family, Ann had already been on medication for 10 days. The difference in everyone's demeanor was clearly evident. Ann was making noticeable advances in her schoolwork, and to everyone's delight she was sleeping through the night with her door closed. Ann could not explain this other than to say that she just did not feel scared at night and did not even need to use the checklist. She said she was tired at night and it was taking too much time to check everything. She preferred to have her parents tuck her in and check on her before they went to sleep. Ann's teacher had completed a behavior checklist the pediatrician had given her to monitor the effectiveness of the medication. Ann's classroom behavior had improved considerably. She was able to stay in her seat and complete her work without interrupting others.

Tom and Betty were eager to gather as much information about ADHD as possible. I gave them the titles of a number of books about ADHD that were written for parents. I encouraged them to join the local parent support group and gave them the name and number of the contact person in our area. It seemed that we had correctly identified the problem and were properly treating it through education, support, and medication. I was unsure of how I could best respond to the needs of the family at this point and simple asked them how they wanted to proceed from here. Ann looked down and I couldn't tell what she was experiencing. I encouraged her to share with me what she was feeling. She said softly that she liked me, that I was really nice, and would it hurt my feelings if she didn't come back for awhile? I was glad that she could risk being that direct with me and assured her that it would be fine. I told her that I really appreciated her willingness to come and talk with me and I was happy that she was feeling and doing better at home and at school. Tom and Betty felt they now had a sense of direction and were gaining a better understanding of Ann's difficulties. Betty said she could easily identify Ann based on what she had learned about ADHD, and she felt relieved to know that there was something they could do about it.

Tom and Betty asked to see me one more time in two weeks to answer any more questions that might arise and to evaluate Ann's ongoing progress. I added that it would be a good idea to discuss Ann's peer relationships. While they were excited over her sudden progress, I wanted to address her difficulties with her peers. Many children with ADHD have difficulty negotiating the give-and-take of relationships; it is a skill that needs to be developed over time with a plan of action in mind. At Tom and Betty's request I discussed some strategies with Ann's teacher, such as preferential seating, sanctioned movement, and monitoring social problem solving, that she could use with Ann in the classroom. The pediatrician had also sent her a package of handouts on working with the ADHD child in the classroom.

When I met Tom and Betty in the waiting room for our seventh session, I was surprised to see Ann with them. Ann smiled broadly when she saw me and tugged on her mother's sleeve to get her attention. They announced that Ann wanted to come in today because she had something she really wanted to show me. We proceeded to my office where Ann could hardly wait for me to sit down before handing me a folder. It was her report card from school. She wiggled in her seat while I opened it. Ann had straight A's and was on the honor roll. In addition, her conduct and study skills grades had gone from unsatisfactory to satisfactory in almost all areas. Mrs. Spring noted that Ann was completing assignments, not disturbing others, and seemed happier. She was very pleased with Ann's progress and said many complimentary things about Ann and her parents' efforts to turn things around. Everyone was pleased and we took some time to enjoy Ann's accomplishments.

Because the end of the school year was fast approaching, I discussed with Ann and her parents some summer activities that would provide Ann with structured situations in which she could interact successfully and in a skill-building way with her peers. Tom and Betty told me that the pediatrician had recommended a two-week summer camp for children with ADHD. Ann seemed excited about the idea, and Tom and Betty were looking into it. Ann also expressed an interest in participating on the swim team at the local pool, and it was decided that she would take swimming lessons until the summer swimming league started. At this time we terminated our weekly meetings. Everyone was pleased with the progress that had been made, and we left with the understanding that Ann and her parents would check in with me as needed.

I saw Ann and her family on two more occasions during the summer. In these sessions I provided more information about ADHD and supported their efforts to work with Ann. Tom and Betty became involved in the local parent support group. Ann finished the school year on the honor roll, and much to her delight she experienced a number of successes on the swim team. She won ribbons and a trophy and was clearly proud of her accomplishments. Ann continued on Ritalin during the summer months as it appeared to help her control her impulsive and aggressive stance toward peers. Her fears and anxieties were no longer present; Ann even had difficulty recalling how fearful she had felt only months before. Tom and Betty decided against sending Ann to camp and planned instead to take a family camping trip.

DISCUSSION

Ann's case was resolved in a satisfactory manner and in a relatively brief period of time. A number of aspects of the case made it an important and memorable one for me.

One of the lessons I learned from this case and continue to learn is that it is at times difficult to resist getting caught up in the parents' sense of urgency when their child is in distress. In Ann's case her parents longed for an immediate solution for Ann's problems. In responding to their anxiety I put pressure on myself to act quickly and without sufficient data.

Another point this case highlighted is the importance of multiple perspectives in the evaluation of childhood disorders. Children can be accurate reporters of their own internal experience but at times have difficulty reporting on their overt behaviors. While parents are an important source of behavioral information, the observations of the classroom teacher are a rich source of data that should not be overlooked. In this case, both Ann and her parents identified internalized problem behaviors as a concern. This led me to conceptualize Ann's problems as an anxiety disorder of undetermined origin. The information provided by Ann's teacher led to a reappraisal of the situation and in this case contributed to a proper diagnostic decision and an appropriate course of action.

Finally, the case reinforced the importance of keeping a flexible perspective on what is happening in treatment. In hindsight I felt that I should have gotten more information before jumping into an intervention with Ann and her family. However, I was able to realign my sights in light of feedback and new information and embark in a new direction on the basis of what I had discovered. Hopefully, this is a skill I will retain and perhaps, if I am fortunate, one that I will be able to pass along to my clients.

Biographical Statement

David B. Baker, PhD, is an assistant professor of psychology at the University of North Texas in Denton, Texas. His teaching and research interests are in the areas of child psychopathology, assessment, and intervention. Dr. Baker is coauthor of The Clinical Child Interview. *A licensed psychologist since 1988, he maintains a private practice in child and family psychology in Denton, Texas.*

2

The Defense Never Rests

Arthur J. Clark

Arthur J. Clark, a school psychologist at the time of this case, describes a sixth grader's relinquishment of denial, rationalization, and blame. Ed was a difficult, resistant young man (Oppositional Defiant Disorder, DSM-III-R *313.81). Dr. Clark chose Adlerian, person-centered, and cognitive-behavioral approaches based on information he had gleaned from projective tests and background provided by parents and teachers.*

Clark effectively explains the therapeutic process in this chapter, and discloses his rationales, doubts, and feelings as he helped Ed move from awareness to comprehension to consolidation over the course of 14 weekly sessions.

The note from the teacher read, "Please attend a meeting with me and two very difficult parents to discuss their son, Ed Reynolds, who is having problems in my class." Prior to joining the conference for Ed, I quickly checked his school records. He had moved with his family from a distant state at the start of the school year. His academic progress was inconsistent, even though his standardized test results were in the above average to superior range. He had an older sister in the eighth grade and a brother in high school. Ed's medical history was unremarkable. An unsigned note in his folder did stand out: "Extremely demanding and involved parents, especially father."

As I entered the conference, I immediately felt the tension between the classroom teacher, Mrs. White, and Ed's parents. Mr. Reynolds was questioning the quality of the school system and its lack of responsiveness to the needs of his and other children. After I made an attempt to provide another perspective on the schools, we finally started to address Ed's issues. Mrs. White stated nervously that Ed's homework was often incomplete and his grades were unsatisfactory in most areas. More importantly, she emphasized, Ed questioned the value of school assignments and expectations.

The next half hour was one of the more unpleasant that I have experienced in my many years in the public schools as a school counselor and school psychologist. Mr. Reynolds went into a lengthy and intellectualized discourse on education. He then interrogated Mrs. White about her philosophy of education, goals for teaching, professional experience, and more. My attempts to return the focus to Ed were quickly dismissed. Mrs. White, a veteran teacher who was highly respected in the school, met the challenge, but with obvious discomfort. As we had been meeting for almost an hour, the "discussion" concluded with a hurried decision for me to meet with Ed for counseling.

CONCEPTUALIZATION

Initially I felt relieved that the meeting was over, but I was also dissatisfied in several ways. I certainly should have been more supportive of Mrs. White. Further, I could have suggested a systems approach to working with Ed, in coordination with his teachers and his parents, or even family counseling. I consoled myself with the realization that family treatment would have been strongly rejected by the parents, who would probably think the school was shifting the blame to them.

I was uncertain how to counsel with Ed but determined to do so as effectively as possible. A further review of Ed's school records unearthed anecdotal statements such as "He has constant excuses for his misbehavior," side by side with remarks about his high academic potential and periodic superior achievement. I also learned that Ed was interested in riding horses, swimming, and the martial arts. Additional information was gained from a discussion with Ed's history teacher, Mrs. Martin.

My immediate goal in meeting with Ed was to establish a relationship that allowed him to feel comfortable in expressing himself openly in an accepting and trusting environment. I have this relationship goal with each individual with whom I work in counseling, but I knew with Ed it would not be easy. In the initial stage of counseling I planned to use rapport- and trust-building techniques from several theories of counseling. Using person-centered therapy, I would attempt to demonstrate empathy, positive regard, and genuineness in my interactions with Ed. Using Adlerian psychology, I would emphasize equality, encouragement, and understanding the purpose of the client's behavior to strengthen our counseling alliance. And using reality therapy, I would strive to establish a climate of mutual participation and commitment, beginning by discussing interests to stimulate involvement. In theory, at least, I felt prepared.

To gain a better understanding of Ed, I decided to do a brief personality assessment using three projective techniques and my observation of Ed's behavior. I thought the projectives would also be useful in establishing rapport due to their task-centered qualities and the intrinsically interesting features of drawing and storytelling. Anticipating resistance from Ed in our initial meetings, I expected to observe his use of defense mechanisms. My task would be to recognize those defenses while providing him with support and understanding that would lessen his reliance on them in a counseling relationship, and ultimately, in his life.

■ PROCESS

A moment before calling Ed to my office for our initial meeting, I paused to think for a moment about what I wanted to do. My main objective was to try to establish a relationship with him, and I did not want to feel rushed about trying to do much else. Ed walked in. Before he had even sat down, he asked a sarcastic question.

Ed: Why am I here?

AC: I can understand why you are concerned about that. You are probably wondering . . .

Ed: When can I go back to class?

AC: Well. (Squirming in my seat, I was thinking to myself, I'm going to have a real run for my money.) I sense that you don't feel that there is any reason for us to meet.

Ed: When can I leave?

This was going nowhere fast, and I needed to do something.

AC: You feel that you are coming along in your classes.

Ed: I am! My work is really getting better.

As of the day before our meeting, Ed was failing in all of his academic subjects. Without this information I would have had no idea that Ed was not telling me the truth. He appeared totally convinced about his improvement in his classes. His denial was entrenched. I was determined to reflect his statements without imposing my evaluation on the truth of his words. I mistakenly hoped this would enable him to be more candid. It was time to shift to my backup strategy of discussing Ed's interests in swimming and horses. It worked and we had a spirited talk.

As our time was drawing to a close, I decided to take advantage of Ed's good mood and at least begin the projectives. As soon as I asked Ed to draw me a picture of a person, he started in again.

Ed: Why do I have to do this?

AC: It will give me a better understanding of you. (After saying this, I thought, Why would Ed want that?)

Ed: I don't have any problems!

AC: You don't like it when people say that you are having difficulties in school.

Ed: I'm sick of it. I thought for a minute that you might be different, but you're on my back like everyone else. I'm going back to class.

We were back to where we started almost 40 minutes before. After a few more minutes of my reflecting Ed's feelings, the bell rang and Ed quickly got up and left my office. I was drained and, to say the least, discouraged. I should have followed through on the drawing—for most clients the figure drawing helps strengthen the counseling relationship. Then again, maybe I had pushed Ed too hard and I should have stayed with his interests. But if we had discussed only those activities that Ed enjoys, our session would have been superficial and I would not have learned much about Ed. And then my worst doubt: Would there be another meeting?

A week passed and I felt relieved when I saw him enter the office area; at least he had decided to show up for his appointment. I wondered about how resistant he would be in our session, and it did not take long to find out.

Ed: I really don't have to see you if I don't want to.

AC: You're pretty upset, and you don't like being told what to do.

Ed: I am! I don't have to do anything if I don't want to.

AC: You hate being bossed around.

Ed: (a long silence) I'm tired and I want to go back to class.

Just when I thought for a moment we were coming together, Ed wants to end it. Acknowledging Ed's fatigue, I attempted to stimulate discussion around the theme of feelings of coercion; Ed would have none of it. I feared our second session was quickly coming to an end and I still did not have much of an understanding of Ed. I decided to try the projectives again.

AC: I can see that you are pretty tired, but we need to complete a few tasks.
Ed: What do you mean "tasks"?
AC: Well, they are kinds of evaluations for self-understanding.
Ed: I don't need any self-understanding.
AC: What I mean is that you are struggling in school and this may help in understanding why.

For a few minutes we went on like this, and Ed finally yielded, mainly, I think, to stop me from explaining further. Once Ed began his figure drawing, he quickly became interested in the activity. He also showed reasonable effort and cooperation on the sentence completion and early recollections. Over the years, I have observed many resistant clients let down their guard after accepting and becoming involved in completing projectives.

Projective techniques are criticized for their questionable psychometric qualities: only moderate levels of validity and reliability, lack of representative norms, and imprecise scoring systems. Yet, even with these limitations, I find the projectives highly revealing of a client's personality dynamics, and they have become an integral part of the counseling process for many individuals with whom I work. I try to avoid speculative interpretations and attempt to generate reasonable inferences or hypotheses from multiple client responses on the projective instruments.

Ed's drawing was revealing; he depicted a person with arms outstretched, no hands, near the top of the page. Arms reaching into the environment suggests a need for affection and acceptance, and placement high on the page indicates uncertainty and lack of support in the environment. Omission of hands is related to feelings of inadequacy. From this, I developed hypotheses about Ed's low self-esteem and his need to be accepted by others in a supportive and caring environment—aspects of Ed's personality that he simply did not demonstrate in his counseling sessions.

As it is with many clients, Ed's sentence completion was illuminating, especially in identifying his use of defense mechanisms. Denial was indicated when he wrote, "I regret . . . nothing" and "I failed . . . nothing." His sentence "My father . . . is nice" was contradicted in a later completion, "I wish . . . my father would get off my back." Ed's use of rationalization was apparent when he wrote, "I failed . . . history because of my dumb teacher" and "Other kids . . . get me in trouble." His opinion of the formal learning process was summarized with, "School . . . is a waste of time."

The use of early recollections as a projective technique is derived from the work of Alfred Adler. The client is asked to recall at least three memories from a period before 8 years of age. Each memory must be visualized in a single, specific event. Ed related his first memory in a subdued tone.

Ed: I spilled milk on the kitchen floor, and my father was standing over me as I cleaned it up.

Ed's second memory also included his father.

Ed: I was learning to ride my bicycle, and my father was teaching me. He said that he would hold on to me, but he let go and I fell.

A third memory depicted Ed at his birthday party.

Ed: I had a nice birthday cake, but only two kids were at my party. There was a lot of stuff to eat, but not enough kids were there.

With each of his memories I asked Ed how he felt, and he replied, "Stupid and mad." Ed's early recollections suggested his sense of incompetency in an unkind environment. His lack of support from people, particularly in his dealings with his father, was evident. His feelings were a mix of hostility and disappointment.

With only a few minutes left in our session, I asked Ed about several of his responses on the sentence completion. He wanted no part of this, and he insisted on going back to his class. With his departure I felt relief but also hope as now I had a better understanding of Ed.

Between counseling sessions, I assessed Ed's projectives and reflected on the direction I should take and even wondered if we should continue to meet. However, I was challenged in two ways by Ed: I felt that I could work with him effectively, and I was intrigued by his defenses. After a discussion with Ed's teachers and a telephone conversation with his mother, I agreed to continue our weekly sessions.

In my next meeting with Ed, I immediately questioned my decision to continue counseling. He was hostile and sarcastic for the major part of our time together. Relentlessly he questioned the value and need for our sessions. At the same time, Ed continued to deny any problems of his own, stating again and again that he was improving in his school subjects, while criticizing his teachers for their incompetence and lack of understanding.

There were times when Ed was blasting his teachers that his statements seemed at least plausible, especially when he gave examples to support his position. Ed recounted a complaint about his history class.

Ed: The book is so stupid. I'm only in the sixth grade and the book is written for high school kids.

AC: (knowing something about the text and the teacher) It sounds like the book is difficult, but Mrs. Martin clarifies a lot of it in class.

What I thought was a sensible statement became lost as Ed continued to employ the defense of rationalization.

Ed: You really don't know what you are talking about. Have you ever read the book? She even said in class that the book is too hard. You can't even understand half of what she says because so many kids fool around in her class.

Well, I knew that Mrs. Martin was having difficulty with discipline in some of her classes. She told me that the book was excessively demanding. Each of Ed's assertions had a sufficient degree of truth to give credibility to his position. He also expressed himself with such conviction that attempting to determine the degree of validity of his statements was a challenge to say the least. As I weighed his responses, what helped me the most was the understanding I had gained from the projectives that Ed employs denial, rationalization, and perhaps, displacement. Secondly, I knew that in any defense there must be an element of plausibility or it would have no deception value.

Our session ended and again I felt discouraged; we had made no real progress in our meeting. I needed to forget about Ed, and I went to see what was in my mailbox. Mrs. Martin had written me a note: "Ed's behavior has deteriorated even further. Now he does absolutely nothing in my class." She was kind to leave out what was implied, "since he began meeting with you." Now the pressure would be increasing from Ed's teachers for him to show some improvement in his behavior.

My discouragement suddenly ended with my fourth session with Ed. He had received a high grade on a class assignment and was delighted to tell me about it. I reflected his pleasure in the accomplishment, and I thought that a turning point had been made in our relationship. It seemed timely for me to disclose how I had also struggled in school with inconsistent progress, but Ed was unimpressed with this and he offered no indication that he cared about my educational history or, even worse, about me. He seemed to deny or ignore the intimacy my words offered, as though his self-preoccupation prevented him from being affected by another person's experiences. Feeling resentful towards Ed, I shifted the topic from myself back to his good grade in class. Once again, Ed spoke with satisfaction about his work. At that moment, even though I apparently mattered little to him, I was able to muster concern for him out of my belief in the intrinsic value and worth of people.

Our next session provided a new low point in our relationship. Ed began in a caustic tone: "You haven't helped me at all and my parents agree with me on this." Although I have been accused of not being helpful from time to time by clients, this occasion was more painful than usual because of the strong effort I had extended on Ed's behalf, and my supposed expertise in working with resistant clients. My participant-observer stance held up long enough for me to state, "Everyone has their preferences." But inside I felt like telling Ed to get out of my office and go tell his parents to find some other counselor to put up with his obnoxious and self-centered behavior. After our session, I engaged in some self-reflection on the topic of countertransference: Why did Ed upset me this way?

Even more intriguing to me was Ed's unyielding mechanisms of defense. How could I continue to be a threat to this young person after a number of weeks of offering him understanding, respect, encouragement, and a reasonable degree of genuineness? What is the tenacity of Ed's defenses that compels him to maintain his guardedness in front of a middle-aged man who has clearly demonstrated that he is on his side? The thought of terminating with Ed started to take on a new appeal.

One of the difficulties in working in the schools is that when counseling fails the client remains on the premises as a constant reminder to the counselor and to all others present. Of course, the counselor, using his or her defenses, can rationalize about the lack of effort that the client expended in the sessions or that the client was not ready to change. I did, however, have to face the fact that unless we established some degree of mutual trust there would be little sense in continuing to meet.

As it was time for our sixth session, I was hoping that Ed would be absent or late for his appointment. Right on time, Ed began, "I've decided that coming here is not so bad because it gets my father off my back some." What a relief this was for me. For the first time in several sessions Ed gave me an indication that the counseling process held some promise of progress. I very much wanted to be precise and accurate in my response to Ed.

AC: You seem really determined. It's important for you to be able to make up your own mind.

Ed: Yeah, I get sick of people telling me what to do. My father thinks that he knows everything.

AC: You resent it that your opinion is not worth much, especially when you are with your father.

Ed: He thinks that I am stupid, and so do a lot of other people.

Ed was making statements that were rich in therapeutic potential. I was gratified that we had reached this point, and I wanted to be sure that we effectively processed what he expressed. In my notes, I wrote verbatim some of his statements. As Ed continued, two related themes emerged: feeling coerced and feeling intellectually inferior. This session with Ed was by far the most satisfying for me. As he confided in me, I felt relieved that a relationship had finally begun to take hold, and my doubts gave way to more confidence in my strategies and interventions. I felt that continuing to provide Ed with understanding and acceptance was essential in reducing his guardedness and developing trust. It was more than satisfying for me to have this assumption confirmed by his response to me in this session. I now had to consider where to proceed in the middle stage in the counseling process.

It was time for me to become more active and to share with Ed what I had learned about him in our six weeks together. In particular, I wanted to focus on Ed's self-defeating and maladaptive thoughts. The work of the cognitive-behavioral therapists, including Albert Ellis, Aaron Beck, and Donald Meichenbaum, would be central in my efforts. I also wanted to challenge contradictions in Ed's behavior, but in a way that would not jeopardize our counseling relationship. Confrontation, a gestalt intervention, would be crucial to me in this attempt.

At our seventh session the focus shifted to Ed's thinking or cognitions, as we entered what I refer to as the integration stage of counseling. As Ed talked about feeling inadequate in school, I confronted him in a supportive tone, "You feel that you can't do that well in the class, but you also tell me that you don't do any of the homework." If I had said this to Ed a few weeks before, he would have responded with anger and indignation. Instead Ed replied in a more resigned way, "Sometimes I'm just a lot of talk." His sense of despair prompted me to disclose how I personally had experienced many difficulties in school, much as I had told him several weeks before. This time he seemed encouraged by my words.

Ed's contradictory behavior was most apparent in his classroom performance. He constantly spoke (although with diminished intensity) about resenting being told what to do, but he also expressed discouragement about feeling "stupid." In a reassuring tone I attempted to relate two prominent and contradictory assumptions Ed had made.

AC: You talk a lot about how important it is for you to make decisions for yourself and that you hate being told what to do. (If there was one conviction of Ed's that he and I had established, this was it.)

Ed: So?

AC: Well, I'm trying to figure it out too. You always want to get your own way, but you also don't like being seen as not very smart.

My attempt to juxtapose Ed's contradictory positions began to make sense to him. If Ed insisted on getting his own way all the time, did this mean he was not being very smart? I was not fully sure where we might go with this, but a softening of either assumption would be a positive change. Ed then began a direct appeal to me.

Ed: I'm not really dumb, you know. A lot of times I fake it so that I get my own way.

AC: (I decided to really open it up.) So often Ed, you blame other people for things when it really is more your own fault.

Ed: (after a lengthy silence) I'm taking a hard look at this. I do have ways to get around things. I just want to be somebody. . . . I'm a nobody.

Ed was expressing such significant feelings that I had a difficult time in responding in effective ways. Staying with what seemed to be working, I continued to traverse the web of Ed's contradictory behavior. Together Ed and I openly explored the numerous inconsistencies in his young existence, and there were many. We were progressing, but I felt that we still were not reaching Ed's more fundamental premises about life, because he continued to engage defense mechanisms when he felt pressured.

Our next session began with what appeared to be a setback, when Ed made statements about topics that I thought we had already worked through: "School really doesn't matter," "I really don't care about anything around here." In a supportive yet firm way I challenged Ed's statements, using cognitive restructuring.

AC: You are giving up any real chance to get anywhere in the future by not trying in school. Why not do what you can about making things better by controlling what you can?

I spoke with deep conviction in my voice because I touched on a topic that has meaning for me, and I was clearly reaching Ed. As I spoke, he was looking at me with an intensity that I had never seen before.

AC: If you want to be somebody in life, you need to put an effort into it. You can't just wish for things to happen and blame other people when they don't work out.

As I went on, I became aware that I had to let Ed respond. I did not want to lose the impact that I seemed to be making on him. With my pause, Ed reacted in a subdued statement, "I look for excuses all the time, rather than do more on my own." This jumped out at me! I asked him to repeat exactly what he had said, so I could write it down in my notes. As Ed spoke the words again, I was aware of the "therapeutic moment" and wished to take full advantage of it.

AC: Ed, you said something that is not easy to say; go on.

Ed: For a long time I've been thinking about how I try to blame everyone else for my problems, rather than blame myself.

This induced a lengthy silence (for me, anything over one minute is lengthy). Ed did not look like he was going to speak but I told myself to be quiet. Finally, Ed spoke: "I'm tired. I really don't want to talk about this much more."

This threw me. Just when I was excited about a breakthrough which could spark a behavior change, Ed said he was tired. What about the therapeutic moment? I certainly wanted to continue, but wondered if I should push Ed when he had expressed so much and now wanted to stop. As it turned out, we did shift to another topic, and although we returned repeatedly to the control theme in our sessions, Ed never again expressed the depth of awareness that he had reached in this encounter.

In our tenth session, Ed began by complaining about how unfair one of his teachers was in her grading. As Ed went on, I thought back on our recent meetings where he appeared to fully realize how he defended himself while avoiding responsibility for his actions. This realization now seemed lost on Ed. I went on to challenge his perceptions through cognitive restructuring, much as I had done in our last session. During our next two meetings the themes of Ed's acceptance of responsibility and avoidance of blaming other people for his problems were emphasized. Ed was particularly pleased when I informed him that his teacher, Mrs. White, told me that he had started to improve in his work and that he was now "enjoyable to have in class."

Only once in this period did we discuss what I thought was a central conflict in his life: Ed's relationship with his father. At one point in an earlier session, he stated that his father liked it when Ed did "lousy" in school. I confronted Ed with my observation that his father seemed interested in how Ed did in school, and said I did not understand his statement. Perhaps I had cut off consideration of Ed's perception at that time, because he did not mention it again for several weeks. This time, when Ed spoke about how his father really did not care about how well he performed academically, I offered an interpretation: "Could it be that you used to do poorly because of your dad's dislike of school that you have heard so much about?" When I said this it seemed rather implausible and Ed did not want to discuss the topic further.

We did not go beyond this attempt to clarify Ed's relationship with his father. It was evident all along that Ed felt both resentment and apprehension towards his father. I thought about Ed's early recollection of his dad standing over him after Ed spilled his milk. Perhaps if Ed had indicated more interest, we would have pursued this further. Ed seemed to be progressing in other ways, so I did not attempt further interpretations to explore developmental conflicts. In retrospect, I am aware that Ed's relationship with his father required further clarification.

■ OUTCOME

The main accomplishments of counseling with Ed were his increasingly accurate and integrated thoughts that developed over twelve sessions. In the final stage of counseling Ed discussed changes in his belief systems with satisfaction: "I still try to blame other people when things go wrong, but I'm getting better at owning up to things." I offered Ed frequent encouragement by emphasizing his control, effort, and capabilities. In particular, I stressed growth in his adaptive behavior and the diminished power of his defense mechanisms: "You are more honest with yourself" (less denial), "You face up to things better now" (less rationalization), and "It's hard, but now you blame other people a lot less when things don't work out" (less displacement).

Meaningful change, however, must be manifested in productive actions. Ed's negative self-evaluation and defense mechanisms were well established, and they did not yield easily to more productive patterns. We used cognitive-behavioral techniques to facilitate purposeful change. Ed tried the Adlerian technique of catching himself each time he began to talk about a negative attribute ("I'm stupid—I must always get my own way"), or a defense (denial, rationalization, and displacement were combined under avoiding responsibility). One week Ed carried a small notebook in his pocket and recorded his behavior. Ed caught himself using such negative talk 19 times. With a decline in frequency of such behaviors over a few weeks, Ed felt a further sense of accomplishment.

My time with Ed was drawing to a close, and we began to talk about terminating counseling in our fourteenth meeting. I felt very satisfied about our work together, especially since I had come so close to giving up early in our sessions.

In a meeting with Ed's parents and his teachers near the end of the school year, I eagerly anticipated a discussion where I expected to receive credit for my good work with Ed. After a review of the academic and social progress that Ed had made, it was time for Ed's father to speak: "I think that most of the improvement with Ed came about because my wife and I enrolled him in a karate class." Somehow it all didn't seem very fair.

DISCUSSION

It is sometimes difficult in the midst of the counseling process to fully appraise the progress of a case. Only after moving through the stages of the counseling process is it possible to accurately assess outcomes. Of course, the most important outcome is how the client progresses in his or her life after counseling concludes. Looking back in my counseling with Ed, I can see that I made some mistakes and avoided others. I can point to many positive elements in the growth of our relationship. In writing about Ed, I chose to present a case in which the outcome was successful rather than one that was less rewarding. I try to learn from my experience and to enjoy the more positive outcomes.

Several times I considered terminating with Ed, particularly early in our relationship. I thought that we were not progressing and would not be able to establish a counseling relationship. Sometimes I become impatient and expect progress, forgetting that the counseling process occurs in irregular gains, delays, and reversals. I also thought about terminating because I was being worn down by Ed's obstinacy and general unpleasantness. If I had allowed termination to occur, both Ed and I would have missed an opportunity to grow.

I find that I need to remind myself that the counseling process is often enhanced by working with the larger system. Reflecting on my first conference with Ed's teacher and parents, I suspect that if I had been more assertive (actually courageous) in my support of Mrs. White, I might have struck a more advantageous service arrangement. For example, working in consultation with Ed's teachers or starting family counseling should have at least been discussed. I made no attempt to establish a team approach, which frequently has more potential for success. Instead, I settled for expecting positive behavior change to occur only through individual counseling.

At different times I felt pressure from Ed's teachers and parents to achieve a quicker behavior change. As a result, I attempted to force the counseling process in several instances by intervening excessively and prematurely. For example, I offered a self-disclosure (about my failures in school) that was too intimate before Ed and I had established our counseling relationship. Even worse, I blamed Ed when this intervention didn't work. Most of the time, I was able to trust the counseling process and remain solidly focused on the relationship.

The least effective intervention with Ed was interpretation. He resisted my efforts to relate his conflicted feelings to his developmental experiences. I was not sure if the strength of Ed's feelings had subsided or if he was defending with restricted affect. Another possibility is that I did not employ interpretation effectively. We had little success in linking Ed's past to his current functioning. Since my time with Ed, I have attempted to improve my understanding of interpretation in the counseling process, especially in working with clients of a young age. This effort remains unfinished for me, but I am intrigued by it.

The conceptualization of the counseling process into three stages provides me with a general direction for client progress. This does not mean that a hypothetical stage is clearly apparent or that the process is irreversible. The sequence of stages, however, does affect the timing of strategies and interventions within each stage. For example, the positive impact of cognitive restructuring depended on my previous challenge of Ed's contradictory behavior through confrontation.

Modifying a client's defenses in a specific sequence within the three stages of counseling facilitates an understanding of how change occurs. In the initial stage Ed became aware that he was experiencing defensive feelings. He increased his comprehension of how and why he engaged defenses in the integration stage. And in the final stage of counseling Ed assumed a more adaptive manner of functioning. Somehow the stages never seem this neat and tidy during the counseling experience, but looking back, one can see that the process of change occurs in a sequential way.

The operation of a client's defense mechanisms has long been a fascinating topic for me. Over the years, I have learned that several strategies are not beneficial, and I avoid using them. The to-be-avoided list in handling defenses in counseling includes tolerating, disputing, and attacking. Tolerating defense mechanisms may be necessary in the beginning of a relationship, but it is unrealistic to expect enduring patterns to change in an emotionally comfortable climate. Examining contradictions and distortions that are inherent in defenses also allows for their cognitive foundations to be clarified. Although in the initial stage of counseling with Ed I was tolerant as he exhibited defenses, I shifted to a more challenging stance in the middle stage and confronted his contradictory behavior. Disputing, in the form of bickering or arguing with a client over the validity or legitimacy of his or her defenses invariably results in a more urgent and intense display of the mechanisms. Attacking or stripping defenses makes a client feel exposed and vulnerable: he or she may fall apart or mount even stronger defenses.

Ed came by the school to visit last year. After he told me that he was doing well, he said, "I don't know how you put up with me. I used to blame my parents, my teachers, and everyone else for my problems except me." It was so good to see Ed again.

Biographical Statement

Arthur J. Clark, EdD, is an associate professor and coordinator of the counseling and development program at St. Lawrence University in Canton, New York. He was employed as a school psychologist in the public schools at the time of the case presented here. Dr. Clark is a licensed psychologist and is the author of numerous articles, including "The Identification and Modification of Defense Mechanisms in Counseling," which appeared in the Journal of Counseling and Development *(1991).*

The Boy Who Trashed His Final

Larry B. Golden

Twelve-year-old Joshua is referred because he told his English teacher, "Let my family see me dead!" He is intellectually gifted and very much an underachiever. Josh has a high-performance younger brother, a mother who expects no less from every member of this competitive family, and a father who brings a large dose of ambivalence to most of life's undertakings.

*Over time Golden changes his initial diagnosis of Adjustment Disorder with Depressed Mood (*DSM-III-R *309.00) to Dysthymia (*DSM-III-R *300.40) as it becomes apparent that Josh's problems will not yield to a behavioral approach. Indeed, after an apparent lifting of depression, Josh creates a crisis by throwing his final English exam into the trash can.*

Golden next moves into the cognitive realm. The assumption of cognitive therapy is that we create our own reality according to how we construe experience. This family has created a protective myth around Joshua that is getting in the way of his attempts to individuate. Golden proposes a new, constructive myth.

Finally, this case illustrates that therapeutic gains usually occur day by day, by putting one foot in front of the other; they are not the dramatic outcome of a single intervention, however deft.

Joshua's parents had come to the end of their proverbial rope. Joshua was a 12-year-old seventh grader. He was exhibiting some very disturbing behaviors: plucking out his eyebrows and "earning" grades of D's and F's, despite an IQ of 130 and good rapport with his teachers. When he started talking about suicide, his parents decided to *shlep* (drag or carry) him to a psychologist.

Joshua's father, Raul, was a copywriter at an advertising agency. His mother, Beverly, was an assistant principal at a public elementary school. Joshua's brother, Sidney, though one year younger, was a little taller, handsomer, and a straight-A student. Sid had skipped a year in school and so both brothers were in seventh grade.

Joshua was reputed to be a talented writer. However, regardless of the assigned topic, he turned his stories to themes about cataclysmic warfare between magical kingdoms. Josh was relatively weak in mathematics. He often failed to turn in work in any of his subjects and was unresponsive to either the carrot or the stick approach.

Joshua was in an English class for gifted and talented (GT) students. Beverly suggested that I call Mrs. Katz, the GT English teacher, who had an especially good relationship with Josh. She said that Josh had a habit of pulling out his eyebrows. He would fall asleep in class. Josh *kvetched* (endlessly complained) about not being liked. Mrs. Katz maintained, however, that while Josh was not popular he was not disliked. He simply didn't respond to other kids and they, in turn, had lost interest in him. She saw him as depressed, withdrawn, and manipulative. She said she had gone the extra mile to help Josh. For example, she would permit him to write about his warfare fantasies instead of insisting that he compose stories on the assigned theme. He was quite willing to talk about personal problems—his "perfect" brother, demanding mother, and angry father. When Josh said, "Let my family see me dead," Mrs. Katz sent him to talk with Mrs. Hernandez, the school counselor.

I called Mrs. Hernandez. Josh had told Mrs. Hernandez of a plan to run away and live in a bat cave near Austin. Josh assured her that the temperature in the cave was a constant 70 degrees Fahrenheit and that the bats, contrary to their terrible reputation, were harmless. Mrs. Hernandez thought Joshua was depressed but not at immediate risk of suicide.

■ CONCEPTUALIZATION

My primary occupation is that of a college professor. I like to theorize and analyze and spout off about most everything. Which is to say, you are in for a lecture. Also, please enjoy the Yiddishisms. I was raised in a culture that is rich in terminology for human *mishugas* (craziness).

Gifted Underachievers

I have maintained a practice with children and families since 1976. After all these years, I usually get to work with the types of people and problems that interest me. I especially like working with gifted underachievers such as Josh. Most adolescents are poor candidates for psychotherapy. They distrust adults as agents of oppression and regard the therapist as their parents' hired gun. "Off my back" is the teenager's battle cry! Gifted children are more verbal than their peers and psychotherapy, after all, is a talking cure. They are also fascinated by their own ruminations and somewhat curious about psychology as a field of study—a hook into counseling that I am not above exploiting.

Typically, gifted children are expected to and expect themselves to accomplish great things. When these high standards can't be reached, low self-esteem is the result. Many gifted students, including Josh, though ranking in the top 5 percent or so in intellectual ability, are quite vulnerable to academic failure.

Sibling Rivalry

Another feature of this case was intense sibling rivalry. Parents are often amazed that their naturally born children are so different. It can be no other way. Siblings choose different paths so as to avoid a head-on contest. This is a workable strategy if there is a wide range of competitive arenas. That is, one sibling can invest in music, another in athletics, and so on. In Josh's family, however, academic achievement was everything and Sidney had a corner on the market.

Parents, meaning well, try to convince the losing sibling that he, too, is loved and that they are proud of him as well. However, love and pride are two different things: "You mean you're proud of my crummy grades!" "Well, no, but we're proud of your, well, uhmmm, you play a terrific game of Monopoly!" Such duplicitous reassurance only supports the losing sibling's view of himself as a psychological cripple in need of phoney parental bolstering.

Later, we will see that Josh's mother believed that he was expressing contempt for her values when he failed in school. It is more likely that Josh's underachievement could have been a statement, to wit: "This is the only game in town and I lose every time. Why try? Grades are stupid, anyway." Classic sour grapes.

Strategic Family Therapy

It's unusual in my practice to get a request for family therapy. Typically, I get a call from a parent, usually the mother, who is worried about a child's misbehavior. I always ask to see the entire family. Other than in cases when a child must escape a grossly dysfunctional family to survive, it makes sense to include the whole *mishpuchah* (the family at large). Family members live with each other, usually love each other, and are certainly trying to influence each other. So why not invite them to participate together in therapy? I explain that I need everyone's point of view in order to fully understand the child's misbehavior. What's more, if I'm to be effective, I will need everyone's help. Joshua's family, like most, was willing to participate.

Of course, there are different varieties of family therapy. This case is an illustration of strategic family therapy. The strategic therapist tries to change only those aspects of the family system that maintain the symptomatic behavior. Therefore, it falls under the category of brief, rather than depth, psychotherapy. The depth, or psychodynamic, approach assumes that the symptom is merely a cover for underlying pathology. However, this kind of excavation can take years, and this family's insurance coverage provided a strong incentive to complete this work within 20 sessions. How many layers of the psychic onion can be peeled in 20 sessions? For the strategic therapist insight is frosting on the cake and not necessary to resolving the presenting problem.

Strategic family therapists are fond of using paradoxical interventions. For example, one could tell an underachiever like Josh to fail every one of his subjects to prove once and for all that he is not his parents' puppet. If the paradox works, his grades will improve. Good old reverse psychology. I don't like this approach. It's basically disrespectful and, as often as not, backfires in some unpleasant way such as a double reverse!

The strategy I prefer is variously called reframing, use of metaphor, and story rewriting. Every family creates its own stories and myths. These family myths, like societal ones, serve a purpose. They help explain the ways of the world, support family unity, and provide guidance for children as they prepare to embark on their own lives. But sometimes a myth outlives its usefulness.

It's almost impossible to use rational argumentation to convince a family to give up its outdated mythology because a myth is based on irrational beliefs. Instead, the therapist must help the family create a new story to replace the old, a story that serves them better.

Diagnosis

Adjustment Disorder with Depressed Mood was my first choice for a *DSM-III-R* diagnosis. This is a relatively nonstigmatizing label that assumes that the patient is suffering short-term depression in response to a stressful situation. When the stress is removed or the patient learns to cope, the mood improves. Later, I changed Josh's diagnosis to Dysthymia because I became convinced that his depression was more or less chronic.

■ PROCESS

Therapy began on May 4 and continued until October 15 for a total of 20 sessions. Therefore, I met Josh toward the end of the school year and stopped working with him early in the next. Typically, sessions were a three-ring circus with time reserved for (a) family counseling, (b) individual counseling with Josh, and (c) parent education and counseling. On occasion, the two brothers were seen together.

The First Seven Sessions

Session 1 (5/4). This session was attended by Joshua, his younger brother, Sidney, and his parents. Joshua said that he was interested in creative writing and classical music. He admitted that he often failed to turn in assignments. Joshua said that his peers saw him as a "nerd," a "geek," and a "dweeb." His parents reported that a medical examination had not disclosed any physical condition that could account for Joshua's difficulties. There was no evidence of alcohol or substance abuse.

Session 2 (5/11). Sid was quick to speak on behalf of his unresponsive older brother. Sid volunteered that Josh's best friend was "Alex the Terminal Weird." Sid, for his part, told me that he enjoyed building model planes, was a fanatic Trekkie (fan of the original "Star Trek" television show), loved computers and playing the flute. He added, "I'm the best in 7th grade in algebra! Oh, I know Josh feels terrible when I say that." A Renaissance sib!

Beverly described her family as "a fierce problem-solving outfit" and was optimistic that Josh's problems would be overcome. That was the good news. The bad news was that she saw Josh as a chip off Dad's passive, never-get-ahead block. In fact, though, Raul had a reputation at the advertising agency as being creative and quirky. He was content to leave the management end of the business to the more ambitious types. Sid, on the other hand, was obviously a go-getter like his mother. In a more egalitarian society, Beverly would have been president of General Motors at least. As it was, she was assistant principal of an elementary school.

Sunday was typically "nag and scream" day for Beverly, but this Sunday Raul, at my suggestion, agreed to take charge. Specifically, he would make sure the boys completed their chores. This would not be the first time I would try to shift responsibility for discipline to Raul.

For his part, Josh agreed to an experiment. At least three days during the week, he would complete his work in history no matter how discouraged or bored or lazy or angry he felt.

On May 15, I called Mrs. Katz, Josh's GT English teacher. She reported a "superficial" turnaround. Joshua was completing his assignments, talking to peers, and, as usual, pestering her for personal conferences.

Session 3 (5/18). Beverly was angry. Josh had led her to believe he was giving it his best shot in algebra, and she felt betrayed when he brought home a failing progress report. She demanded a full disclosure. Josh admitted, "I'm failing and I'm not trying." A contrite Josh agreed to complete three chores without even being nagged. Beverly was also angry with Raul. His monitoring of the boys' chores had been half-hearted. They agreed to another therapist injunction: No nagging or punitive measure in regard to the boys could be undertaken prior to both parents consulting with each other. The intent was to encourage Raul to share the disciplinary burden with Beverly. Working together, they could achieve a balance; at odds, they would polarize and undermine each other.

Session 4 (5/25). Josh said that he was trying his best in algebra. He declared that he would try out for the school baseball team next year. I found it hard to picture Josh as a jock.

Session 5 (5/29). A lackluster, low-energy session with Josh. Will he follow through on his promises and thereby, hopefully, pull himself out of depression? I wasn't feeling very optimistic.

On May 31, I received three calls within minutes of each other from Beverly, Mrs. Hernandez (the counselor), and Mrs. Katz. They told the same sorry tale—Josh walked up to Mrs. Katz's desk and dumped his final English exam in the trash can! Later, she retrieved it. Josh had thrown away a C paper that would have earned a passing grade in the course. Instead, he failed GT English for the semester. He also failed history and algebra, though without the benefit of a dramatic flourish such as ditching a final exam. Beverly wanted Mrs. Katz to count the trashed final. Fortunately, she refused: "I've rescued Josh all year." However, Mrs. Katz deferred to me. If the F would activate Josh's suicidal tendencies, she would reconsider. I didn't think that Josh was suicidal and advised her not to count the trashed exam. Mrs. Hernandez, the school counselor, said that Josh could retake English and algebra during summer school and thereby pass to the next grade. However, if Josh went to summer school, the family would have to cancel plans for a Disney World vacation.

Session 6 (6/5). Gloom and doom. Beverly and Raul were mystified and scared. Why! Why would anyone throw a passing final exam in the trash? Why a preference for failure? How have *we* failed?

I asked each family member to tell me how they would account for the fact that Josh had trashed his final exam.

Josh said, "I don't know." His statement sounded genuine.

Sid shrugged, "He's weird."

Half seriously, Raul said, "Einstein failed seventh-grade math and went on to discover the theory of relativity." But in a more analytical mood, he guessed that Josh had simply given up in his losing rivalry with Sid.

Mom's theory was, "He's shooting the royal bird at our values. He's rejecting everything we believe in and hold dear, the importance of education and trying your best."

I had little use for the family's lame explanations for Josh's motives. I wanted an explanation that would be empowering, not discouraging. If Sid was correct in his assessment, then there was little hope. Even Freud knew of no cure for being weird.

Raul seemed to think that Josh's intellectual gifts would enable him to go on to great things (such as the theory of relativity) despite a minor setback like failing the seventh grade. However, Josh was no Einstein (it would be fair to assume that Einstein's IQ was somewhat in excess of 130). Dad's concern about Josh's discouragement over Sid's relentless achievements deserved serious consideration. I suggested to Sid that if he would fail a few subjects, that would certainly be a shot in the arm for Josh's self-esteem. Sid refused.

Beverly's view, that Josh was rejecting the family values, did not offer a productive lead either. It connected Josh's failures to the vaunted adolescent propensity for rebellion against authority, a tide I had no hope of turning.

No one suggested the role of marital tensions in Josh's behavior, nor did it occur to me at this point in time. Was Joshua subconsciously fighting Raul's battles with Beverly? I would deal with this issue later in therapy.

Any one or all of the above assessments of Josh's motives for trashing his exam could have been correct. On the other hand, since no one knew for certain what the motivation really was, least of all Josh, I decided to invent a motive that would help me do my job.

Session 7 (6/12). Now it was time to plug in my *spiel* (story) that, God willing, would explain Josh's behavior to everyone's satisfaction. I addressed the family thus: "Imagine an Olympic athlete. The judge is about to hang the gold medal around his neck, but the athlete steps back and declares, 'I can't accept this award. I've been using steroids to boost my performance.' How would you judge such a person?"

The family consensus was that, while the athlete's use of steroids was reprehensible, declining the gold medal was an honorable and courageous act. I told them that I saw Josh's trashing his final exam as a similar act of conscience. I explained: "Josh uses his reputation as a psychological cripple to get unfair advantage. He *kvetches* to his teachers about how Sid makes him feel stupid, how his mother loves Sid more than him, drops hints about suicide, and plucks his eyebrows. His teachers provide loads of sympathy and demand less of him than the others. When Josh threw his exam in the trash can, he was making a statement, 'Enough is enough. I cannot accept a grade I did not earn!'"

Everyone liked my version. Josh basked in the glory of his gutsy choice. Now Josh's parents could shift their guilt for Josh's failures to his very recently broadened shoulders.

Of course, Mom stopped trying to get the teacher to credit him for the trashed exam. I pointed out that Josh would not tolerate such rescuing.

Josh was left with no reasonable alternative other than to pick up the burden of manly responsibility I had fashioned for him. He agreed not to solicit therapy from his teachers; one therapist was enough for anyone. Mrs. Katz was relieved to hear that she was out of the psychotherapy business and could resume her chosen occupation as a teacher.

As for Sid, he was advised to *shlep nachus* (bring home honors that would reflect well on his parents) as he'd always done, assured by me that Josh had the raw courage to bear up under his younger brother's success.

The Remaining Thirteen Sessions

I wish I could say that my clever story about the Olympics resolved Josh's problems of underachievement, low self-esteem, and depression. In fact, my reframe gave the family a different perspective, one that enhanced everyone's self-esteem. However, the school year was over, and Josh would have to await the start of summer school to demonstrate any renewed commitment to academics. Much work remained. Which is to say, like most of us, Josh took one step backward (at least!) for every two forward.

There were several obstructions besides Josh's brute inertia. I knew that I would have to do something to defuse the sibling rivalry. As things were, Josh would rather fail than risk a head-on contest with Sid. Further, long-standing marital problems had surfaced.

Defusing Sibling Rivalry. In an individual session, Josh told me that he thought that his parents loved Sid more than him because Sid was an academic superstar. I pointed out that Josh was mistaking gratitude for love. When Sid looked good, Beverly and Raul looked good. Sid brought home the bacon, and his parents were appreciative.

"So what do you want from them, Josh?" I asked. "Love? Would you believe them if they told you that they loved you as much as Sid?"

"Not really," said Josh.

I told Josh that I thought that his parents already loved him enough, maybe too much.

Josh decided that love was hard to define. Instead, he would attempt to win his parents' respect. I told Josh that I didn't think he would have to match Sid's stellar performance to do this. But he would have to become a *mensch,* a man of his word, a person others could depend on.

Josh was eager to tell his parents of his quest for their respect. I advised against a premature spilling of the beans: "Go for it! Maybe they'll notice."

I wanted to make the competitive nature of this family explicit and thereby less destructive. In a conjoint session, I asked the family members to line up on a winner-to-loser continuum. Sid was numero uno, then Bev, then Raul, with "the dweeb" bringing up the rear. Then I asked the parents to objectively evaluate and compare each brother's abilities as if they were judges at a county livestock fair. Of course, Raul and Beverly didn't get far with this crude exercise. It focused unpleasantly on the way that both boys (indeed, even the parents) were seen as the family's prize steers! It was also true that these parents loved their children. But the distinction between unconditional love and pride in a child's achievements had become blurred. In relation to Beverly, Sid saw himself as a *nachus* machine, Josh as a source of bitter *tzuris*. (*Nachus* is the joy children bring to their parents through their positive achievements, while *tzuris* is the heartache children cause their parents through misbehavior.)

In a session that included only the boys, I asked for a disclosure of slings and arrows, verbal and physical, that each brother employed against the other. I wanted to get these weapons out on the table where they could be dealt with. Sid told of Josh's constant physical attacks over the years. These had stopped in recent months. I'd love to attribute the cessation of violence to counseling, but I suspect it had much more to do with the fact that Sid was now as big as Josh. In the realm of verbal weaponry, Josh's best shot was to call Sid "mama's boy" or "fag," while Sid would retaliate with "loser" or "psycho." They agreed not to use these epithets against each other for one week. So as not to leave them naked and unarmed, I gave each brother a secret and terrible name to use in case of dire need. Josh was instructed to lambast Sid with *schlemiel* and Sid was to smear Josh with *shlamozel*. (Both are Yiddish words that mean "jerk," more or less.) The intervention had the desired effect; it took the sting out of the verbal cuts.

Encouraging Joshua to Accept Responsibility. Josh told me of a dream in which he forgot his books and registration card on the very first day of summer school. You don't have to be Carl Jung to interpret this one: Josh was worried that he would mess up his big chance to prove himself. Beverly and Raul were also anxious about summer school. I was too. In Josh's presence, I asked Beverly and Raul if they wanted to assume responsibility for Josh's passing summer school. They declined. I asked them if they held me responsible (God forbid). They let me off the hook as well. So who would be entitled to the credit or blame for passing or failing? The man himself!

As summer school got under way, I assigned Josh the task of keeping a daily log of his progress in both of his summer school classes, English and algebra, and issuing brief weekly reports to his parents. Grades aside, these (hopefully) truthful, dependable reports would accrue to Josh's status as a *mensch*.

In his first official report Josh predicted an A in English and a B in algebra. By the fourth week, however, Josh had downgraded his estimate to an A and a D. His final grades after the six-week summer term were an A and an F. *Oy gevalt*!

Josh was promoted on the condition that he repeat and pass algebra during the fall term.

Nail biting had taken the place of eyebrow plucking when Josh was in his anxiety mode. But he wanted to stop being anxious, not merely substitute one symptom for another. He asked my advice. I told him that maybe a little anxiety wasn't so bad. He decided to substitute clicks with his ballpoint pen for nail biting.

I helped Josh compose "awful angry notes" to send to Beverly when she got on his case. How did Woody Allen put it? "I don't get angry, I just grow a tumor." For Josh, substitute an F for the tumor! Beverly said that she would much prefer Josh's nasty notes to his being passive-aggressive.

Marital Issues. I scheduled a parents-only session in preparation for the new school year. I urged that the home-school team go into action at the first indication of serious goofing off and vigorously pursue evidence of same. Raul was worried that Josh would feel that he wasn't trusted. Trust, shmust! Parents should understand that their teens are in the business of outfoxing them. Raul agreed to do the detective work and check on Josh's schoolwork, but his heart wasn't in it.

I knew that trust was also an issue between Beverly and Raul. Raul felt bossed around by Beverly. He handled this in a passive-aggressive manner by not following through. Consequently, Beverly saw him as unreliable and untrustworthy.

While Beverly and Raul had not contracted for marital counseling, I observed that their issues were getting in the way of Josh's progress. I pointed out certain parallels between Beverly's feelings towards Raul and Josh and their reactions to her.

Raul complained that he had sold out his dream of being a novelist to earn a living as a hack at an ad agency. He wanted to blame Beverly for this disappointment. Beverly, however, was angry, even despairing, about Raul's lack of ambition. He had languished as an advertising writer while others had risen to managerial positions and partnerships. Beverly saw the same self-defeating tendencies in Joshua. She was astonished that Raul still had a yen to be a novelist since he hadn't written anything but advertising copy since he was in college.

"That's the point," said Raul.

"So whose fault is it?" asked Beverly.

"I wonder if Joshua will ever take a risk," said I.

Raul corrected me, "Raul, not Joshua."

My slip wasn't lost on either partner. Raul and Josh—they were the two *schlemiels*. I asked Raul if he would tolerate one of my lectures. He said that he would. My message to Raul was that he could set a good example for his sons and win his wife's respect by being a *mensch*. Either get to work on a novel or give it up, but stop blaming Beverly or the advertising agency. What's more, I told him to stand up to Beverly and stop being passive-aggressive in their relationship.

I asked Beverly if she could imagine feeling good about Josh settling for B's or Raul not advancing his advertising career. She replied that B's would be OK but not wonderful and the same went for Raul. Josh was smart enough to get A's, and Raul was capable of advancing himself. Still, she had been in the education business long enough to know that there are different kinds of smarts. Josh's and Raul's dreamy world view and their ambivalence towards academic and career achievement would not yield A's or promotions no matter how hard they tried. Were Josh and Raul quirky guys who didn't fit the common mold? Or were they bent on resisting Beverly's push for excellence even at the expense of their own advancement? While there may have been some truth in both scenarios, I suggested that she buy into the quirky guys idea for the sake of peace and quiet in the family.

This session was as far as either parent wanted to go with marital counseling.

■ OUTCOME

Josh predicted a good first six-weeks report card. The parents promised a celebration of some sort if Josh's prophecy came true. So what do you think happened?

Good news! Mostly B's, no D's or F's. I praised Josh to the sky for delivering on his word, a more significant indicator of maturity than good grades.

As often as not, I don't hear from clients after termination. In this case, Beverly kept me posted with occasional notes for about six months. The gist was that Josh was doing well, Sid was doing great, and she and Raul had found some peace of mind. Here are two of the notes.

> *Note (12/9).* We survived the second six weeks. Josh slipped a bit—95 down to 78 in French and 80 to 70 in algebra. He knows we are disappointed, and for what it may be worth, I think he's putting out a bit more effort. I guess you could say that we are trying to ride the tide. Sid turned out another superb performance—six A's! I've enclosed one of our family photos; the boys mentioned that you might like one. Please know we will feel free to call you at the first sign of a real crisis; we'll handle the small everyday ones!

> *Note (1/21).* Things running fairly smoothly. Josh brought home a progress report for algebra—89 average! Long may it continue. He wants to go to France this summer in an exchange program so he knows he must keep his grades up. We let him set the parameters, and he suggested an 83 minimum in everything. Now we wait and see. Sid was the school team alternate to the Math Counts competition at the University of Texas, and he placed fifth among all alternates who competed. Hubby and I are continuing to enjoy the challenges of adolescence. We're still able to smile, a positive sign.

My sense of these two notes was that the bitter, baffled reaction to Josh's miserable school performance had abated. There was an ironic acceptance of the *tzuris* that parenting holds in store. And, of course, Josh was passing his subjects, working up to *his* expectations and current capabilities.

DISCUSSION

My initial attempt at getting rid of Josh's negative behaviors resulted in superficial changes and set the stage for a dramatic crisis—trashing the final exam. The reframing of Josh's self-defeating behavior as an Olympic myth had positive results. Josh had been saddled with a myth that he was a psychological cripple, needy of external support. I meant it when I had told Josh that his parents loved him too much. Their well-meaning attempts to bolster his self-esteem only demonstrated that he was needy of special help. The trashing of the exam could easily have been the "nail in the coffin," confirming this family's worst fears about Joshua and themselves. The Olympic myth portrayed Josh as being irrevocably committed to a course of autonomy, no longer willing to accept undeserved advantage.

One myth that therapists are stuck with is that one brilliant therapeutic stroke can reverse years of complex behavior patterning. This particular myth is canonized at professional conferences where one witnesses dramatic "cures" by the great gurus of psychotherapy. True cures? Maybe yes, maybe no. For my part, therapy is a little bit of this, a little bit of that, and then maybe a partial solution.

This family was in many respects a mirror of my own family of origin. I, like Josh, had a hard time making a comeback from a one-down sibling rivalry. It's important to know that Sid (and my brother) also paid a heavy price, for he was never sure if he was valued for anything other than his achievements. Working with a client and a family that is similar to your own is tricky business. To the extent that therapists are aware of their own family dynamics, they can bring the benefit of personal experience and insight to their work. However, ignorance can lead to problems with countertransference and projection. For this reason I believe that counselors should get therapy for themselves intermittently throughout their professional lifetimes.

Biographical Statement

Larry B. Golden, PhD, is associate professor of counseling and guidance at the University of Texas at San Antonio. He is a licensed psychologist and has maintained a part-time private practice since 1976. He specializes in counseling with children and families. Dr. Golden has published several books, including Psychotherapeutic Techniques in School Psychology *(1984),* Helping Families Help Children: Family Interventions with School-Related Problems *(1986),* Preventing Adolescent Suicide *(1988), and* Ethical Standards Casebook *(1990).*

Help! But Don't Get Close

Lauren J. Golden

Eight-year-old Cindy arranges to be referred to Lauren Golden, her mother's therapist. Golden assumes that she has a head start, given Cindy's desire to be in therapy as well as prior knowledge of Kate, Cindy's mother. In fact, Cindy is highly ambivalent. She craves an honest relationship but has good cause to fear intimacy.

*Golden struggles with a precise diagnosis. She sees Separation Anxiety Disorder (*DSM-III-R *309.21) as well as Dysthymia (*DSM-III-R *300.40) as plausible descriptors of Cindy's condition. But Golden isn't entirely comfortable with either. Instead, she commits to the existential view that Cindy is a unique being who can best grow in a relationship that eschews categories and expectations. Golden recognizes her good fortune in that her work with Cindy is not time limited by an insurance policy. We see this case unfold over a four-year period.*

Cindy, a tall, coltish 8-year-old with the most compelling smile you could imagine, asked to talk to her school counselor after he had visited her class. They spent four cheerful, chatty meetings discussing friends, school, and teachers before she hinted about her parents' divorce and her discomfort in her relationships with her mother, father and 13-year-old sister. Her secret agenda was never explicitly revealed but began to become clear when she told the counselor that she didn't want to hurt his feelings but she thought she would be more comfortable talking to a woman ("You know, girl talk") and proceeded to ask him if he knew a therapist named Lauren Golden. Curious as to where this was leading, he answered that he did, indeed, know a therapist by that name and asked Cindy if she knew her.

Cindy: Yes, my mother sees her every week.
Counselor: Does Lauren seem like a person you would like to talk to?
Cindy: Maybe.
Counselor: Have you mentioned this to your mother?
Cindy: (There was a pause as Cindy's expression darkened.) No.
Counselor: How would you feel if I talked to her about you and about Lauren?

Cindy gave the school counselor permission to call Cindy's mother, Kate, who was receptive to the idea of Cindy seeing Lauren.

So Cindy and I began to work together. But it was at least two years later that I learned she had planned the whole thing. Having observed the positive change in her mother's mood after she had started therapy, Cindy planned her strategy in order to get what she herself needed.

At that time I had been treating Cindy's mother, Kate, for about three months for depression. She had divorced her husband five years earlier when Cindy was three. Kate had devoted time and energy to finishing medical school. She completed her residency in psychiatry and found a position in a private clinic that specialized in geriatric treatment. During her years in school her life was a juggling act as she strove to combine study and motherhood. She made use of babysitters and various arrangements with her parents to care for Cindy and her older sister Ellen. Cindy and Ellen maintained regular contact with their father, Don, who was a university professor in a city about a four-hour drive from where they lived with their mother. Academic success, achievement, and status were significantly valued in this family. Both sets of grandparents were teachers. Both parents had graduate degrees.

In therapy, I had learned that Kate had experienced tremendous conflict in her relationship with her own parents. She began to gain insight into and relief from this struggle while, paradoxically, feeling driven to prove herself "good enough" in their eyes. She was the anxious product of a critical, manipulative, needy mother and a moody, enraged father. Their frequent arguments suffused the household with unresolved tension and depression. Kate frequently scurried to attend to her mother, who dramatized her need for control with relentless sick headaches.

As a newlywed, Kate had delighted in a new sense of freedom. Her husband, Don, offered her a sheltered life within the familiar world of the university campus in which she reveled until she began to feel the weight of Don's subtly expressed conditions. Where she had initially felt somehow uplifted by his emotional support of her, she began to feel beaten down by his covert belittlement and disregard. Her despair grew and took hold during her pregnancy with Cindy. Three years later and without her parents' support, Kate found the strength to leave Don.

I learned from Kate that Cindy often developed headaches or stomachaches to avoid going to school and that she performed below grade level. She suffered daily anxiety over peer relationships as well as tearful fights with her sister. Kate described Cindy as frequently irritable and prone to temper tantrums.

The nature of Cindy's fights with her sister, Ellen, became more apparent during a joint session with the two of them. As they were getting seated in my office one afternoon, Cindy earnestly made an effort to please Ellen by admiring her shirt. Ellen rolled her eyes and responded incredulously, "I've had this shirt forever!" Translation: "If this is the first time you're noticing, there's something terribly wrong with you, dummy!" This was the type of message that trickled down to Cindy from each member of the family. The distressing sense of inadequacy felt by their father and mother was internalized by Ellen who, like her parents, compensated with impressive scholastic achievement. Through Ellen Cindy became a convenient target for the parents' unconsciously sanctioned scapegoating. Accepting her role in this destructive, crazy-making charade, Cindy obliged with irrational outbursts while her sister sat back with righteous disdain.

Cindy was desperate in her desire for Ellen to be happy for her, which, of course, would show that she cared. Over and over, with ever renewed hope she would share happy news with Ellen only to have those hopes dashed. The experience and pleasure of a good grade or an exciting field trip was predictably spoiled for Cindy. Ellen's spoiling methods didn't vary. She either corrected Cindy in some way or belittled her. I could visibly see Cindy wilt when this happened.

■ CONCEPTUALIZATION

As a therapist, I find it both appalling and fascinating to see the writings I've studied come alive before my eyes. In *Envy and Gratitude* (1975) Melanie Klein describes the etiology of envious rage and the hostile effort to spoil another's pleasure ("If I can't have it, you can't either"). Although Ellen appeared to be the more favored of the two sisters, her deprivation and hostility were quite evident. Eric Berne so masterfully detailed the neurotic repetition of destructive interactions in *Games People Play* (1964). Here was

Cindy so anxious to be loved and, not ready to deal with the reality of her family members' inability to love, setting herself up again and again to be hurt as in Berne's "Kick Me" game.

My assessment of Cindy evolved as I began to put the puzzle pieces of the family dynamics together. Using a psychodynamic and systems orientation, I decided that Cindy's depression and anxiety were the result of several interwoven circumstances and factors.

The development of Cindy's insecurity and mistrust certainly had its origin during her first three years when she experienced the instability of her parents' marriage and divorce. Feeling abandoned by her father and dependent on an emotionally dependent mother, Cindy had no one strong to rely on or identify with. Thus, she was left with an unresolved attachment to her father and much identity confusion. Perceiving her mother's neediness and anxiety, Cindy learned to suppress any genuine expression of feelings. Burdened with tremendous hostility and feelings of hopelessness, Cindy became increasingly moody and irritable. The reinforcing cycle of Kate's anxiety and Cindy's irritability gave rise to Cindy's temper tantrums and somatic complaints.

But there was more to the picture. As my detective work continued, it became apparent that Cindy was chosen as the family scapegoat, the target of projected inadequacy. All children feel a realistic sense of inadequacy, but it dissipates as they learn and grow. However, children who grow to adulthood without a sure sense of having felt valued and accepted feel a more emotionally scarring sense of defect or inadequacy. For both Kate and Don, who could never measure up to their parents' standards, this was their emotional legacy. And they used Cindy to help them maintain their own psychic equilibrium. Thus, I saw Cindy in a double bind where performance and intellectual achievement were valued but she was neurotically needed by the family system to be the inadequate one. Guided by the unconsciously communicated needs of her parents, Ellen identified with her father and used her intellect to continually one-up Cindy, joining in her parents' collusion.

Kate's complicity was manifested in her inability to deal with Ellen's abuse of Cindy, who was left feeling unprotected, unworthy and, of course, inadequate. I'm sure Cindy also felt quite motherless.

Finally, in her relationship with her father, Cindy was a victim of his generalized lack of regard for women. This, in turn, affected her sense of value as a female and caused her to be mistrustful and fearful of boys and men.

I am sometimes frustrated with the focus on diagnosing. There are always more layers to a problem than an objective diagnosis can describe. Cindy was a diagnostic enigma. The events of her first few years supported a diagnosis of Separation Anxiety. Her avoidance of school, fear of the dark, somatic complaints, and anxiety before visits to her father would have easily justified this diagnosis. However, the symbiotic system that exacerbated her distress pointed more to Generalized Anxiety and Dysthymia. Cindy's avoidance of school and her poor performance there related less to separation anxiety than to the anxiety associated with her unconscious acceptance of the role of the inadequate member of the family who was doomed to ongoing disapproval. The demanding school environment represented the antithesis of anything that Cindy might experience as gratifying. Her inner conflict and psychic pain must have been excruciating.

My initial goal for Cindy was to provide a therapeutic relationship where she could learn to trust me. Once this was established, I hoped she would feel safe enough to begin expressing feelings appropriately so that we could work on building her self-esteem. Resolving her oedipal conflict, eliminating her scapegoat role, and reducing her identity confusion were equally important goals. Finally, interested in planting the seeds for future independence, I wanted her to learn how to nurture herself.

To facilitate a trusting relationship I was acutely sensitive to Cindy's negative transference reactions which set off a need to control. After a lengthy period of testing and resistance she learned that she could request how she wanted the session to be. Sometimes she would choose what she wanted to talk about or she might ask me to pick the topic or activity. Taking a walk was one of Cindy's favorite choices. I learned that whatever I did or said had to allow Cindy much latitude. She would rarely answer a direct question.

■ PROCESS

One of my goals for both Kate and Ellen was to help them resolve their own feelings of inadequacy so that the scapegoating would dissipate. I worked with all three individually and saw them conjointly as well. Cindy's father was unwilling to participate although I sent him carefully worded reports. Because he was very much a part of their life, I felt it important that he be aware of his daughters' problems and progress.

Cindy never really had a presenting problem. She adeptly accomplished her own objective by getting the school counselor to make the arrangements for her to see her mother's therapist. At that time she only made passing comments about the true problems she faced, but I am convinced that she was shrewd enough to know that she had to have reasons to be referred.

Cindy came into therapy with a fundamental dilemma: longing for a relationship but distrustful of intimacy. Any secret objective I may have hoped to accomplish was sniffed out with a great gift of practiced intuition learned in her dealings with her manipulative mother. Cindy had to feel in control of the session and yet would experience much conflict, as she also wanted desperately to please me. When stumped, she would either be silent or talk nonstop in an effort to distance herself from the conflict. Although Cindy was keenly alert to any agenda that wasn't her own, she didn't feel free to assert what she wanted or needed.

Cindy had very negative reactions to questioning. To begin with, her mother was a very intellectual type of person, much impressed with academic jargon. She was also an inexperienced psychiatrist. Poor Cindy had endured every half-baked counseling technique in the book! As a consequence, she hated psychological questions and would relentlessly foil my attempts to focus sessions. In the four years I worked with Cindy, she never let me be a therapist!

Cindy experienced her mother's most intense questioning when she felt the most needy and most longed for her understanding. It was her neediness that fueled Kate's anxiety which, in turn, led to the insistent "therapizing" and questioning that left Cindy feeling profoundly isolated, controlled, and hostile. The problem was particularly spotlighted when Cindy suffered a headache. All Kate could see was her own needy and emotionally draining mother. If only she could have made her mother feel better, she wouldn't have to feel so anxious. Years of accumulated resentment and frustration were directed at Cindy as Kate impatiently attended to her. With this background Cindy experienced unexpected relief when I was able to communicate understanding. Often, however, my efforts to understand, whether by questions or just gentle reflecting, caused her to recoil as she feared the familiar threat of her mother's intrusive anxiety. The paradox was continually with us. While seeking control, she wanted me to show leadership. While desiring a connection, she pulled away.

A session that was to be a turning point in our relationship began in typical fashion. I could see that Cindy was troubled and anxious but was clearly trying to distract both of us. She walked around my office looking at the photos, books, and bric-a-brac and asking an endless stream of questions. I let her go on for awhile to see where her comments might lead. None of her questions related to any particular topic or to each other. Nor did it matter how I answered. She continued this evasive behavior and, I believe, could have continued it for the duration of therapy!

I had tried all kinds of approaches. Today, I decided to be direct as I might be with an adult. Even though I had tried this before with Cindy and was met with either silence, a change of subject, or obedient answers to please me, I tried again.

LG: Cindy, I really don't want to do this anymore. Can you put into words what's bothering you? (Cindy does not respond.) Do I scare you?

Cindy: Where is your cat?

LG: I know you're avoiding my questions. Are you mad at me for some reason, or did I hurt your feelings?

Cindy: I feel fine.

LG: I think that you don't like questions. They must be very troubling to you.

Cindy: (Cindy starts to cry but quickly controls her tears and responds angrily.) There's nothing wrong!

LG: I can tell that you're not happy about something and you do have a right to tell someone.

Cindy: (after a long silence) What do you mean "a right"?

LG: That it's OK for you to say what you need to say, that you are allowed to talk about anything that is important to you.

Cindy: What if I don't have anything important to talk about?

LG: You can tell me that, too. Did you feel you *had* to have something important to talk about?

Cindy: I thought that's what I was supposed to do.

LG: Well, I'm sure glad you told me that. I'm sorry if I gave you that impression. If you don't have anything important to talk about, you can tell me what else you might like to do. That's called having rights.

Cindy: Can I tell you about my teacher?

With that simple question, I finally felt that the ground was fertile for trust to grow. The change in Cindy was visible as she experimented with the new freedom I had offered. If she didn't have to take care of me and worry about pleasing me, what were the possibilities? I truly looked forward to seeing them unfold for Cindy.

Therapy took another significant turn during a session when Cindy was particularly quiet and fidgety. After a few minutes I felt her silent plea to try again to connect with her. Our relationship had become more relaxed as she came to discover that the only agenda I had was to be her friend and that I didn't want to control her. On a deeper level, however, her inner wounds were a festering secret needing very gentle surgery. I felt she was ready for an exploratory probe.

LG: I think there's a little girl inside of you who sometimes feels afraid and unhappy, and I was wondering what she wants and how we might give her what she wants. (Cindy stopped fidgeting, took a breath and sat up just a little. She kept her head down.) I also think, for us to help her, she needs a name.

Cindy: (after a long pause) Belinda.

LG: What a lovely name. I would enjoy getting to know her. (I was always stretching to avoid questions.)

Cindy: Why?

LG: Because I enjoy getting to know little girls.

Cindy: Even if they're bad?

LG: I don't believe any little girl is bad. If Belinda feels she's bad, we really need to help her. That's a very unhappy way to feel.

Cindy: Belinda thinks she's bad.

LG: I wonder where she got that idea.

Cindy: She's a pest. She gets in bad moods.

LG: Oh, I know what you mean. Well, that doesn't bother me. I'm sure she has a good reason for her bad moods. Everybody has bad moods.

Cindy: My mother doesn't like bad moods.

LG: Yes, I know. She has difficulty with them. Maybe that's how Belinda has gotten the idea that she's a pest.

Cindy: Maybe. (I believe this was the first time Cindy was open to considering her mother's problems as being related to her own.)

LG: Until your mother learns more about bad moods I think it's only fair that you and I try to understand Belinda's bad moods. Would you be willing to help me with that?

Cindy: OK.

Offering an alliance with Cindy along with some distance from her feelings gave her the safety she needed. From that time forward we often talked about Belinda—her moods, feelings, wishes, and frustrations. It was very touching to see this youngster learning to nurture the grieving little girl inside. Belinda had much to grieve about, and as long as they were Belinda's problems, Cindy was able to talk about them. Over time she was able to refer to her own feelings but easily shifted the focus back to Belinda to help her deal with more threatening emotions. Moving back and forth from the intensity of significant issues to the lightweight chitchat of clothes and hairstyles, we began to paint the mural of Cindy's real-life experience so that, together, we could face it.

Cindy so longed for her father's approval. She literally was a Cinderella character during visits with him as she took on the role of maid and was on the outside looking in while her father and Ellen enjoyed an exclusive, intellectual camaraderie. After one of these visits Cindy described a typical oedipal-type wish dream in which her mother had died and Cindy was going to live with her father. While Cindy felt the yearning to live with her father and "take care of him," Belinda felt anger toward him. With much patience, Cindy, Belinda, and I began to sort out this contradiction.

School was another source of much sorrow for Cindy. She said Belinda was dumb and that was all there was to it. When I told her that things can happen to people to make them feel dumb even though they really aren't, I got her attention. We began looking for clues to discover what had happened to make Belinda feel dumb.

The process of Cindy's therapy was uneven and disheartening as well as joyful and hopeful. Some days it was boring and so seemingly meaningless that I felt guilty taking my fee. But somehow we covered the important diversity of subject matter that makes up a child's life and creates that healing bond between child and adult. She described friendships, losses, and popularity. She asked about menstruation and her mother's birth control pills. We wrote very expressive letters not intended for mailing. We played chess and looked at old photos. I made a little Belinda doll out of yarn.

Cindy learned to say no to her father. We celebrated when she graduated to a higher-level reading book. Sometimes we referred to our sessions as "heavy." She learned to say no to me.

Nearing the end of therapy, Cindy very proudly announced that Belinda was no longer her little girl. When I asked why that was, she said, "Because she grew up!"

■ OUTCOME

Learning her rights and joining me in understanding and nurturing her "little girl," Cindy began to express herself more openly and to explore the possibilities of our relationship. She discovered that I wasn't trying to control her and that she could exercise many prerogatives. She became more aware of her family relationships, realizing how she felt controlled and abused. She learned how to express these concerns to her family. Instead of remaining acquiescent and hostile she began to have a voice in her family and fought back when she felt depreciated or manipulated by her sister and mother.

As Cindy's ability to express herself grew, so did her sense of personal power and worth. Joint sessions with her sister Ellen and her mother gave Cindy the opportunity to risk dealing with her feeling of being abused. She came to understand how her school problems were related to her unhappiness at home, and over a two year span her schoolwork steadily improved until she was finally and firmly at grade level. She gained sufficient confidence to protest to her father when he tried to belittle her or manipulate her into serving him. When we first had ventured into looking at her conflicts regarding her father, Cindy found strength in seeing herself as Belinda's protector. Out of her understanding of her father and his "little boy" inside, she was able to see his inadequacies and his limited ability to be the ideal daddy she wished for. Cindy's mother became more able to assume her correct role as mother. Up to that point she had colluded in the family scapegoating by allowing Ellen and her ex-husband to belittle Cindy. Kate would no longer condone that behavior. Kate had achieved insight into her own dependency needs and how she, also, had used Cindy.

As Cindy's self-esteem continued to grow, she chose more emotionally healthy friends. She literally beamed when she told me that she thought she was smart, and we enjoyed many sessions talking about her countless future possibilities, which included college and modeling. To me these two goals were particularly meaningful because Cindy had come into therapy feeling stupid and unattractive.

Terminating therapy was somewhat of a celebration for Cindy. Gradually, she had begun to trust Kate as she experienced her mother's growing strength. Separating from me was timely. We laughed about her expressed relief and appreciation that I showed no need for her to maintain ties with me.

DISCUSSION

Cindy was a patient who tested the limits of my humanity and relatedness rather than my knowledge of therapeutic theory and technique. I was reminded of a well-worn admonition among social workers: "Be where your client is." My major challenge with Cindy was to be where she was and then allow the relationship to evolve from there at whatever pace necessary. Having so much advance information by virtue of being Kate's therapist had an unfortunate effect. I wanted to help Cindy more quickly than she was ready to trust and accept help. Thus, I am certain Cindy experienced me as another controlling adult with specific expectations. She resisted me just as she resisted her mother who impatiently needed to "fix" Cindy to calm her own anxiety. The one piece of information Kate had not been able to give me would have been the most beneficial. But she herself was unaware at that time that she drove Cindy crazy with her psychiatric questioning and analyzing.

Believe me, I began figuring it out quickly! I didn't have to be a wizard to realize that even the most innocuous question was greeted with blunt resistance. Because Cindy had been so aggressive and seemingly motivated in maneuvering her referral to me, I wrongly assumed she would be more accessible. Even during the first session, after some initial pleasantries, I began to suspect there was more to this young lady than met the eye.

I had had some excellent training in various therapy modes for children. I tried them all! From Virginia Axline's client-centered play therapy to the Jungian sand tray to art therapy—I went the gamut. Cindy would have no part of it. She knew I would gain information that she was not ready to give or to face.

Mostly, though, I put my goals for Cindy on the back burner and just became her friend. With the luxury of not having an insurance company or agency policy undermining the evolution of a relationship with time-limiting restrictions, we began to proceed at a comfortable, realistic pace.

Although Cindy grew tremendously, she would need continued support and, perhaps later on, further help in resolving her fear of males. Her understanding regarding her relationship with her father proved invaluable to her, but she was only able to grow as far as her mother had. Kate struggled to come to terms with her own mistrust of her father and men. She had finally achieved independence in relationship to men and was able to date and have comfortable male friendships. Kate's terror of intimacy, however, remained an obstacle even though she felt more hopeful.

We had come full circle. I remembered the school counselor quoting Cindy's request for "girl talk." Loosely translated, this was an expression of her fear of men. Both Cindy and her mother had reached a stopping point in therapy but with the understanding and my recommendation that at the appropriate time in the future they each work with a male therapist to help them experience a corrective relationship.

Clark E. Moustakas, in *Psychotherapy with Children: The Living Relationship*, describes the therapist's relationship with the child as "the essential dimension, perhaps the only significant reality" in the process of growth. The teachings of both Dr. Moustakas and my personal mentor, Ida W. Klinger, had particular relevance in my work with Cindy as they share a similar belief that the quality of the relationship is the "curative" factor over and above any therapeutic technique or psychological theory. Cindy craved relatedness. I will be forever grateful to her for insisting that I relate to her and to be where she was.

REFERENCES

Axline, V. M. (1947). *Play therapy*. Boston: Houghton Mifflin.

Berne, E. (1964). *Games people play*. New York: Random House.

Klein, M. (1975). *Envy and gratitude*. New York: Dell.

Moustakas, C. E. (1959). *Psychotherapy with children: The living relationship*. New York: Ballantine.

Biographical Statement

Lauren J. Golden, MSW, a licensed, clinical social worker in California, has been in private practice since 1975. She received specialized training in play therapy and spent several years in psychiatric training with Ida Watkins Klinger and J. H. Klinger, who studied under Freud in Vienna. In addition to conducting her clinical practice, she is a field liaison with the San Diego State University School of Social Work. Lauren and her husband Ken, who is also a clinical social worker, conduct training seminars for mental health professionals.

The Worried Boy

Sharon Gordetsky and Joan J. Zilbach

An extraordinary aspect of the case of 9-year-old Cyrus is his creativity in expressing his feelings and needs. Unfortunately, Cyrus's creativity is in shut-down mode as a result of his potent psychological defenses. However, as therapy unfolds, Cyrus demonstrates an ironic sense of humor as he learns to master his impulses. He is a fierce competitor, expressing aggression through competitive games.

Cyrus's therapist makes a relatively straightforward diagnosis: Separation Anxiety Disorder (DSM-III-R 309.21). Some separation anxiety is normal in young children, but Cyrus's excessive fears threaten to sabotage his healthy development. Further, dangerous unresolved aggression makes it all the more difficult for Cyrus to freely explore and express his emotions. He is a prime candidate for child-centered play therapy. Drs. Gordetsky and Zilbach bring impressive knowledge of child development to their understanding of this child. It is obvious that Dr. Gordetsky, the therapist (and presenter of the case), is touched by this special therapeutic relationship.

Cyrus, age 9, was referred to my private practice by his parents after his mother, Rachel, had discussed her concern about his anxiety attacks with her own individual therapist. When asked how she would account for her son's anxiety, Rachel related two incidents. When he was 4 years old, Cyrus was locked in a bathroom at nursery school by another child. After this incident he showed signs of nervousness. When he was 5, he got lost at a museum. Following the museum episode, Cyrus would cry even when Rachel took her hands off the grocery cart he sat in while she was shopping. Cyrus had no difficulty going to school, doing well in his classes, or making friends. Rachel and Frank (Cyrus's father) described him as being creative and sensitive.

The presenting problem was that Cyrus would become anxious when one parent was away from home, especially his mother. At these times, he would express fear that the absent parent would not return. Several times a week, Cyrus would wake up in the middle of the night and check to make sure that his parents were still there.

Rachel was a professional artist. As an adolescent she became pregnant by her boyfriend and was sent away to have the baby and release him for adoption. Feeling like an outcast, she returned home to graduate high school and immediately left to attend art school in another state. Many years later she married Frank, an established scientist 25 years her senior, who was previously married and had four grown children.

Cyrus was born after a three-hour delivery. Almost immediately, Rachel experienced a severe postpartum depression: "I cried for a month and felt a sense of doom." She nursed Cyrus for four months but found nursing to be excruciatingly painful, "like knives through my breasts." Her pediatrician recommended that she stop nursing.

After Cyrus's birth his mother's PMS (premenstrual syndrome) worsened. She experienced severe mood swings around her menstrual cycle and had difficulty getting out of bed in the mornings. By the time Cyrus was two years old, Rachel felt angry with the whole world. Rachel told of an episode when she lost control, threw Cyrus in a crib, and called a hot line for help. It was then that she sought treatment for herself and began her search for the child she gave up for adoption.

Rachel said that her relationship with Cyrus was volatile. When she and Cyrus fought, she said, "I really scare him, and then we both cry." They would then promise to stop fighting.

Cyrus's developmental history was unremarkable. He had no history of significant medical problems or illnesses. However, Rachel reported that he had had a fear of noises since infancy. She would have to leave the kitchen to tear a piece of tinfoil or he would become upset. School fire drills terrified him.

At 20 months of age Cyrus was clingy, according to Rachel. He would cry when she left the room. Cyrus happily attended nursery school with the notable exception of the time when an "aggressive" little girl in his class locked him in the bathroom and told him she was never going to let him out. It took the teacher a long time to calm him down.

Diagnostic Interviews

Cyrus was an adorable, stocky, freckle-faced 9-year-old. At the diagnostic interview he came across as friendly and verbally precocious. He separated easily from his mother and entered my office. He said that he knew that he was there because he worried too much. When I asked him what he was worried about, he said, "My mother has PMS."

He took no initiative to explore the play materials. I asked him to draw a picture of a person and then a family. For a reputedly creative youngster, the drawings he produced were rigidly constricted. The figures had large cerebral heads in profile. When I asked Cyrus to make three wishes, he said that he wished that (a) his mother wouldn't get so mad, (b) he could stop worrying, and (c) his mother and father would live longer.

Cyrus told me that one time his mother forgot to tell him that she was leaving the house and that he would be left with his father. "My father got very angry with me because I cried," he said. Cyrus said that his mother was in a group that helps mothers find children they gave away for adoption and that his mother had found her son living in New Hampshire. He said, "I've met him; he's very nice." Cyrus complained that he saw Rachel only "about every two weeks"! In fact, Cyrus and his mother spent a great deal of time together, but his strong sense of rejection overshadowed this fact.

Cyrus asked, "Am I the most serious case you've seen?" I assured him that I took his worries and all of his feelings very seriously. I told him that next time I would ask him to take some tests that would help me figure out how to help with his problems.

At the next session I administered the Rotter Incomplete Sentences (elementary school form) and the Thematic Apperception Test (TAT). Even the relatively simple task of completing sentences prompted distancing and distracting maneuvers. For example, Cyrus meticulously went over the page to check punctuation before beginning to respond. There were 28 partial sentences to complete, and Cyrus responded to 8 of them around his worries. For example: "It's scary . . . when Mom leaves," "My father doesn't . . . like it when I worry," and "Nobody knows that . . . I worry so much."

The TAT projective material provided a deeper look at Cyrus's worries. Responding to the card that depicts a latency-aged boy sitting and staring at a violin on a table, Cyrus made up a story in which his aggressive feelings immediately lead to abandonment and death:

> This boy was feeling kind of low. He had violin practice. He was staring at the violin and something happened. It smashed into 50 pieces! His music teacher had leukemia and couldn't come. Then he woke up and found out it was a dream.

Cyrus put the card away, and I asked him to tell me more about how the boy in the picture felt. "Very low. He realized that his teacher had been dead for five years and actually out of business for five years."

Throughout testing, Cyrus ignored specific stimulus material. He would leave the pictured females completely out of his story. He would ask what the numbers and letters on the backs of the cards meant.

In another story Cyrus told of a young doctor coming to the rescue of an older doctor. The older doctor was in a terrible hospital. The younger doctor "couldn't let him die and told the men who were operating on him the correct procedure."

■ CONCEPTUALIZATION

Following these diagnostic interviews, I met with Cyrus's parents. They were surprised that the creativity they saw in their son had not been apparent to me. I viewed Cyrus as a youngster desperately trying to keep himself and others under control; if things got out of control, someone might get lost or killed.

Both parents thought that Cyrus would benefit from psychotherapy and agreed to participate in parent and family meetings. We would begin with weekly sessions and evaluate his progress together in occasional parent sessions.

Cyrus met the *DSM-III-R* criteria for Separation Anxiety Disorder. I viewed Cyrus's constant worrying as the overt expression of unconscious conflicts about aggression. In addition, I thought that his symptoms represented unresolved ambivalence toward both parents, especially his mother. Rachel had been unable to consistently provide a "holding" environment for Cyrus's aggression as a toddler. The child inevitably strikes out at his or her environment, and the parent's responsibility is to confine and control this aggressiveness without aggressing back.

I theorized that the interruption of Cyrus's developmental progress had begun in the second year of life. In therapy I intended to provide a safe, contained space in which Cyrus could redo earlier developmental steps. In therapy Cyrus could express negative feelings that he was too frightened to directly express to his parents. I believed these feelings needed to be expressed primarily in action rather than words, as a toddler or preschooler would be most likely to do. Therefore Cyrus's treatment, as it unfolded, was a treatment of action and affect played out through games, mutual fantasy play, and verbal humor. Despite Cyrus's highly developed intellect and verbal skills, talk about problems and feelings was minimal.

■ PROCESS

Cyrus eagerly agreed to come to weekly sessions. At the start of our early sessions, Cyrus asked, "What do you want to do today?" He was guarded. I helped him develop a worry rating scale with 1 indicating "not worried at all" and 10 being equivalent to "terrified." He could use his fingers or write notes to show me how worried he was.

After several sessions, Cyrus initiated a competitive style of play. Shoot the Moon was a favorite game. It required patience and skill to maneuver a small metal ball down narrow metal bars with the goal of loading them into slots worth different points. Cyrus delighted in beating me. However, toward the end of the hour when he was assured of a big win for the day, he would encourage me to take shots over and insist on taking a turn for me. It wasn't until months later that he commented on this tendency to help me, "I feel sorry for you." I should point out that I never intentionally lost to Cyrus. He beat me fair and square!

As Cyrus felt safer, he dared to express undisguised aggression toward the steel ball. He invented tortures for the ball when it did not obey his command and land in the 1,000-point slot. Cyrus wrote newspaper-type headlines announcing these dreadful tortures to the public, including being shot with a pistol, having its head chopped off by a guillotine, and being electrocuted. He built elaborate torture devices which were employed dozens of times over the next weeks.

Observing that this aggression towards a steel ball was tolerated, Cyrus felt ready to take me on more directly, and the next several months saw games of office basketball and volleyball. We moved the tables and chairs out of the playroom. Then Cyrus would remove his shoes and prepare for battle! He would cheat by changing the rules for his benefit. He made up leagues and mascots. He planned the schedule for weeks ahead announcing which of his teams would play mine. Aggression would emerge as "spike balls" and "bombers." At these times, I would remind him of our safety rule. I would then structure the play to allow his aggression to emerge, but simultaneously to contain it so it would not threaten either of us. For example, if I scored a point in volleyball, Cyrus would be furious and throw a "bomb" very near my head. I instructed him that when he got so mad that he needed to throw a bomber he should announce, "Bomber." I would then step aside so he could throw the ball at the wall behind me as hard as he wanted. At times he would tease, saying "Bomber" softly and throwing swiftly. I learned to be vigilant!

Five months into treatment, Cyrus introduced "The Game of Murder." He drew a large picture of a person and then threw balls at it. After each throw, he would draw in the wound he had inflicted. Soon the person was in a head-to-toe cast with blood dripping from its nose and mouth. Then he redrew the injured person as a "hippie" while he and I were designated as "rednecks." His hippie was complete with bandanna and peace symbol. Since hippies were about two decades before his time, I asked Cyrus where he had learned about them. "My mother was a hippie when she lived in Tennessee with the rednecks."

It was almost time to end the session and Cyrus was looking at the ceiling. He wanted to know if the room was soundproofed. I assured him that it was. After the session, Cyrus told his mother about the hippie game with me present. She looked at the picture and immediately associated: "That's just like me when I lived in Tennessee." Cyrus and his mother left discussing where they would go for dinner.

As summer approached, Rachel told me that Cyrus's separation problems were less severe and that Cyrus had asked to spend a month at an overnight camp. He had a friend who was going to this camp, but as things turned out, Cyrus attended a different camp session. In our family meeting he denied any anxiety about being away from home. Rachel discussed strategies for preparing the whole family for the separation, while Frank seemed unconcerned.

Following the summer vacation, Cyrus telephoned to confirm that his appointment would be on the same day and time as before. I scheduled a meeting with Cyrus's parents to hear their impressions.

Rachel described what dropping Cyrus off at camp was like for her: "I cried my eyes out, but he didn't notice because it was raining." She admitted that the separation was difficult for her and that she cried the first three nights he was gone. However, she and Frank thought that Cyrus had adjusted well to camp. He had signed his first three letters from camp as follows: "Your anguished son," "Your homesick but happy son," and "Love, Cyrus."

In general, Rachel and Frank were happy with Cyrus's progress. However, Rachel was frustrated with endless "morning battles" before Cyrus left for school. Frank said that Cyrus behaved better when Rachel wasn't at home.

In his first several sessions back Cyrus resumed the competitive games. He wanted to know if I had practiced volleyball while he was gone. I asked if he was worried that I might have improved enough to beat him! One time he brought a tape recorder and played the Rolling Stones' song "Mixed Emotions" repeatedly. We sang the song as we played ball against one another, and during the game we talked about having mixed emotions toward people you loved.

Cyrus told me that he had been homesick at camp and cried the first two nights. He felt embarrassed because no one else cried. He told me about his letters home and laughed as he imagined his parents reactions at reading them. On his "worry scale" camp got an 8 to start but was a 2 by the end.

I asked Cyrus what he thought could be done about the "morning battles" with his mother. He said he wanted her to wake him up at 5:30 but was resistant to my idea for a family meeting.

He then wanted to play Monopoly. His playful, provocative style was very much in evidence. He wanted to pinch both of my cheeks when I collected money from the bank. Worse, he deliberately gave me less than the amount of money due me. Of course, I didn't let him get away with it! I also commented on how much he loved to tease. "My favorite thing," he responded.

Typically, toward the end of sessions where he had won, he gave me extra points or extra turns. "I feel sorry for you and don't want you to feel bad." I assured him, truthfully, that it did not make me feel either bad or mad.

At the next session we celebrated Cyrus's 10th birthday. During our party he told me he had had a bad dream. He dreamt that he had been at camp for months and wasn't going to be sent home. He remembered crying and yelling but to no avail. Prior to this dream, Rachel told me that she had had a screaming battle with Cyrus. She felt that this fight could have caused the dream. This was an eerie repeat of interactions that had occurred when Cyrus was two years old that had also frightened them both. And just as Cyrus became more clingy after the early incident, he once again experienced separation anxiety which was manifested in his dream. The fact that his anxiety expressed itself in a dream was important because in the past his anxiety symptoms had tended to generalize to day-to-day situations.

Since Cyrus had been symptom free for about six months, his father suggested he take a break from therapy. I thought an abrupt break would not be best and we agreed to wind down over several more sessions.

Cyrus had been in treatment over a 14-month period, including interruptions. "I still like it but two times ago I didn't want to come. I wanted to get ready for the cooking show with my friend." I had known about this; it was the first time that Cyrus had told his mother he didn't want to go to therapy.

I asked Cyrus why he didn't just tell me that he didn't want to come that day. He said, "I didn't want you to think I didn't like you." I assured him that I knew he could like me and still want to do other things on Thursdays.

During the following session, Cyrus drew a picture of his "prototype of the electrodome."

Cyrus: This invention could save the world.
SG: How would it do that?
Cyrus: It would harness all the potentially lethal energy into its storage tank where it couldn't hurt anyone.

Using detailed drawings, he demonstrated how the invention could work. For perhaps the first time in his treatment, Cyrus spent the entire session spontaneously talking. The topic switched to the subject of AIDS. He drew a picture of a doctor who bore a striking resemblance to his father.

Cyrus: Even if he cuts himself with a needle he would only have a 10 percent chance of getting AIDS so he'd be safe. Teenagers get AIDS because they never believe anything bad will happen, but in about 50 years there will be a cure and you could get a shot like a flu shot. Maybe they'll even have some herbal medicine for it.

Cyrus changed the topic again, this time to John Lennon, one of his heroes.

Cyrus: I'm wearing black because of something that happened 10 years ago. John Lennon was weird when he was a kid (Cyrus considers himself somewhat weird). But the Beatles were the greatest. What's your favorite Beatles song?

During this session, despite wearing black clothes (to mourn the termination of therapy?), Cyrus communicated his feelings of hopefulness. Bad, destructive things can be contained. Lethal energy and AIDS can over time be controlled. John Lennon, "a really weird kid" created something great that lives on in people's memories.

Cyrus arrived for his next session with food.

Cyrus: We'll have a little party each week and then a big party the last time. How long have I been coming here?
SG: How long does it feel like?
Cyrus: It feels like six weeks.
SG: It's been about one and a half years but you didn't come for a long time over the summer.
Cyrus: My parents saved a lot of money this summer.
SG: Do you think they were happy about saving money on your therapy?
Cyrus: Well, they didn't mind paying. They were worried I'd have a nervous breakdown. Only kidding. Did I tell you I might take trombone lessons on Thursday afternoons?
SG: So now I'll know what you're doing when you aren't here.
Cyrus: Yes, you will.

During our last few sessions we played almost all of our favorite games, the "oldies but goodies." He freely expressed his competitiveness and anger and openly expressed ambivalence towards me and towards termination. "I don't like you," he said when I retrieved the bonus-point pick-up stick, "but I also do like you."

At the end of this interview Cyrus turned off the lights and closed the playroom door leaving me alone in the dark. When I opened the door, he was standing there grinning.

SG: You want to go upstairs ahead of me?
Cyrus: I can go by myself.

Before the next to last session I met with Rachel. She reported they had had a fight the previous morning and she took away his baseball cards for a week. He left for school furious at her, but he returned later that day, apologized, and said he understood how she felt. Rachel said that Cyrus expressed feelings more freely, and she reported feeling less guilty, herself, when she set limits.

Cyrus talked about his anger with his mother's "stupid headaches and PMS." He had talked to me about his mother's PMS during our very first session together while we were exploring his worries. However, this almost final session was so different! He talked about his anger at his mother directly with much less conflict and anxiety attached.

He played basketball aggressively and flung the ball over my head. I reminded him of the safety rules. He then became more contained and controlled his aim.

Cyrus: I guess I'm ready to move on. So do we have a final diagnosis, "no longer psychotic"?
SG: Did you feel crazy when you first came?
Cyrus: Only joking.

Cyrus came to his last session with his father and a basket of flowers. He brought drinks and chips, and I had bought him a huge chocolate chip cookie. "I'll eat a little bit every Thursday," he said, thereby assuring both of us he would still be taking in my nurturing.

He made several attempts to draw a picture of us. "Can it just be any therapist?" he finally asked. I left the room to get him a color marker he wanted. When I returned, he hid behind the door and waited for me to find him. As we sat eating together, I told him that his parents gave me permission to write about our meetings together for a book.

Cyrus: Just say I'm the nicest, most compassionate little boy, and I never set fire to the office building.

I explained a little about the book and that I would call him by another name to respect his privacy. He told me it was fine to use his real name. I said I wouldn't do that, but he could choose the name I would use. He then created an elaborate system of rolling dice and matching the number thrown with a corresponding letter of the alphabet. This intellectualization of an emotional issue took a very long time.

Cyrus: We have no time left, do we?
SG: I know it's going to be hard for me to say good-bye today.
Cyrus: You'll write my story in the book?
SG: How do you feel about having the story of our therapy in a book?
Cyrus: Fine. (Then he sang a line from a Beatles song) "I'm in love with you and I feel fine." (long pause) Oh, just call me Cyrus.

■ OUTCOME

The treatment was marked by a progression of increasingly direct expressions of aggression in play, from office basketball to "tortures." After about a year of treatment and summer separation, Cyrus was able to verbalize aggressive feelings and their complications. Cyrus actively used both dramatic play and the transference relationship with his therapist to directly express and then resolve an earlier developmental impasse that at times left him overwhelmed by anxiety.

His mother and father were cooperative in their part of their son's treatment. Rachel, in particular, possibly because of her own treatment, recognized aspects of Cyrus's difficulties in her own intrapsychic problems. By the end of treatment Cyrus's expression of aggression had become developmentally appropriate. His worries and separation anxiety were diminished.

DISCUSSION

The case of Cyrus illustrates the use of play in the treatment of separation anxiety. Cyrus came to treatment when he was 9 years old, but his separation difficulties had a long history. Though he had progressed in many developmental areas, by the time he was 4 to 5 years old, his worrying when apart from his mother was significant. Referral took place when the mother's own therapist encouraged her to pay attention to her son's difficulties. Diagnostic interviews and psychological testing indicated that Cyrus had difficulty expressing aggression, which was confirmed by the parents. The termination session revealed his sadness at leaving treatment and yet his readiness to move on.

About one year after Cyrus's last session, I happened to meet Cyrus and his mother at a shopping mall. "Oh, Dr. Gordetsky, I've been thinking about you," he said. "I think I have to come back." Rachel confirmed that, unlike the summer following treatment, this summer Cyrus had had a difficult time at overnight camp and she had intended to call me.

I wondered if Cyrus would need to reenter treatment. Although an intellectually gifted and verbal youngster, Cyrus communicated his problems and arrived at their solutions through his play material and transferential relationship to me. Cyrus had not been able to directly use words to express formerly unconscious material. Freud taught that unconscious conflicts need to become consciously expressed and accepted before a cure is possible. Without verbalization there could be little insight. How specifically does this need to happen with young children? I wasn't sure, but as with many of our theoretical questions, our clients help us find the answers.

This time, with the benefit of another year to grow and develop, Cyrus was able to *talk* about his problems. He told me, "When I came last time we played, now we need to talk." Cyrus's earlier treatment, in which his aggressive feelings and actions were both accepted and contained, provided a solid foundation. Now that he was 11 and at a different stage of cognitive development, he was ready and eager to continue.

Cyrus said that he only needed to come back "for a little while." He thought that perhaps we had ended too abruptly the first time. We reminisced about his former treatment. We talked about how he loved to "really beat me" in our games. I tried an interpretation: although he enjoyed beating me, I thought that it also made him worry, and suggested that he felt worried when he expressed aggressive feelings toward me and other people he counted on. He then volunteered that he worried about being mad at his parents because if something happened to them it would be his fault, "just like I killed them myself." I was impressed with this clear elucidation of a hidden fear! Now Cyrus could openly talk about disturbing thoughts and feelings without overwhelming guilt and anxiety. This had not been possible earlier in treatment.

This case served to remind me that psychotherapy, like life itself, has its own developmental course. I feel grateful to have played a positive role in the unfolding of a child's personality.

Biographical Statements

Sharon Gordetsky, PhD, is the chief psychologist at Parents' and Children's Services in Boston, Massachusetts. She is a consultant in family therapy with the Department of Child Psychiatry of the Cambridge Hospital at Harvard Medical School. She has written several articles and book chapters on the integration of child and family treatment.

Joan J. Zilbach, MD, is a child psychiatrist and family therapist in private practice. She serves on the clinical psychology faculty of the Fielding Institute in Santa Barbara, California. Dr. Zilbach is the author of two books on family therapy with children, Young Children in Family Therapy *(1986) and* Children in Family Therapy: Treatment and Training *(1989).*

6

Mandy: Out in the World

Barbara Herlihy

*Barbara Herlihy presents the case of an 11-year-old girl who comes to her already burdened with a severe diagnosis: Schizoid Personality Disorder (*DSM-III-R *301.20). Herlihy uses a child-centered approach in individual counseling with occasional family interventions. The medium of music becomes an important way of connecting with this unusual child.*

Herlihy deals with two basic therapeutic issues. First, Mandy is emotionally withdrawn from family and peers and seems to have always been so. She seems quite content when alone in her bedroom playing the flute. Does the therapist have a right to tamper with Mandy's chosen approach to life? If we can agree that it is appropriate to modify pernicious behavior in another person, does it follow that it is desirable, or possible, to change a personality *trait? Second, when Herlihy's work with Mandy bogs down, her impulse is to refer Mandy out to someone, anyone, with more experience in treating personality disorders! Do such impulses emanate from a keen awareness of professional ethics or from a hidden source of resistance within the therapist? It is fascinating to "overhear" a seasoned therapist wrestle with these issues.*

When 11-year old Mandy walked into my office, I was struck by her pale, almost ghostly appearance. She was tall for her age and very thin. Her long, straight hair was ash blonde, and her face was so pale that I wondered whether she was allergic to the sun. At her mother's prompting, she piped a reedy and barely audible hello. My first impression, one that would mislead me for some time, was of a child who was not only wraithlike but very fragile.

My contact with Mandy was preceded by a phone call from Donna Alvarez, her middle school counselor. Donna occasionally referred to me, in my private practice, a child whose counseling needs went beyond what she could provide in the school setting. She told me that Mandy's mother, Ann, had requested a referral. She had provided a list of referral sources, and Ann had selected me and asked Donna to call me and share background information. Donna described Mandy as a loner who had no close friends and who always ate lunch alone in a corner of the school cafeteria. She had no record of discipline problems at school and had been absent on several occasions for extended periods of time. Her grades were above average: mostly B's, a few C's, and an occasional A. She had performed well enough on the Cognitive Abilities Tests (CogAT) to be eligible for placement in the gifted and talented program but had lacked the needed grades and teacher recommendation.

Based on the information from Donna, I had formed a tentative picture of Mandy as extremely shy and possibly school phobic. During my initial meeting with Mandy and Ann, I gained no information from Mandy that would add to the picture. Despite my best efforts to include Mandy, Ann did all the talking.

Ann's concern about Mandy was deep and abiding. As she described their home life, it became apparent that Mandy was a loner within the family as well as at school. Mandy's typical after-school routine was to close herself in her bedroom and do her homework until dinnertime, emerging only for the meal with the family. After dinner, she would retreat to her room to finish her studying, practice her flute, or listen to music until she went to sleep. She rarely went outdoors, and never invited a friend to the house. Occasionally, she would receive a phone call from a schoolmate asking for help with a homework assignment. Mandy willingly gave the help but didn't linger on the phone to socialize. Ann's frustration was evident when she stated, "Mandy doesn't communicate with us. I don't know how she feels, what she thinks. I can't even get her to tell me what she'd like for dinner!"

As Ann continued to relate various anecdotes, a pattern was emerging. She would have extended periods of being patient, encouraging, and protective of Mandy. Then she would snap in frustration, yell at her daughter, and seek outside help. I imagined that Mandy knew the pattern well and didn't trust the patient and supportive mother, and that each of Ann's outbursts was driving her further into herself. It seemed like Ann needed to detach from her daughter; this was an easy prescription to give but a very difficult one to follow for a parent who was so intensely concerned.

Ann's further comments revealed that the problem was long-standing. Over the past three years, she had taken Mandy to one psychologist and two psychiatrists. Mandy had been hospitalized twice. At this point, I requested and received permission to contact the previous therapists. Then, speaking directly to Mandy in Ann's presence, I repeated my explanation of confidentiality. I asked Ann to give me some time to get to know Mandy. Ann gave her daughter a hug, to which Mandy responded as limply as a rag doll, and left the room.

Mandy and I had about 15 minutes together in the remainder of the first session. She spent most of the time with her head bowed. School was "OK," she "didn't know" how she felt about coming to see me, and my open-ended questions were met with a shrug. I was not surprised by her reluctance to communicate with me. I simply attempted to provide a safe climate and to convey both verbally and through my body language a calm acceptance. Since her mother crowded her with intensity, she needed to feel my respect for her personal space. She said "OK" to my invitation to return the next week, although I believed she was bowing to her mother's wishes rather than expressing her own desires.

■ CONCEPTUALIZATION

As I gathered information from the other helping professionals who had worked with Mandy, it became apparent that her condition was difficult to diagnose. The psychologist, whom Mandy had seen when she was eight, had tentatively made a diagnosis of Avoidant Disorder of Childhood with an accompanying anxiety disorder, based on her shrinking from contact with people, her inarticulate and often mute response in the therapeutic setting, and reported impaired social functioning in peer relationships. He also noted that therapy had not been deemed effective.

The psychiatrist whom Mandy had seen two years ago sent his records. He had recommended hospitalization and had continued as her primary therapist during her inpatient treatment. He had diagnosed Mandy as schizophrenic. She had told him that she "saw another face in the mirror," and he had also noted her flat affect, impaired interpersonal functioning, social withdrawal, and emotional detachment. He had prescribed an antipsychotic medication but noted that "its only effect was to make her sleepy." Mandy had been minimally compliant with the 21-day treatment program.

The other psychiatrist, who had worked with Mandy 10 months ago, called me when he received my request for information. He related that he had initially made a diagnosis of Schizotypal Personality Disorder but later changed it to Schizoid Personality Disorder. He, too, had recommended hospitalization, and Mandy's parents had complied. Again, as with the previous psychiatrist, he had found no medication to have a positive effect. Her hospital stay had been brief. When Mandy's parents came to visit, she cried and begged to be taken home. Her parents withdrew her from the hospital after six days.

I was left with a variety of possible diagnoses, all sharing similar characteristics. The diagnostic criteria for Schizoid Personality Disorder seemed to come closest to describing Mandy. According to the *DSM-III-R,* a person with this disorder neither desires nor enjoys close relationships, including being part of a family, almost always chooses solitary activities, rarely if ever appears to experience strong emotions, has no close friends or confidants, and displays constricted affect.

Although this diagnosis seemed possibly appropriate, I felt reluctant to consider it. I didn't *want* it to be correct. My experience with personality disorders, aside from my clinical training, was rather limited. The vast majority of my clients in private practice, adults and children alike, came to me with a keen interest in self-exploration and the capability of translating awareness into behavioral change. Therefore, improvements were often rewarding for them and me. My impression of personality-disordered individuals is that their world view and subsequent behavioral patterns have become so entrenched, they may not desire change. They often enter counseling only because their loved ones are troubled by their symptoms. This seemed to be the case with Mandy; her mother sought help for her, and Mandy seemed to acquiesce in a resigned way.

The prognosis for this disorder is quite limiting. The *DSM-III-R* states that males are usually incapable of dating and rarely marry, while females may passively accept courtship and marry. Social relations remain severely constricted, while occupational functioning may be impaired except in work conditions of social isolation. This seemed such a bleak outlook for an 11-year-old child. Nonetheless, it was my initial, tentative diagnosis.

PROCESS

As we began our second session, Mandy sat with her head bowed, her hands in her lap. She responded with silence, a shrug, or "I don't know" to my attempts to make contact. We were sliding into a question-and-answer session that was going nowhere. I became increasingly aware of an anxious knot in my stomach. The knot reminded me of an interminable hour I had endured during my practicum experience at the master's level. At that time my client was a reluctant 9- or 10-year-old boy who refused to verbalize. I watched the tape spin around on the recorder and knew that my professor was not going to be impressed with a tape full of silence. I filled the tape with the sound of my voice, wondering if I was saying the right thing, thinking the hour would never end. I had gotten a terrible grade on that performance and didn't need to repeat it here and now.

Since talk therapy was proving unproductive, I changed strategies. Mandy seemed relieved to be offered some manipulatives. She would draw or use materials when given a specific suggestion, although she initiated nothing on her own. At the end of the hour, when we were both engaged in putting things away, I asked her again how she felt about coming to see me. When she responded with a shrug, I offered, "I'm trying to imagine how I would feel if I were 11 years old and my mother kept dragging me around to see counselors." As I expressed my feelings, Mandy stopped her tidying-up activities, and for the first time looked straight at me. I finished by saying, "So, I don't know whether I'd want to come back." After a pause, Mandy said, "I want to come back." I felt encouraged as she left. She had made one definitive statement, and it was a beginning.

As our third session progressed, my hopes began to fade. Once again, Mandy was compliant with suggestions as we sat together in the play area, but she just seemed to be going through the motions. I couldn't find a way to connect with her at any meaningful level. Several strategies, including art activities, a sand tray, various games, and companionable silence, were met with passive acquiescence.

At one point Mandy brushed back her long hair and I caught sight of her earrings. I commented on how pretty I thought they were, and how unusual. Then, since the thought occurred to me, I went on to tell her that my best friend had a daughter who was about to have her 13th birthday. I wanted to get her a small gift, and I knew her ears were pierced like Mandy's and that she also enjoyed wearing unusual earrings. Did Mandy have any advice that might help me with my shopping? To my surprise, she had a great deal to say. She described at length the styles that were popular with girls her age, what stores would have the best selection, and so forth. I was genuinely grateful for the help, told her so, and was rewarded with a shy smile. In that moment, we had contact with each other. We had connected, but the contact was not sustained. For the remainder of the session, Mandy reverted to passivity when I failed to initiate a direction. She seemed to be lost deep inside herself. I wasn't sure she was even aware of my presence.

With Mandy's agreement, our fourth session was a family session. My hope was to gain some insights by observing the family dynamics. Mandy's father, Brad, entered my office first and sat on the sofa. As Mandy followed and sat down next to him, he draped his arm behind her over the sofa, his fingers barely touching her shoulder. Ann and 15-year-old brother took individual chairs, while her baby sister, a toddler, made straight for the toys I had placed on the floor.

Ann dominated the conversation. Brad mostly listened, although he spoke clearly and assertively when addressed directly. Her brother Michael, an average student who was very involved in athletics, was eager to be heard. He was concerned about fairness issues within the family, such as whether he could drive the family car when he turned 16 and the division of household chores. As we explored such topics, I was able to suggest to Ann that perhaps she was exhausted from taking charge of so much within the family. It appeared that she was taking responsibility for all the decisions—dividing the chores, determining the allowances, enforcing the rules.

Not only did this seem to be a heavy burden for her, but it wasn't doing the others any good. If she continued to take responsibility for them, they wouldn't learn to take responsibility for themselves. She seemed grateful for the suggestion, and the session began to focus on strategies for shared decision-making in which Mandy, her brother, and her father could make some choices and be accountable for them.

As the session drew to a close, I thought it had been rather productive. If Ann could ease off on her intense efforts to "fix" Mandy and force her to join in with the family, perhaps Mandy would move into the space that was created. The unspoken dynamics of the family's interactions, however, interested me more than their words. The toddler told the family story at a nonverbal level. Throughout the session, when she needed help with something—putting her shoe back on, putting a toy together—she went to her mother. When she wanted attention, she came to her brother, her parents, or me. When she just wanted to be held, she went to Brad. In the entire hour she never approached Mandy.

Mandy and I had two more individual sessions, neither of which yielded any discernible progress. I began to question my competence and brought Mandy's case to my consultation group. Without giving away Mandy's identity, I described my client, the counseling process, and my frustrations. I wondered aloud whether I should consider referring Mandy to someone with more expertise. One of the group members asked me, "Who, besides Mandy, frustrates you?" "Her mother," I replied. "She goes through periods of being patient, protective, supportive and encouraging. Then when Mandy doesn't change, she throws up her hands and takes Mandy out to an expert to be fixed." I felt a rueful smile form on my face. "Aha," I said. "Let me own that. *I* have been patient, supportive, protective, and encouraging. Now that *I* see no change, I'm considering sending her off to an expert." I decided, for now, to persevere.

Ann, obviously upset, followed Mandy into my office at the beginning of the seventh session. "You two need to talk about Mandy's report card," she declared, waving it in her hand. Mandy had gotten an F for the marking period in language arts. It was the first time she had ever received a failing grade. Ann explained that the major grade for the marking period had been based on a speech that the students had to give in front of the class. Mandy had refused to do it. She had stayed home from school on the last three days when she might have been called on to give her speech.

After Ann left the room, I said, "I remember that my parents were upset, too, the first time I got an F. Do you want to talk about it?" Mandy shrugged. By now, I understood that a shrug meant the topic could be explored. When Mandy didn't want to pursue a subject, she would shut down with bowed head and frozen posture. Working with a set of drawings of faces (smiling, neutral, frowning, sad, and so on), Mandy conveyed that she believed she had made the right choice. While getting good grades was important to her, she could not and would not stand before the class, make a speech, and stand up there while it was critiqued. Mandy had made the choice and accepted the consequences, although it made her sad that her mother was angry.

I glanced at the report card her mother had placed in my hand, and noticed that Mandy had received an A+ in music. When I asked about that, Mandy smiled the broadest smile I had yet seen. She loved music and played the flute. When I asked if she would bring her flute next time and play for me, she smiled again.

Thus, it was in our eighth session that I found an entree into Mandy's emotional world. She arrived with her flute and immediately unpacked the instrument. At my invitation she began to play. As I listened, at first I was amazed at her technical proficiency. Then, I sat back and let the music affect me. Mandy had selected Pachelbel's Canon in D, a mournful, evocative piece. When she finished, there were tears brimming in my eyes. I said, "I felt so sad listening to that." Mandy looked mutely at me, and I saw that her eyes were glistening too. I added, "Sometimes I think music expresses feelings much better than words ever could." Mandy nodded in agreement. We had a focus for our session—sadness. And I had learned to communicate with Mandy by indirection.

As we worked with various materials, I discovered that it made her sad when her family worried about her. On the other hand, she didn't want to change to make them happy. When she drew a picture of her family as her parents would like it to be, she drew the five of them sitting on a sofa in front of a television. When she drew the family as she wanted it, she drew her mother in the kitchen, her father in front of the TV, her brother behind the wheel of a car, her baby sister asleep, and herself alone in her room playing the flute.

Our next two sessions followed the same format. Mandy played her flute, and we focused on the feelings the music had expressed. It seemed clear to me that we had developed a working relationship, within the limits of Mandy's expressiveness. I was tempted to kick myself, just a bit, for not making use of the flute sooner. The information about her love of music had been there from the beginning.

Despite these inroads, in Mandy's larger world nothing changed. I touched base with Donna Alvarez, her school counselor. Since I had begun working with Mandy, spring had come. Now Donna saw Mandy at lunchtime, eating her bag lunch alone on the grass outside the building. She reported that Mandy continued to go through her days essentially alone. At home Mandy continued to retreat into her room.

It was time for me to reflect on the goals of counseling. Whose goals were to be met? What Mandy's parents wanted was clear. They wanted her to join with the family and to have a "normal" social life with friends and activities. What did Mandy want? She had given me some clues. She now looked forward to our sessions and seemed to enjoy spending time with one person who would let her express herself in her own way. She wanted to please her parents. However, she didn't seem to want to make the kinds of changes that would accomplish that. Was she able to connect with others as a result of her disorder? Was she unable to but needed to learn some social skills? Or was she truly content to be as she was? What was in Mandy's best interests? It was time to get clarification from Mandy.

I was looking for an opportunity to raise the question, and I managed to create one in our next session. It began, as usual, with Mandy playing a selection on her flute. It was a piece I didn't recognize. When I asked about it, Mandy told me that the composer was someone whose music had been unappreciated while he was alive. I commented that it must have been hard for him, knowing the kind of music he wanted to create but also knowing that others didn't want to hear it. I suggested that, perhaps in some ways, that composer's situation was like her own. He, too, was out of synch with the way other people wanted him to be. She gave me a curious glance.

I went on to say, "Mandy, you are *of* this world—you've been born into it and you are alive. But I get the impression that you live very little *in* this world, among its people. You seem quite content to be by yourself. And that's OK, if it's what you want and it doesn't bother you to be alone a lot. What happens, though, is that it seems to bother other people. It causes problems for your teachers, who have to give you lower grades when you don't participate in group activities or speak in front of the class. Possibly, it bothers people who'd like to be your friend—when you don't reach out to them, they drift away. And it bothers your parents when you don't join with the family."

I paused to gather my thoughts, and was aware as I did so that Mandy was staring straight at me, her brow furrowed in concentration. Never had I seen her look so intense. I waited. Perhaps two minutes passed. Then, with a decisive nod of her head, Mandy said, "OK." She immediately got up, went to the drawing table and picked up a sketch she had started last week. She was drawing a jazz ensemble. The faces and figures of the musicians were roughly sketched, but their instruments were carefully and precisely drawn. She worked on it, silently and with great concentration, for the rest of the hour.

After Mandy left my office, I was left to ponder that brief period of intense concentration. I thought something had happened, but I wasn't sure what. Was I creating a "significant moment" out of nothing more than a furrowed brow, a nod, and a simple OK?

The answer began to emerge a week later, when Ann called to say she had to work late and needed to reschedule Mandy's session. She reported that Mandy had come out of her room for a couple of hours twice during the week and had watched TV with the family. She had even volunteered to go with her brother (who now had his driver's license) when he ran some errands on Saturday.

Since we were unable to reschedule the appointment, I didn't see Mandy until the following week. Mandy came in and played the flute, but this time she had an agenda of her own. She wanted to ask her music teacher for private tutoring after school and wasn't quite sure how to go about it. We strategized together about how she might ask the teacher.

One evening later in the week, Ann telephoned, saying, "Something has happened. I don't know what to do." She went on to relate that she had come home from a stressful day at work to find the dishes in the sink and the beds unmade. She had lost her temper and yelled at Mandy before she realized that it was Michael's turn this week to do the dishes and make the beds. "So, what happened then?" I asked. I was confused. Mandy's mother sounded as much elated as she did upset. She replied, "Mandy yelled back at me!" I could hardly believe my ears. It was hard to imagine Mandy standing up to her mother and yelling back. Yet, apparently that was exactly what had happened. Her mother and I were both aware that it was a real breakthrough in Mandy's expressiveness. Ann was concerned, though, that if things were not resolved between them Mandy might retreat back into her shell. After talking it over, she decided to allow a cooling-down period and then apologize to Mandy for yelling before she had her facts straight.

I asked Mandy about the incident the next time I saw her. I asked her how she felt about it. She shrugged and said, "OK," with her shy smile. She seemed to feel no need to pursue the topic. She hadn't yet approached her music teacher and wanted to rehearse it again. She had asked her parents about it. They were in favor of the tutoring and had offered to contact the music teacher for her. "How do you feel about that?" I asked. Mandy shook her head. I said, "This is something you want to do for yourself." She nodded in agreement.

Two weeks later, Mandy's parents asked if they could join us for a few minutes at the beginning of the session. Her mother had a piece of paper in her hand, and for a moment I feared that it was another report card. It turned out to be an application for a summer music camp. Mandy's music teacher had given the class a brochure describing this two-week residential camp in a neighboring state. Her parents were apprehensive about the idea; Mandy had never been away from her family overnight. As we discussed it, Mandy was quietly insistent that she wanted to go. Her parents finally agreed.

I saw Mandy only sporadically in late spring. She had arranged to have after-school tutoring with her music teacher which was scheduled during our usual appointment time. Summer arrived, and she was gone for two weeks to music camp. By the time she returned, I had gone on my vacation. When I returned, her family had left town to spend their annual month at Mandy's grandparents' beachfront cottage.

It was early August before I saw Mandy again. She didn't bring her flute. We spent much of our time catching up on how her summer had gone. She had enjoyed music camp and hoped to go again next year. Ann was teaching her to cook and they were spending time together in the kitchen. She was looking forward to school starting in the fall. Very hesitantly, she explained that she would have a busy year with after-school music tutoring. She was also taking piano lessons. When I suggested that maybe she was trying to tell me that she might not have time to come to see me, she replied that her parents thought she should keep coming. I told Mandy that the choice was hers. She didn't have to come back, and she didn't have to stay away. My door would always be open to her if she decided she wanted to talk with me occasionally. She smiled and said she thought she was finished. When her parents came to pick her up, I called them in and we discussed the decision to terminate counseling. They accepted it, although with some reluctance. As they got up to leave, Mandy shyly presented me with a cassette tape, saying that she had recorded a selection she had played for me on her flute.

As they left the office, I realized that Mandy had intended the tape to be her farewell present to me. I inserted it into my tape recorder. The sound of Mandy's flute filled the room. She had recorded Beethoven's "Ode to Joy."

■ OUTCOME

Throughout the fall semester, I stayed in touch with Mandy periodically by telephone. School was going well, she said, and everything was "OK" with her family. She was still very involved with her music. When I half-jokingly suggested that she might be a famous flutist some day, she discounted the notion. She didn't want to perform for others. She was looking forward to high school. She was planning to take lots of math and science because she wanted to become a pharmacist.

With Mandy's permission I touched base with Donna Alvarez who reported that she had recently seen Mandy in the school cafeteria sitting at a table with a group of girls. Donna said that, in the brief time she had observed, she had not seen Mandy contribute anything to the conversation but it was obvious to her that Mandy was included. When she saw Mandy in the halls, Mandy was sometimes but not always alone. She had checked on Mandy's progress with her teachers. Two of them told Donna that they occasionally had the students do small-group activities and Mandy had participated in her quiet way.

■ DISCUSSION

Although I haven't seen Mandy in more than a year, I sometimes reflect on my work with her. Her case reminds me that while diagnosis can illuminate it can also limit our thinking. On the one hand, conceptualizing Mandy's condition as a personality disorder helped me to understand that she may not have been uncomfortable with her isolation even though it concerned those who cared about her. On the other hand, this diagnosis may have led me to expect less of Mandy than she was capable of accomplishing. Did her diagnostic history and my own attempts to categorize her condition lead me to assume she wasn't able to express her feelings directly? Should I have referred her? Might she have become more communicative had she worked with a therapist more skilled in personality disorders?

I also find myself asking, as is often the case with child clients, whose interests were served in counseling? Certainly her parents were pleased with the results. Mandy now behaves more like a "normal" child and is more a part of the family. Her teachers are pleased. She is a bit more integrated with her peers and is a more willing participant in classroom activities. But what of Mandy herself? She didn't request counseling to begin with and was sometimes a reluctant participant in the process. Unlike other clients, I doubt that she will ever articulate to me new self-understandings and positive feelings about herself. Mandy remains a mystery. Were her changes only in her external behavior and only to get others "off her back"? Or does she feel better about herself and her ability to be out in the world?

When I try to imagine Mandy as an adult, I tend to picture her living alone and working as a pharmacist. She is content to deal with prescriptions rather than with people. She continues to enjoy her music and remains in contact with her family. I find it hard to imagine her married with children of her own.

I could be completely wrong. Adolescence, a time of tremendous changes, is just ahead for Mandy. In any event, the answers will come from Mandy herself. If she changed just to please her parents, she will probably revert to her social isolation when she becomes an independent adult. If she likes it out in the world, she will stay there.

Biographical Statement

Barbara Herlihy, PhD, is associate professor of counselor education at the University of Houston at Clear Lake. She is a licensed professional counselor in private practice and a former school counselor. She has authored two books, The Ethical Standards Casebook *(1990) and* Dual Relationships in Counseling *(1992).*

Billy, the Teddy Bear Boy

Terry Kottman

Four-year-old Billy expanded a negative incident associated with a teddy bear into a full-blown phobia of all stuffed animals, dogs, and cats, and even bubble gum (Simple Phobia, DSM-III-R *300.29). Billy's mother was accustomed to previewing birthday parties and school activities in order to prevent any chance sighting of the feared objects. Terry Kottman uses an Adlerian approach with Billy. She sees Billy for play therapy and regularly consults with his mother. From this perspective, she frames Billy's phobic behavior as a bid for power.*

We meet Kottman as a young and enthusiastic therapist. With the benefit of hindsight and years of experience, Kottman sees how she was intimidated by adult family members who were unwilling to examine their responsibility in maintaining Billy's dysfunctional behavior.

I was a doctoral intern at a university-sponsored community outreach clinic when I first heard about Billy Bass. When his mother, Darlene, called the clinic, I happened to be on telephone duty. She had a list of questions she wanted to ask about the qualifications of the student counselors who worked at the clinic. When she discovered that I was the intern with the most extensive experience working with children, she began to ask me a series of questions about my background, beliefs, and knowledge of phobias. Darlene wanted to make sure that the counselor she hired to work with her 4-year-old son had the "proper experience" because she had "diagnosed the problem as a teddy bear phobia." When she found that I had not worked with any young children who were presenting phobic reactions, she told me that she wanted to search for a more experienced counselor because this was "going to be a very difficult case to cure." This was fine with me. By that time I was thoroughly intimidated by Darlene's barrage of questions and her seemingly impossible-to-cure child.

Time passed. I worked with many interesting children and their families during my internship. I devoted much of my energy to developing a method of working with children that combined the techniques and concepts of individual psychology with the practice of Adlerian play therapy. Every once in a while, when I was on telephone duty, I would remember the "Teddy Bear Boy," but I did not give him a great deal of thought.

About six months after our initial conversation, Darlene called the clinic and asked to speak to me. She informed me that she had not yet found a counselor practicing in the area who could meet her "stringent criteria of experience with phobic children." She seemed almost panicked. She said that Billy's phobia had reached crisis proportions: "He has gotten worse and we can barely leave the house any longer." I asked her to be more specific, and the story of Billy, the Teddy Bear Boy, emerged.

Darlene reported that until recently Billy had been the "perfect child." She said, "He still never makes a mess. He always does what he is supposed to do. He is not like other children—he is very responsible, respectful, and mature. He just has this one quirk that started last year and we can't seem to get him to stop." Darlene traced the "quirk" to an incident that happened when Billy was three years old. He was playing with a small teddy bear when he fell down and cut his knee. He screamed and cried, and his mother had reacted promptly with comfort and a bandage. His mother, wanting to help the situation, scolded the teddy bear for tripping him. Thereafter, Billy cried every time he saw the teddy bear. Eventually, his mother threw it out, but he started reacting with screaming and crying to every teddy bear he encountered.

Though he was originally just afraid of teddy bears, the list of things that frightened Billy grew and grew. By the time his mother called the second time, Billy was fearful of all stuffed animals, dogs, cats, talking dolls, and assorted other objects. When he saw any of these objects, either in stores, at preschool, or at other children's homes, he started screaming, crying, and shaking and would not be consoled. The only way to stop his reaction was to remove the object or to take him far enough away from the object that he could no longer see it. As time passed, Billy's list of frightening things grew even more, and he had attacks of uncontrolled hysteria more and more frequently. The situation progressed to the point that the family's activities revolved around the need to avoid teddy bears, stuffed animals, dogs, cats, talking dolls, and all of the other things that Billy feared. Darlene had started previewing stores to make sure that they would avoid the aisles that displayed teddy bears or any of the other feared objects. She also previewed birthday parties, other children's houses, and various preschool activities to make sure that Billy would not encounter any of the objects that triggered his attacks. Darlene wanted me to begin working with him immediately.

Before I met with Billy, I asked his mother to come in for a couple of sessions by herself. During these two sessions with Darlene, I began to gather some background information. I also talked to her about the fact that I would need her help in order to help Billy and the family. Although she really wanted me to "just fix Billy," I told her that I would need to see her for parent consultation every week. I would divide the 50-minute session between a 30-minute play therapy session with Billy and a 20-minute parent consultation with his mother. She was reluctant to agree to this, but I explained that she knew much more about Billy than I did and that I would need the valuable information only she could supply. I also pointed out that she could have a much greater impact on him than I could since she lived with him 24 hours a day, 7 days a week and I would only be seeing him once a week for less than an hour. When I told her that I might need to see her husband and her mother-in-law, she said she would talk to them about this, but that she could not make a commitment for either of them.

Billy was an only child. Darlene had been close to 40 years old when he was born, and she told me during our first conversation, "Billy's birth was a miracle. We thought we couldn't have a child, but there he was—a beautiful baby." She reported that she had quit her job as a "very successful" accountant when Billy was born. She had decided to stay home to "be a good mother," and she was devoting all of her considerable energy to Billy's upbringing. Both of her parents were dead. An only child, she reported that she had never had much contact with her extended family. When I asked her about her activities and contacts outside the family—old friends from her job and the like—she looked confused. She seemed to be surprised that I would ask such a question and replied, "I really don't have time to pursue other interests. Taking Billy to preschool and his lessons and cleaning the house take up all my time."

The Bass family lived next door to Billy's widowed paternal grandmother, Estelle, who had retired when Billy was born to "help out." Darlene stated that her mother-in-law came over to "check on things" several times a day and had "very strong views" on how children should be raised. It seemed to me that Billy's mother felt that Estelle was more of a hindrance than a help. However, even when pressed, she would never confirm this hypothesis. Darlene seemed to have ambivalent feelings toward Estelle. She reported that her mother-in-law was rather critical of the way she handled discipline and had repeatedly expressed the belief that if she would just "whip him every time he carried on like that" Billy would stop reacting to the feared objects. However, Estelle was also the most consistent contact Darlene had with another adult. Darlene seemed to value the chance to talk about Billy and his problems with someone, even if it was someone who disapproved of the way she was handling the situation.

Darlene reported that Billy's father, Steve, worked as a troubleshooter for an international banking consortium and traveled during the week on business, coming home only on the weekends. During these weekends, Steve spent much of his time writing reports for the bank on his week's activities and drilling Billy on readiness skills—the alphabet, counting, and color names. Darlene reported that they had already enrolled Billy in a kindergarten class in a very prestigious private school for the following year and wanted him to "be ready to succeed in school."

When I asked Darlene about her relationship with her husband, she said that it was "fine." However, when I probed for details about how they managed to maintain communication and a level of marital intimacy, with her husband being gone so frequently, she seemed to get anxious and changed the subject. She would tell me very little concrete about their relationship. Asked specific questions about activities they enjoyed together during the weekends, she said they "spent quality time with Billy." She could not think of a single activity that they had done as a couple without Billy since Billy was born, even though Estelle always wanted to babysit.

CONCEPTUALIZATION

According to Adlerian theory, there are four goals of misbehavior: attention, power, revenge, and inadequacy (Dreikurs & Soltz, 1964). From an Adlerian perspective, the goal of Billy's behavior was power. He used his fears to assert some element of control over others and his environment. There are two types of power-oriented behaviors: active and passive. While Billy's method of gaining power had started passively, with his desire to avoid one particular teddy bear, his behavior had quickly escalated to a more active mode. By having hysterics whenever he encountered one of the feared objects, he discovered that he could control the decisions and behaviors of others.

In my experience, children who believe that they must be in control either have little power in their interactions with others—especially parents and other family members—or have an overwhelming amount of power in their interactions with others. Billy had very little control over many aspects of his own existence. Either his mother or his grandmother still chose all of his clothes, dressed him, coaxed him to eat, cut his food for him, told him when he had to go to the bathroom, brushed his teeth, and generally kept him from making any move toward independence or individuation. At the same time, through his fears and the accommodations that people made for them, Billy controlled the actions of his family, most of the activities in his preschool, and many of the interactions in his small circle of friends.

Steve never attended a counseling session. Darlene reported that he was not available because of the demands of his job. Whenever I asked Billy's mother to bring Estelle to a session, she agreed to ask her, but she always arrived at the session with an excuse for her mother-in-law's continued lack of involvement in the counseling process. Consequently, I worked exclusively with Billy and his mother. I had five primary goals with Billy and his family: (a) to help Billy learn to appropriately express his feelings, (b) to help Billy realize that he did not have to use his fears to control situations and other people, (c) to help Billy learn new ways of interacting with others based on something other than the need for power, (d) to help Billy's parents and his grandmother let go of some of their control of Billy and let him have some appropriate power in his own life, and (e) to help Billy's mother cultivate some other interests in life besides Billy and reestablish an identity other than "Billy's mother." I assumed that once Billy realized that he could have control of many of the usual things 4-year-olds can appropriately control, he would not feel the need to use his fears to assert power over other people and situations.

■ PROCESS

Before my first session with Billy, I met twice with his mother. The initial session was a time for me to hear her story, assess the background and family information, and to begin building a trusting relationship with her. She had done a remarkably successful job of intimidating me when I talked to her on the telephone. Therefore, I decided that I needed to see her several times without Billy to establish some therapeutic leverage, so that she would not be totally in control of the course of therapy. One of the main things I had to decide during these initial parent consultations was the direction I wanted to take with Billy. My first response to Darlene's diagnosis of a phobic reaction was to consider abandoning play therapy and trying systematic desensitization or some other behavioral technique that has proven successful with phobias. However, as I talked with her, I realized that I did not agree with her assessment of the problem. An Adlerian interpretation of Billy's behavior as a bid for power made much more sense to me and fit with my theoretical orientation. I decided that Adlerian play therapy combined with parent consultation was a viable intervention strategy for the problem presented by Billy and his family.

Adlerian play therapy combines the concepts and strategies of individual psychology with the techniques of play therapy (Kottman & Warlick, 1989; Kottman & Warlick, 1990). It is a four-phase process that first involves building an egalitarian, therapeutic, accepting partnership with the child.

After establishing this trusting relationship with the child, the play therapist begins to explore the child's life-style. In Adlerian terms, life-style is a person's general orientation to life—the basic convictions about self, others, and the world and the behaviors based on these views that a person uses to gain significance and a sense of belonging (Manaster & Corsini, 1982). After developing an understanding of the child's life-style, the play therapist uses various therapeutic strategies to help the child gain insight into that life-style. The final phase of counseling involves a process of reorientation and reeducation. The play therapist helps the child learn new and more appropriate ways of gaining significance and interacting with others. In Adlerian play therapy, the counselor works with the child, using play media as a means of communication, and with the parent(s), using parent consultation and education, individual counseling, marriage counseling techniques, and any other available method of changing the child's social system.

I am not sure what I expected, but I was surprised at Billy's appearance when I finally met him. Billy was a slight child with great big brown eyes, an imposing frown, and an exquisite vocabulary. He talked and moved like a wizened 80-year-old man. I introduced myself and greeted him by name. I knelt down so that I could be at his eye level and remarked on the cartoon characters on the T-shirt he was wearing. I did this in order to disarm him because I was afraid that he would add me to his hit list of feared objects.

He did not seem timid at all. He frowned even more deeply at my frivolity when I asked him about his T-shirt and began to interrogate me about whether his mother had told me that he was afraid of teddy bears, stuffed animals, talking dolls, bubble gum (this was a new one since I'd last talked to his mother), and numerous other objects. I answered that she had told me and suggested that it was time to go to the playroom. We began walking down the hall toward the playroom with Billy continuing his non-stop questions and comments: "So, she told you that I'm afraid of teddy bears. Good. It's important for people to know that. I generally don't go to new places until she makes sure they don't have anything I'm afraid of there. You don't have any teddy bears or stuffed animals in this playroom, do you? You can't chew gum when I'm here. Neither can that lady at the front desk. Is she your secretary? Does she know I'm afraid of teddy bears and stuffed animals? If you don't remember to keep all of the things I am afraid of away from me, I will scream and yell and you will all be very sorry that you didn't do what I said." I reflected his feelings by saying, "You want me to know that you're afraid of all those things." I also began making guesses about the underlying message in his statements and his purpose in telling me all of this by saying, "You really want to make sure that I do exactly what you tell me to do. It sounds like it's important to you to be the boss."

When we got to the playroom, Billy did not look around the room to make sure that none of the feared objects were there. He stood very close to me and reiterated the entire list of things he feared. He also listed all of the situations that he found intolerable and what happened when he encountered any of them and told how it was his mother's job to "make sure I don't even see any of those things." He did this without breaking eye contact or taking a breath. I had decided to take all of the toys on the original list out of the playroom, and none of the toys that were left in the playroom were on the expanded list of forbidden objects.

Billy continued this pattern for the first four or five sessions. He was extremely serious, never smiling or showing any kind of emotion. He had the most intense eye contact I have ever experienced—he always looked me straight in the eye. He talked nonstop about all the terribly frightening things in the world and how "everyone" must help him avoid them. He described these terrifying things and his reactions to them in a flat voice, with no facial expression or body language indicating any kind of emotion. Although I usually ask children why their parents have brought them to play therapy, there was no reason to ask Billy. He repeatedly told me that the play therapy was "supposed to make me stop being afraid of things, but I don't think you can."

I used these sessions to begin to build a relationship with Billy. Most of my responses to him consisted of reflection of his feelings, restatement of the content of his comments, and guesses about the purposes of his behavior, which was almost exclusively designed to control my behavior and the behavior of other people in his life. As Billy gradually began to play with some of the toys in the playroom, he repeatedly demonstrated his dependence on adults by asking me to do things for him, such as turning on the water or opening the doctor kit. I made it a practice never to do anything for Billy that he could do himself, making encouraging statements that I believed he could do these things for himself. When he attempted to do things independently, I encouraged his efforts, regardless of the outcome of his attempts.

Billy very seldom did anything even close to breaking the playroom rules. When he did, usually by pointing the dart gun at me, I stated the limit in a nonjudgmental way, reflected his purpose (which usually seemed to be testing my reactions to his behavior), and encouraged him to generate his own alternative behavior by saying, "I bet you can think of something else you can shoot that would not hurt anything." Occasionally, he would complain that he could not think of anything else that he could do, but when I chose not to argue with him or try to coax him, he always thought of something else to do that was acceptable to both of us.

At the end of most of my play sessions, I tell the child that it is time for us to clean up the room together. I let the child decide who is going to pick up the various toys. I say something like, "What do you want me to pick up? What are you going to pick up?" This reinforces the need for action and builds a cooperative venture. Because Billy was so overcontrolled, by his family and by himself, I decided not to use this strategy with him. I wanted him to have the experience of being allowed to make a mess if he wanted to do so without having to worry about an adult's reaction. I wanted him to experience the fun and freedom of being a child without feeling overly responsible.

As time went on and Billy began to feel more comfortable with our relationship and the playroom, he gradually expanded his repertoire of behaviors. He still did not play with many of the imaginative toys, preferring to play games and role-play structured situations. During this stage I continued to work on building a trusting relationship, but I also began to explore Billy's life-style. In order to do this, I asked him some questions about his interactions with his parents and his grandmother, trying to understand Billy's perceptions of his family atmosphere, his family constellation, and this method of gaining significance in the family. I also observed his interactions with his mother and his play in our sessions. Billy seemed to recognize that the family had an atmosphere of high standards, in which it was assumed that every member of the family would be responsible and achievement oriented. He said, "I have to do well in school or my parents will be very disappointed in me." This statement seemed to produce a great deal of anxiety in him, and he stood very close to me for the entire session after he related this to me. Whenever he was playing, Billy watched me very closely, as if to determine how I was reacting to his behavior. He often looked at me as if to say, "Do I measure up to *your* standards?" I interpreted this to him by making comments such as, "Seems like you're wondering if it was OK with me that you did that. It's important to you that people like what you do. In here, it's up to you to decide what to do."

Billy told me many times that he was "the only son and the only grandson. That is a very important job." He seemed to feel very pressured by this position in his family. His behavior during the first two phases of counseling seemed to be almost a parody of the typical ways many only children act (Pepper, 1979). He was definitely the center of attention with me. On days when I talked to other children in the waiting room, he got angry and frustrated and talked in a loud voice, demanding my exclusive attention. He never talked about other people during our sessions, even the members of his family, except in the context of their interactions with him. He seemed to believe that he did not need to extend any effort himself to have things turn out the way he wanted them. He just needed to let the adults in his life know his wishes and he would get what he wanted. Whenever those wishes were not granted, he got angry and refused to cooperate. Our relationship was different from all of his other relationships. For the first time in his life, an adult was not controlling him or being controlled by him. He frequently seemed confused by my insistence that in this relationship we would share both the attention and the power.

Based on my analysis of his family atmosphere, birth-order position, and the goals of his behavior, I began to formulate some hypotheses that summarized Billy's life-style: "I am not very powerful, but I need to be powerful to be significant and safe. Other people are frequently more powerful than I am, and they will try to control me. The world is a scary place in which you are either powerful or powerless. The best way to cope with the world is to make sure that I am in control—of myself and of other people."

Because I had now developed an understanding of the purposes of Billy's behavior and his life style, I moved to the insight phase of therapy. My aim during this phase of the play therapy was to share that understanding in such a way that Billy could gain insight into his life-style and begin to make some changes in his behavior. I began to disclose what I thought were the purposes of his behavior, using tentative hypotheses to share my inferences about his need for power. I made guesses such as, "You really like to tell me what to do" or "You always want to make sure you're in charge and that things happen the way you want them to happen." He usually affirmed these guesses, sometimes verbally and sometimes nonverbally through a recognition reflex, such as a nod or a smile. However, when he did not affirm them, I chose not to pursue these statements. By not insisting that he confirm my guesses, I was letting him absorb the information I was trying to communicate at his own pace and in his own way.

During this stage of the therapy, Billy seldom mentioned his fears. He was a rather harsh and authoritarian teacher, and I was a compliant child. I used what I call the "whisper technique" of role-playing when we did this. This strategy gives the child control of the direction of the role-play. I use a stage whisper voice, which is obviously different from my normal voice and from my playtime character voice, to ask the child to direct what I do and say. For example, Billy would say, "I'm the teacher and you're the student. You will write on the board." I would whisper, "What should I say?" or "What should I do?" and then comply with his instructions. During these interactions, I would interpret his purpose in the form of tentative hypotheses, by making guesses like, "I bet you feel safer when you're in charge, telling me what to do."

We also played lotto and bingo at his request. He made up the rules for the games that we played. If he started to lose, he would change the rules to insure his victory. Although sometimes I agreed to his changes and other ways of controlling our interaction, at other times I would tell him that I was choosing not to do that particular activity his way and suggest that we negotiate what we were going to do. Occasionally, I began to suggest that he did not always have to be in control, that sometimes it might feel good to not have to be in charge. He usually ignored these comments, and I did not insist that he acknowledge them or agree with me. I simply wanted to plant the idea that he did not always have to be in control. I continued to encourage his own strengths and ability to make decisions.

I frequently use storytelling and metaphors with children to help them became aware of their life-styles and to show them that there are different ways of gaining significance than their usual method of interacting with others (Kottman & Stiles, 1990). I asked Billy to tell me a story, so I could use mutual storytelling to suggest some alterative behaviors. He flatly refused to do this and insisted that he did not know how to tell stories. In a later session, I tried to tell Billy a story about a lion who got very tired of making everyone in the jungle do what he wanted by roaring every time they did something he did not like. Billy told me that it was a dumb story. He said, "That lion should have just roared louder and everyone would have done what he wanted." After this interchange, I gave up on trying abstract, metaphoric approaches with Billy and stuck to concrete interpretations and statements.

I began to point out similarities between his behavior in the playroom and his behavior in other settings. I made guesses about the fact that he probably liked to be in charge of situations at home with his mother and his grandmother and at school with his teachers and classmates. I also used tentative hypotheses to suggest that he was using his fears to control other people. His interactions with me were gradually changing, such that he was not always having to demonstrate that he was more powerful than I was. I wanted to help him generalize this behavior to his relationships with others, so I started making statements about the fact that he did not always have to be in charge with other people and he could still be safe and significant.

During these first three phases of the play therapy, I was also working with Darlene. We were focusing on her need to control Billy's behaviors, on her relationship with her mother-in-law, on reestablishing her personal identity as someone other than simply Billy's mother, and on her parenting skills. I tried to help her explore the underlying factors involved in her need to control Billy, but she balked every time I asked about her family of origin or made a guess about her own personal past having anything to do with her present life or her parenting. She would not acknowledge that her personal issues were a significant factor in her relationship with her child, her husband, or her mother-in-law. Since I was having difficulty getting past this resistance, I decided to settle for her agreement that her continued tight control over Billy's behavior would have to stop if she wanted Billy to stop having hysterics every time he saw a teddy bear.

Although Darlene also refused to discuss the dynamics of her relationship with her mother-in-law, she did acknowledge that she felt hurt by Estelle's continued criticism and interference. She decided that she needed to establish some firmer boundaries to protect herself from this pain and to give Billy some relief from the constant pressure of having "two women telling him what to do." Darlene reported that she had requested that her mother-in-law not come over to the house unannounced and not do things for Billy that he could do for himself. She even gave Estelle a list of things that Billy could do for himself, such as choosing his own clothes, brushing his teeth, and deciding what to wear.

I wanted to help Darlene cultivate some other interests outside of Billy and reestablish her identity as a person in her own right. This would reinforce her willingness to let go of some of her control of Billy and his behavior. However, she was less receptive to these changes than she had been to the changes in her relationship with her mother-in-law. She seemed reluctant to try to contact former colleagues and old friends, saying that "they were busy and probably wouldn't be interested in my life now." I made some tentative guesses about how she was using Billy's fears and the curtailment of her own activities and interactions to protect herself from being vulnerable in relationships. These met with total denial and hostility. She said that she "just didn't believe that good mothers have interests other than their children." She did agree to joining a "Mother's Day Out" at their church, and she also volunteered to do some of the accounting for the church. Initially, this was as far as she would go in letting go of her solitary role as Billy's mother.

I introduced Darlene to several Adlerian parenting strategies to replace the alternately autocratic and submissive styles of discipline on which she had previously relied. I taught her how to determine whether a problem was hers or Billy's and how not to let Billy's problems become her responsibility. I explained the four goals of behavior, the feelings that are the basis of the goals, and how to recognize them. We discussed the ways Billy was using his fears to gain power and to feel significant and safe. I suggested that she begin to encourage Billy for his efforts rather than praise him for finished products. I pointed out that she could use the same strategy she had suggested to her mother-in-law and not do things for Billy that he could do for himself. I taught her how to present Billy with choices, rather than always trying to control his behavior. I suggested that she use logical and natural consequences rather than punishment and taught her how to set limits and negotiate consequences (Dreikurs & Soltz, 1964).

As Billy's need for power became less frantic, we moved into the reorientation-reeducation phase of the play therapy. Whenever Billy wanted to take control of the interaction or tried to control my behavior, I suggested that we use problem-solving techniques, such as brainstorming or negotiating, to reach a compromise solution in which we could share power. I encouraged him for trying to do things that he previously had refused to try, such as painting and making clay figures. I also encouraged him for making decisions for himself without trying to coerce me into telling him what to do or how to do it. He was much more willing to try to do things that were physically challenging, such as shooting the dart gun or hitting the punching bag. I pointed out his attempts at these previously shunned activities and his improvement in physical dexterity and self-confidence.

Eventually, with Billy's permission, I asked his mother to join us in the playroom. I modeled different ways of interacting with Billy for his mother. I coached Billy's mother through several different interactions with him. I encouraged them to begin to play together, to take turns sharing the power, and to negotiate solutions that did not disenfranchise either of them.

Although I had repeatedly suggested that Darlene needed some time to work on her own issues, she steadfastly refused to consider the possibility that she might need some personal counseling. However, during the reorientation-reeducation portion of our parent consultation time, we discussed her relationship with her husband and her feeling that she was "not a particularly important part of his life." We talked about her lack of friends and her loneliness. We also discussed the importance of having family time devoted to fun and togetherness, rather than to achievement-oriented activities. I pointed out that there was a relationship between these personal and family issues and Billy's problem, but she was completely unwilling to acknowledge that there was a connection. Despite her continued denial, however, she slowly began to make changes in all of these areas.

OUTCOME

Gradually Darlene began to establish an identity outside her identity as Billy's mother. She started taking several classes at a local university and made some friends. As Darlene began to "get a life," she gradually stopped living Billy's life for him. She let Billy take care of himself more often and let him make more of his own decisions. She got better at redirecting Billy's attention, rather than giving in to his fears. She also started setting limits on how much time she was willing to spend with her mother-in-law and on how much input Estelle had into Billy's life.

Billy also made some changes. He gradually became more like a 4-year-old boy and less like an 80-year-old man. He started to occasionally laugh and act silly. Billy began to play with other toys in the playroom by himself, without always needing to have me play with him. He made several friends at preschool, and his mother reported that he seemed "much happier, but now he makes some messes at home and doesn't always do what he is supposed to do." I took this as a healthy sign and tried to reframe this childlike behavior for her so that she could see it as growth in a positive direction.

Nine months after I started working with Billy, he began to give up his fears, one by one. Each week he would announce that next week he did not think he would be afraid of one of the things on his list of terrors. He started with bubble gum, even insisting that I bring some gum into the playroom so that we could each chew a stick. The last fear to go was teddy bears. Billy had stopped throwing tantrums in order to make sure he did not ever have to be near a teddy bear, but he was still telling his mother and me that he was afraid of them. Then one week, Billy went to a birthday party where the host was twisting long skinny balloons into animals. Billy decided that teddy bears made of balloons "weren't really the same as regular teddy bears" and brought one home. That was the beginning of the end of his very last fear. After Billy let go of this final fear, his mother and I decided that he need not continue to come to play therapy. Although I wanted his mother to continue to work with me, she said that she "really didn't see the point. After all, Billy is cured now."

DISCUSSION

When Billy's mother first called, I envisioned myself having to develop some kind of elaborate behavior modification plan for his alleged teddy bear phobia. This never happened. As a matter of fact, we spent a small fraction of the many hours Billy and I were together actually talking directly about the issue of Billy's fears. The method of dealing with the fears from the perspective of the purpose they served in Billy's life worked beautifully.

I think I could have taken this strategy even further had I considered the reason for the family's willingness to cater to Billy's fears: By focusing on Billy's problems, Darlene, Estelle, and Steve could all avoid examining their own personal issues and the problems in their relationships with one another. Although I tried to address these problems with Darlene, I could have been more effective and efficient if I had worked directly with the entire family. I could have enhanced the therapeutic process by doing concurrent family therapy with all three generations of the Bass family.

As time passed, I realized that there were some obvious problems in the martial relationship between Steve and Darlene. I did not pursue this issue very strongly, and retreated in response to Darlene's reluctance to talk about their relationship. I could have helped Billy and his family more effectively if I had conducted some type of couple counseling in conjunction with the play therapy. Darlene was adamantly resistant to exploring her own family of origin and to having any other member of the family participate in the counseling process. By letting her decide who was going to participate in the sessions and letting her control what we discussed, I gave up a significant portion of my therapeutic leverage. If I had been more comfortable with owning my power as the counselor and had decided for myself who to include and the direction of the counseling, I might have had an impact on Billy *and* his family. At this point in my development as a counselor, I was still very hesitant. This lack of faith in my own therapeutic instincts prevented me from being as effective with this family as I could have been. Since that time, I have discovered that trusting my intuition and relying on my power as a counselor can enhance the outcome of the therapy process.

REFERENCES

Dreikurs, R., & Soltz, V. (1964). *Children: The challenge.* New York: Hawthorn/Dutton.

Kottman, T., & Stiles, K. (1990). The mutual storytelling technique: An Adlerian application in child therapy. *Journal of Individual Psychology, 46,* 148–156.

Kottman, T., & Warlick, J. (1989). Adlerian play therapy: Practical considerations. *Journal of Individual Psychology, 45*, 433–446.

Kottman, T., & Warlick, J. (1990). Adlerian play therapy. *Journal of Humanistic Education and Development, 28*, 125–132.

Manaster, G., & Corsini, R. (1982). *Individual psychology: Theory and practice*. Itasca, IL: F. E. Peacock.

Pepper, F. (1979). The characteristics of the family constellation. *Individual Psychology, 16*, 11–16.

Biographical Statement

Terry Kottman, PhD, is an assistant professor in the Department of Counselor Education at the University of North Texas in Denton, Texas. She is also director of the Child and Family Resource Clinic at the university. Dr. Kottman is the author of articles on Adlerian play therapy, storytelling, and metaphors, and assorted other techniques of working with children that have appeared in Journal of Individual Psychology *(1989; 1990),* School Counselor *(1990),* Journal of Humanistic Education and Development *(1990), and* Elementary Guidance and Counseling *(1990). She has made presentations about Adlerian play therapy at the local, national, and international level.*

8

Will He Choose Life?

J. Jeffries McWhirter

This case study consists of a single interview. It is a detailed account of an assessment of suicide potential. As McWhirter probes for crucial information, we are privy to the process by which the clinician arrives at a conclusion as to whether or not 12-year-old Mark is at risk of suicide.

McWhirter explores such factors as family history, depression, and religious beliefs as they correlate with suicide risk. Client confidentiality is discussed as a related issue.

I have published a number of articles and book chapters on the topic of youth depression and suicide prevention which have had a curious impact on my small private practice. I find myself at times, more often than I might wish, called upon to assess suicide potential. Of course, this kind of responsibility weighs heavily. I listen carefully to a teacher or parent or young person as I try to answer an important question: What is the probability that this particular youngster will choose death over life?

Most mental health professionals will be confronted with this question at one time or another. I assume that they confront, as I do, their own underlying fears: Will I be sufficiently perceptive to discern whether the youngster is a potential suicide? Can I provide alternatives to prevent a suicide attempt? What can I tell the parents to help them help this youngster? It occurs to me that providing a step-by-step review of an actual suicide assessment interview might be helpful to other mental health professionals. My format here provides excerpts from an interview and my accompanying comments as I try to determine suicide potential in a client.

CONCEPTUALIZATION

This case is based on an initial assessment interview that I conducted with Mark Thomas, a 12-year-old middle school student, and his mother, Sally. Sally contacted me regarding Mark's thoughts about suicide after a consultation with Mark's school counselor. Prior to the following interview, I had a telephone conversation with Sally regarding Mark's suicide thoughts, his previous therapy experiences, and their current family situation. I learned that Mark lived with his divorced mother and a younger sister. He had frequent and consistent contact with his father, who lived with his second wife a short distance from Mark's home.

I had also received a call from Mark's school counselor, Paula, whom I had known and worked with for 15 years. Paula's estimation was that an evaluation was definitely called for. She said that Mark had low self-esteem, was having peer adjustment problems, and that there had been previous suicide experiences in the family. Apparently, Mark's mother had made a suicide attempt, and her sister (Mark's aunt) had killed herself some years earlier. Because Paula is not an alarmist, I took her assessment seriously and made an effort to schedule an appointment with Mark as soon as possible after I received his mother's phone call.

In a suicide assessment interview the therapist needs to establish rapport and a therapeutic alliance very quickly. I believe that showing empathy, warmth, and genuineness and practicing good communication skills (as described by Carl Rogers and Allen Ivey) are essential in an assessment interview and in the beginning stages of therapy. Having establishing rapport, the therapist can proceed to specific assessment questions to determine suicide potential.

■ PROCESS

Mark arrived at my office accompanied by his mother. He was neatly and appropriately dressed and was cooperative throughout the interview. He displayed adequate interpersonal skills but subdued affect. He presented himself in a serious fashion and was open about his personal life.

Mark told me that he had strong academic skills. He saw himself as intelligent, based on the fact that he was enrolled in several honors classes. Mark described himself as an accomplished instrumental musician. He was worried about his lack of athletic ability and his image with peers. Mark told me that he was called a "nerd" because his peers thought that he studied all the time. In fact, he expressed an aversion to his teachers and classes. Problems with his mother also surfaced.

JJM: So why did your mom want you to see me?

Mark: Because we've had a lot of communication difficulties. I guess she feels that I don't talk to her enough, but she just asks me to do things. It's always, "Here, Mark, do this. Mark, do that."

JJM: Is she right about you not talking to her enough?

Mark: Not particularly. Whenever she wants to know anything, I tell her. Mostly stuff that I think is personal I keep to myself. Most of the time she blames me for things.

JJM: Could you give me an example?

Mark: Yeah. I think it sort of is my fault though. One weekend I was going on a camping trip and she never asked if I needed to go buy stuff I needed for the camping trip. I didn't tell her because I forgot. But, if she would have asked me, I would have remembered. So my scout leader called me and I asked my mom, and she goes, "Why didn't you tell me about this before? Now I've scheduled some things."

Comment. Some of Mark's conflicts have begun to surface. He implied that his mother was to blame for their poor communication and then immediately shifted the blame to himself, perhaps indicating low self-esteem and self-punitive thoughts. Adolescent suicide attempters display less positive self-esteem than nonattempters, and their negative thoughts and attributions are an important part of their problem.

JJM: Things aren't going well with your friends. You mentioned being criticized . . .

Mark: No, those are not friends but stoners that criticize. Ninety-five percent of school is made up of stoners and the rest are jocks.

JJM: Are you a jock or a stoner?

Mark: Neither, I'm a nerd.

Comment. In Mark's school, "stoners" were youngsters who were perceived to use drugs and alcohol. Drug and alcohol use are prevalent among suicidal adolescents. Although I did not inquire directly, Mark's response suggested that he was not using drugs. On the other hand, he appeared not to have a very extensive peer network and felt alienated. Mark described an incident that supported this view in which two younger friends agreed to meet him but left him stranded. Loneliness and lack of social support are correlated with suicide attempts.

JJM: Do you get down in the dumps?
Mark: No. I get depressed when I can't figure out something or do something.
JJM: Like what? Math, you mean?
Mark: Yeah, math, science, stuff like that. And when I get tons of homework piled up on me and it's all due the next day.
JJM: You seem overwhelmed. But you're not down in the dumps?
Mark: No. There's no reason to be.

Comment. I was frankly surprised at Mark's answer about depression. Most youngsters will admit to depression and to thinking about suicide when asked. Had I pressed too deeply or too quickly? Was Mark unaware of being depressed, or was he aware but unwilling to admit it to me? Or was Mark really *not* depressed? Keep in mind that the relationship between depression and suicide during adolescence is not straightforward. Suicidal behavior may result from depression, but a child need not be depressed for suicide to occur. And, of course, depression does not always lead to suicide. Depression remains, however, the most common denominator among both suicide attempters and completers.

Mark portrayed his father as being permissive but short-tempered. He described his big-brother role with his younger sister. Their relationship alternated between teasing and fighting and Mark's acting like her parent. This led to Mark's discussion of feelings about himself.

Mark: I have sort of low self-esteem. I mean you got to feel good about yourself.
JJM: What do you mean?
Mark: I don't feel good about myself. But I feel that God put me on earth for some reason, for something special.

Comment. A belief in God and the possibility of an afterlife tends to motivate against suicide. I was pleased that Mark coupled his belief with the view that he was put on earth for a reason. Lack of purpose in life is correlated with suicide attempts and completions.

JJM: You have some purpose being here on earth.
Mark: Some purpose, yeah.

JJM: But you haven't figured it out yet?
Mark: No. I'm waiting for that day to come.
JJM: Does it seem hopeless?
Mark: Yeah.

Comment. A feeling of hopelessness is characteristic of suicidal children. Of course, *hopeless* was my word, not his. It seemed time for a direct assault on the possible intention of suicide.

JJM: You've talked about low self-esteem, and you've talked about being lonely, and about not being able to figure out your purpose in life.
Mark: Yeah.
JJM: And even though you say you are not depressed, it sounds like school's not going well and home's not going very well. Maybe this will sound funny coming out of the blue, but have you thought about doing anything to hurt yourself?
Mark: Yeah. Lots of times.
JJM: Tell me about it.
Mark: I thought I'd kill myself once.
JJM: When was that?
Mark: A couple of years ago and again maybe three months ago. I didn't like the way band was going. My teacher was always critical. And really, it wasn't my fault. I got so many detention passes because other people wouldn't leave me alone.
JJM: So you were getting in trouble.
Mark: Yeah. I wanted to drown myself in my pool. But I figured I shouldn't do it. That action would hurt my mom. So I didn't do it.

Comment. A central question for the suicide candidate is, "How will you do it?" The vagueness or specificity of his or her plan helps determine the extent of the risk. By asking this question one can also determine the reversibility of the action and the seriousness of the client's intent. Mark's plan of drowning in his swimming pool was relatively low risk compared to using a gun. His concerns about his mother's feelings also boded well.

I wanted to know if he had considered the range of suicidal possibilities open to him. Second, I wanted to know how often Mark had had suicidal thoughts and whether these thoughts were a recent phenomenon. Had he been contemplating suicide for a long time? Third, I wanted to see if there was a link between the specific suicide ideation and other events in his life.

JJM: Why the swimming pool? Why drown?
Mark: Because the swimming pool is a way out. I mean I couldn't stab myself. I can't stand the sight of blood . . . or pain.
JJM: Have you thought about other ways?

Mark: I thought of strangling myself one day, but there was no place to do it. I thought about many ways to kill myself, but then I thought, "No, there's no reason to."

JJM: When was this?

Mark: Oh, about two or three months ago. Then I started doing better and I stopped thinking about it.

JJM: Two or three months ago it sounds like you were going through hell.

Mark: Yeah.

JJM: Had you thought about killing yourself even before that?

Mark: No, except that time two years ago.

JJM: How would you have drowned yourself?

Mark: Oh, just in the bathtub.

JJM: Any other ideas?

Mark: Yeah. I thought of diving off a bridge onto the freeway. But I figured I'd just end up in the hospital.

Comment. It became clear to me that Mark had not developed a specific plan. Drowning oneself in a bathtub or swimming pool, while possible, is unlikely. More lethal methods had been rejected. His concern about the pain of the act and about botching it and ending up in the hospital weighed against a suicide attempt.

JJM: If you were to take your own life, what would come after, would there be anything for you after that?

Mark: I don't know.

JJM: I don't think any of us know, but what do you think?

Mark: I would probably get stuck in the middle as a ghost, trying to redeem my life so I'd get through it. I'd have to work out bad stuff, like stealing. I stole something, but I had to return it.

JJM: No kidding?

Mark: Yeah.

JJM: You mean you *had* to take it back?

Mark: I didn't get caught. I felt so bad, I had to return it. I returned it, and I said "Thank you very much, here it is." I felt relieved.

JJM: So you believe that even if you were to kill yourself, you would still have to come back and make up for things that you did wrong?

Mark: Yeah.

Comment. Mark had a well-developed superego and a belief that suicide would not be an end to his responsibilities to make things right. I wanted to reinforce this attitude. A strong sense of responsibility to family and friends motivates against suicide.

JJM: What about right now?
Mark: I'm doing better. My schoolwork is shaping up. I got a couple more friends. I do more things.
JJM: What would have helped you when things were really bad?
Mark: Maybe people listening to me. I need to say my problems. I didn't want to talk to my mom because she gets too emotional.
JJM: Well, that's what counselors are for! I'll be here if you want to talk. But there's something I want from you right now. I want an agreement, a contract that you will not do anything to hurt yourself during the time that you and I are talking to each other.
Mark: OK.
JJM: I'll give you a phone number, and if you need to talk, you give me a call. I want you to agree to talk to me before you do anything to hurt yourself.
Mark: OK.

Comment. The formal signing of a contract makes the commitment more concrete. The contract buys time for the client to consider solutions and to learn new skills.

After I met with Mark, I interviewed Mark's mother, Sally. I wanted her impressions of Mark's suicide potential, and I wanted to know more about the family's suicide history. I also wanted to discuss a therapeutic contract.

JJM: How are things with Mark from your perspective?
Sally: Well, I had thought that they were going pretty well. He's basically a good kid. Does well in school. Mark has always been reticent, reluctant to try anything. Cautious to the extreme.
JJM: Not impulsive?
Sally: Right.

Comment. Impulsivity is a major concern when assessing suicide potential. Mark's obsessive need to think things over would function as a safety check.

JJM: Would he have known of anyone who has committed suicide?
Sally: Not that I know of. My sister did about 10 years ago. And she was 25. She was always a bit bothered. Sue had a gun and ammunition because she had intended to kill her husband and herself. It was a strange death. She was left-handed and was shot right-handed, and so I have never

accepted the fact that she killed herself. But I have accepted the fact that her intentions were there. So it was either a scuffle or something went on, or whatever. And I did not tell the children because I thought Mark's father might use that against me. And about five years ago I tried to kill myself. I was depressed over where I was, financially strapped. I ran my car in the garage for a quarter of a tank of gas.

JJM: But you didn't die.

Sally: It was a dumb thing, in my garage. I wasted $5 of gas before I realized what I was doing. I turned the car off and then broke down. It was kind of like, you know, it was a weird thing. Being alone and being in such despair . . . and me driving home and thinking, "I don't care anymore, I don't care who I hurt, I don't care who it touches, I've just had all I can take, I can't deal with another thing." So I know when someone is to that point of desperation that they can't be talked out of it. You almost have to be held down until it passes.

JJM: Would Mark have known about your attempt?

Sally: No. A couple of friends knew.

JJM: And you're surmising that he doesn't know about his aunt?

Sally: He asked me what happened, and I said it was an accident because I felt that that was not a lie, but I didn't need to tell him all of the facts. Quite frankly, because I didn't feel like I knew them all. And I couldn't be objective about Susie's death, and so when they asked about it, they asked if it was a car accident, and I said it was an accident. I have never lied to them, but I have not given the whole picture.

Comment. In this family suicide was seen as a solution to problems. Unfortunately, suicide tends to run in families. I hoped that Mark was unaware of the actual incidents.

Sally: What are your impressions? Am I in a crisis situation with this child?

JJM: I don't think so. I've asked him to sign a contract with me that he not do anything, but I don't think that you're in a crisis situation right now. He's going to need to attend to feelings of loneliness, feeling like he's not really fitting in at school. These are important self-esteem issues, and I do think that counseling can help. I would suggest that I see Mark for 10 sessions. In time, I'll know more about Mark's suicide potential.

Sally: All right. But he does lie. I do warn you about that. He's done that with me a couple of times and it's real hard to catch, but then he has come to me almost immediately, "I told you something that is not true." So, my perception is that he is basically honest but he will lie.

JJM: I would suggest another appointment in three days.

Comment. Ordinarily I do not see clients so soon. Even though I did not think Mark was at immediate risk, I was worried about Sally's comment about lying. Better to be safe than sorry. I was convinced that if Mark could talk through his stresses and conflicts, alternatives would emerge. An important factor in suicide is the individual's dichotomous thinking patterns which tend to limit alternatives. I wanted to teach Mark to expand his black-or-white perspective to shades of grey.

Mark returned to the room. He signed a contract that stated that he would not do anything to hurt himself during the time we worked together. I asked him to call me should he feel especially depressed.

OUTCOME

I worked with Mark on a weekly basis. After three months we moved to twice-per-month meetings. Mark reported that he was feeling better and that his conflict with his mother had become less intense. He said that there had been no recurrence of suicidal thoughts. Sally said that she saw improvement in Mark; he smiled more and his attitude was more positive.

DISCUSSION

I concluded that Mark was not actively suicidal. Therefore, I got a written contract from Mark stating that he would not attempt suicide, and I set up an appointment to begin therapy with the goal of reducing depression. But what if I had assessed Mark's situation as acute? What steps should be taken if a child is evaluated as actively suicidal? In that case, the child must be supervised constantly until the crisis passes, usually about 24 to 72 hours. Help the child and the family find ways to lessen the pain. If communication can be opened and stress can be eased, the immediate and overwhelming sense of hopelessness will diminish. Finally, both medication and hospitalization are possible courses of action.

Confidentiality with youngsters this age is a difficult issue. Parents want and need to know some information, even though the right of confidentiality resides with the client. The basic rule that I follow and which I explained to Mark is that I try to do what is in the client's best interest. I honor confidentiality unless I think the client is in clear danger.

Biographical Statement

J. Jeffries McWhirter, PhD, is professor of counseling psychology at Arizona State University and maintains a private practice in psychology. He is designated as a diplomate in counseling psychology by the American Board of Professional Psychology. He was a senior Fulbright-Hays fellow (1977-78) at Hacettepe University, Ankara, Turkey, and a senior Fulbright scholar at Catholic College of Education in Sydney, Australia (1984-85). Dr. McWhirter has published widely on the topic of at-risk youth, adolescent depression, and suicide, including a book, The Learning-Disabled Child: A School and Family Concern *(1988).*

9

The Girl with Painful Steps

Barbara Peeks and Ray L. Levy

This case presents an 11-year-old girl who walks on crutches because her right leg is swollen and sore to the touch. The cause of her affliction (Conversion Disorder, Single Episode, DSM-III-R *300.11) is unknown and doctors are baffled. As a last resort, the orthopedic surgeon refers Jenny to Ray Levy, then a psychology student intern. The physician's poor opinion of psychology is no secret, and figuring out how to cure Jenny and simultaneously impress the doctor gives Levy quite a headache.*

Levy is committed to a family therapy model but hampered by the fact that the parents are separated and living on different coasts. The father, who is visiting, is due to return to his home in two days. His imminent departure makes Jenny's symptoms—and Levy's—much worse.

A call to Barbara Peeks leads to her serving as Levy's supervisor in the case. The method of treatment is strategic family therapy in which the child's social situation is reorganized to eliminate the cause of her symptoms. Peeks chooses a behavioral metaphor for the precipitating event, and she formulates directives for Levy to give the family (he writes them down on 3-by-5-inch cards to insure accuracy and puts them in his pocket). Rather than attempt to change Jenny, Peeks and Levy design a plan to change the conditions, interactions, and relationships in her environment. We leave it to you, and the orthopedic surgeon, to evaluate the results.

The Therapist's View

The head of the orthopedic surgery department approached me in the hallway: "I have a case for you—one of your types." He was known to look down on psychology as a profession, and he would refer a patient only as a last resort. Eleven-year-old Jenny, he continued, had experienced leg problems for one year. Etiology was unknown and, in fact, her symptoms had baffled her doctors for some time. Finally, she had been admitted to a children's hospital the previous week to undergo diagnostic tests in addition to the physical therapy she had been receiving for several weeks. Still, her doctors could find no basis for her problem. Thus, as a last resort, she was referred to the psychology department, where I was serving as a student intern.

The doctor described the symptoms Jenny was experiencing. She walked on crutches because her right leg from the midcalf down was swollen and sore to the touch. Her left leg had similar symptoms but less severe. She had limited flexion and mobility and was in extreme pain, yet a diagnosis proved difficult. Sympathetic reflex dystrophy was ruled out because of the bilaterality of her symptoms. In addition to five weeks of physical therapy, a myriad of tests and physical treatments had been tried to determine the cause of and relieve the pain, including casting her leg. Jenny's pain would temporarily abate but not disappear.

Her disorder clearly was hindering and negatively affecting her life. She had been a cheerleader but due to her symptoms had dropped out of the squad. Moreover, her social life became more limited due to her lack of mobility. On further investigation of the situation, I found that Jenny's parents were separated. Her father was living on the West Coast; her mother and the children were residing on the East Coast. Her father came to visit every six to eight weeks; he was visiting at the present time but was leaving in two days. When I talked to Jenny alone, she was very open and sociable with me until I inquired about how things were at home. When I asked her about her parents' separation and her feelings about her father, she began to cry and stated that she wanted to go back to her room. She got up on her crutches and hurried out of my office. I followed her to her ward where she found her father and collapsed in his arms crying.

Her father later came to my office and in a sad manner told me about his estranged wife. He said he still loved her, but she insisted on running around with other men. He told me that his wife's father had become ill a year ago. At about the same time he had become so severely depressed about their marital problems that he decided to send his wife and children to the opposite coast to live with her parents. He sincerely related how concerned he and his wife were about Jenny and said they would be willing to be a part of her rehabilitation.

That night I went home with a terrific headache as I tried to figure out how I was going to simultaneously impress the doctor and cure Jenny in two days. Jenny's symptoms were clearly related to her father's imminent departure since her symptoms had recently exacerbated, which they always did when he was about to leave.

I wondered if I could relieve Jenny's pain using hypnosis. While I might have been able to alleviate some of the pain in this way, I knew that unless I did something to affect her environment (i.e., her parents), the relief would be only temporary. I had recently begun reading *Leaving Home* by Jay Haley (1980) and *Strategic Family Therapy* by Cloe Madanes (1981) and had attended a workshop presented by the authors. It was there that I met Barbara Peeks, who had been trained by them. We went to lunch, she told me about some of her cases, she advised me on one of my cases, and she gave me her card. Wanting to give strategic family therapy a serious try, I decided to contact Barbara to see if she would serve as my supervisor.

The Supervisor's View

"Ray Levy? Who is Ray Levy?" I asked myself. "Oh, yes, we met in Washington, D.C. We had lunch together." "Would you be willing to help me?" he asked. "I'll be glad to help," I replied, happy to know that I had sparked an interest in family therapy in a young therapist. He was anxious to do a good job and concerned that this would be the last opportunity Jenny's parents might have for conjoint therapy. Ray was in a doctoral program that was teaching psychodynamic approaches to problem situations, which he did not feel suited the particular characteristics of this case. He lacked training in family therapy techniques and was asking me for supervision.

According to my notes of Ray's first telephone call, he presented the following facts about Jenny and her family. Her pain was from her lower calf to her foot, and it was moving up her leg. The symptom began soon after her mother and siblings had left her father to move to the grandmother's town. Jenny was a middle child of five (ages 14, 13, 11, 6, 5). The father was living on the opposite coast and was presently visiting; he was 34, a bricklayer, and called himself "pathetic." The parents have been married 14 years. The father said that his wife runs around and is a pathological liar. Both parents drink. The father was so depressed a year ago that he sent his wife and children to his wife's parents. The maternal grandfather recently died.

The most startling aspect of the situation that Ray described was the fact that one of the doctors involved with Jenny had described Jenny's worst scenario as amputation of the leg. Here was a child who might lose a leg, and I had just accepted responsibility for phone supervision of a therapist I did not know! I was uncertain of Ray's abilities, knowledge of family systems, his willingness to be directive, or even if the information he had presented to me was correct. But I did know that he was willing to try new approaches, as evidenced by the fact that he had used my interventions with his other case. Knowing the doctor's lack of respect for psychological intervention, I felt he would not attempt another referral for Jenny to the psychology department if Ray was unsuccessful with the case. The medical community had almost given up on Jenny, and I felt sympathy for her situation and respect for the young therapist who was willing to tackle such a difficult case. I would try my best to help Ray. I solicited his pledge to follow my directions as closely as possible, even if he did not understand strategic family therapy in all its details.

CONCEPTUALIZATION

The Supervisor's View

Strategic family therapy is a directive therapy that seeks to reorganize the child's social situation to eliminate the cause of the child's symptom(s). A directive is developed based on the type and severity of the problem and the goal of therapy. The type of directive that is chosen is also influenced by the therapist's understanding of the behavioral metaphor. The directive should ideally eliminate the presenting problem and also alleviate or change the problem in the larger social situation, which is hypothesized to be the source of the child's problem.

Parents who seek a mental health professional for therapy trust and expect the professional to be expert in the area of solving children's problems. They come to therapy seeking advice, direction, and solutions for problems they themselves have not been able to solve. Parents will readily follow a therapist's advice and direction if the therapist takes proper care to involve them in establishing a plausible definition of the problem and reasonable treatment goals.

It was essential for me to be certain that Ray understood the importance of each directive and why he was asking the family to take each action. Without presenting him with a semester-long course in family therapy, I emphasized the following ideas:

1. He must focus the entire session on what everyone in the family could do to help Jenny. In other words, he had to insure that every action he recommended was designed to eliminate Jenny's symptoms, not to provide insight or allow the family members to express feelings.
2. He must believe that Jenny's symptoms were benevolent and protective and that subconsciously she was attempting to help solve some larger problem that was causing distress for her family.
3. He must be in control of the session, must believe in the effectiveness of the directives he proposed, and must convince the family members to take action to help Jenny.

Before a strategy can be developed to solve a problem situation, a hypothesis for the cause of the problem must first be formulated. It is helpful to think about (a) problems evident in a child's social situation and (b) behavioral metaphors.

Ray's initial outline of Jenny's problems included (a) her father's depression and low self-esteem, (b) family transitions (i.e., a move and the grandfather's death), (c) the parent's marriage and separation, (d) the parents' drinking, and (e) her mother's lying and infidelity. One of these problems, a combination of these problems, or as yet undetermined problem(s) may have been the social conditions that contributed to Jenny's symptoms.

Thinking in terms of behavioral metaphors permits the therapist to gain a better understanding of the child's problem in the family context. Just as a literary metaphor gives the reader an understanding of a new concept or idea, a behavioral metaphor helps the observer understand a specific social situation. Jenny's symptoms, considered as a behavioral metaphor, represented someone's inability to step forward or move without pain. My task was to develop a hypothesis about the cause of the problem in terms of metaphor. Who was represented by the behavioral metaphor? What situation was represented by the behavioral metaphor? What series of interactions was represented by the behavioral metaphor?

With the information Ray had provided thus far, I tentatively hypothesized that the parent's marital difficulties were a very important consideration in understanding Jenny's situation. The parents had been separated and living on opposite coasts for a year. I thought that leaving her husband had been a painful step for Jenny's mother, since Jenny's painful steps had begun shortly after the separation. However, her mother, for some reason, would not or could not move back to rejoin her husband.

Ray did not have any information about the relationship between the mother and grandmother or about the family's response to the grandfather's death. All of the parents' individual and marital problems may have been solvable; however, their living on opposite coasts provided little opportunity for problem resolution. Before developing a therapeutic plan, I had to know why the mother would not return to her husband. Had she already decided on a divorce? Was she involved in another relationship? Was she worried about her widowed mother? I called Ray: "Ray, you need to find out why Jenny's mother is not willing to rejoin her husband to resolve their problems."

The Therapist's View

Barbara had explained that I should think of the problem of Jenny's immobility not as originating within Jenny's psyche but as representative of another problem. My goal for the next session was to uncover the missing information about Jenny's family situation. According to Barbara's directions, I thanked the parents and grandmother for coming with Jenny to the session and emphasized the importance of our working together to help Jenny focus her complete energy on healing. I asked for more details concerning various relationships and situations in the family. Notably, as the family talked about the grandfather's death, I discovered that the grandfather had engaged Jenny's mother in a deathbed promise to care for the grandmother. Mother and grandmother talked and cried about grandfather in a fond way, clearly missing and loving him.

The other thing that Barbara asked me to do during this information-gathering session was to have Jenny sit between her parents while they reassured Jenny that every problem would be handled by them alone and that Jenny was to devote 100% of her energy to the rehabilitation of her legs. She was notably excited and smiling, and appeared to be quite content sitting between the two of them.

PROCESS

The Supervisor's View

"A deathbed promise! That's it," I thought. Jenny's mother can't leave her own mother because she promised her father on his deathbed that she would care for her. And how could she care for her mother if she reconciled with her husband and returned to the opposite coast? Although the parents had marital problems and problems with depression and alcohol, the grandfather's death had risen to the surface as the primary social-situation problem. The mother's deathbed promise prevented her from rejoining her husband, thus precluding any solution of their marital problems. I could now better understand Jenny's leg pain. The pain that prevented her from walking initially represented her mother's pain in leaving her husband, and now was expanded to represent her inability to move forward because of the emotional pain that would be caused by violating the deathbed promise. Jenny was immobilized by her painful steps, and her mother was immobilized by the emotional pain her departure would have caused her own mother.

Ray now had one more session with the family while Jenny's father was still in town, which meant I had to develop for him a one-session cure that would (a) relieve Jenny's symptoms, (b) release her mother from the deathbed promise, (c) insure the grandmother's welfare, and (d) bring the parents together to solve their marital problems.

I gave the following directives to Ray to engineer our one-session cure.

1. Ray should invite Jenny's grandmother to the next day's session. Although she was going through a grieving process and did have some minor health problems, Ray described her as being physically and emotionally self-sufficient. I said to explain to her during the session that although the doctors were uncertain about the cause of

Jenny's physical symptoms they felt certain that the mind and body work very closely together. When Jenny's mind is preoccupied with worries about her family, she has less energy available for the physical healing process. The emphasis should be that Jenny needs 100 percent of her emotional energy to focus on her physical healing.

He should explain to Jenny's grandmother that it is impossible for her daughter to return to her husband to resolve their marital difficulties because of the deathbed promise she has made to her father. He should simply ask the grandmother whether she needs her daughter to remain at her home to care for her. If she says no, which was my assumption, he should ask her to hold her daughter's hand and release her from the deathbed promise to look after her. He should direct the grandmother as she tells her daughter, "I understand the promise you made to your father was because you both love me, but you don't need to sacrifice your life and marriage for my sake." He should have Jenny's grandmother state in no uncertain terms that she is perfectly capable of caring for herself.

2. To insure the grandmother's welfare and the mother's peace of mind, Ray should make certain that the mother's sister, who lived in the same town, would care for the grandmother. He should ask Jenny's mother to talk to her sister privately and in detail about whether she would accept the responsibility of caring for their mother, a responsibility she had assured her father that she, herself, would accept.

3. Once Jenny's mother felt released from the deathbed promise, the parents would need a plan for how they would reconcile. I told Ray to direct the parents to go to a place in the area that had been important to them during their courtship, make a three-month plan for their lives, and communicate that plan to Jenny. It was my belief that once released from the deathbed promise, Jenny's mother would plan to return to her husband and attempt a reconciliation. And once her mother was able to leave Jenny's grandmother, Jenny's psychosomatic symptoms, I believed, would stop.

4. If the parents decided to reunite on the opposite coast, Ray should recommend that they immediately seek marital therapy. He should assure them that he would refer them to someone who would continue the work that he had begun. He and I agreed that we would go to any lengths to find a therapist on the opposite coast who had a strategic point of view.

The Therapist's View

At the second and final session that Jenny's father could attend before his departure, I had to effectively implement the directives that Barbara had proposed (what pressure!). I wrote all of the directives Barbara had given me on 3-by-5-inch notecards and put them in my pocket. This was a serious case and a new procedure that I did not intend to bungle. This is what transpired.

1. Although Jenny's grandmother contended that her daughter did not remain with her because of the deathbed promise (something I would have believed had I not consulted with Barbara), she did understand the importance of absolving her daughter of her promise. She said she wanted her daughter to be happy and to work on her marriage. They held hands, cried, and recalled grandfather's love that had prompted the promise. Jenny's grandmother reassured her daughter that she could care for herself.
2. Jenny's mother agreed to seek her sister's help in monitoring her mother's health and happiness.
3. The parents had been talking about how they had grown up, met, and dated in the area, so I asked them to go to a place that was meaningful in their courtship to talk about a three-month plan for their lives. During the session they were turned toward each other, and they continually looked at each other. It was my belief that they had no intention of separating and that they were still very much attached to one another.
4. I told the parents that if they chose to reunite on the opposite coast for the purpose of reconciliation I would make certain they were referred to an excellent marital therapist.

OUTCOME

The Therapist's View

When Jenny, her mother, her grandmother, and two of the other children came to my office one week later, I was amazed. Jenny walked into the room without crutches! She was limping slightly but was able to apply weight to her leg. She reported that her pain level had dropped by 50% and she looked 100% better! Jenny appeared happier and reported that she had played with her cousins and even played in the swimming pool without feeling much pain in her foot.

Jenny's mother reported that she and Jenny's father had gone to a state park, where they had spent romantic times during their courtship, and discussed their marital and financial problems. When her father returned to the West Coast, the couple had an undefined plan for the future but had thoroughly discussed their difficulties. Jenny appeared to be somewhat oblivious, at least overtly, to the specifics that were being discussed. However, as evidenced by her new posture and stance in life, she was very aware that there had been changes in her family.

I asked Jenny's mother if she would encourage weekly contact between the children and father by providing writing supplies and stamps. Although the father's depression was never addressed, I was sure that he missed his family and that he would certainly feel better if he had constant communication with them.

Another session was scheduled, but the family did not come or call. I phoned soon after the missed appointment and Jenny's mother stated that Jenny was doing well and was not experiencing any pain. She also reported that she and her husband had decided to get back together and she was preparing to move the children back to the family home.

Later, I saw the referring doctor in the hallway and mentioned Jenny's progress. He was pleased but not nearly as excited or impressed as I was. But then, this was a doctor who felt psychology had no function in our society. The occupational and physical therapy staffs were also very pleased, but each felt that their interventions explained Jenny's progress. Overall, I was very depressed that I was not getting the recognition I wanted and felt I deserved. Being a therapist, I was beginning to understand, was not going to be an easy task. Barbara was clear in her direction that I should give the credit for Jenny's improvement to the family, as they were the ones who helped her the most.

When I spoke to the family two years later by phone, I learned that Jenny had not had any recurring symptoms and was doing well, and the parents were still together. They had not received any other therapy, although I had given them the name of a therapist in their city.

Five years after this case I find myself immersed in the strategies and theory of brief therapies, especially strategic family therapy. My thinking has completely shifted from a one-person, psychodynamic orientation to a systems perspective that enables me to think of problem situations and conditions in an entirely different way. I look for the causes of problem behavior in the social situation, rather than in the individual. Jenny and her mother have stepped forward in life without pain, and I have stepped forward in my understanding of human behavior with excitement!

The Supervisor's View

It was a relief to hear that Jenny's symptom had abated by 50% in one week's time. This was an indication that the strategies developed to change the organization of Jenny's social situation were appropriate and that she most likely would recover very quickly. We can never be certain what directive or combination of directives began the change that included the remission of Jenny's symptoms. We can only surmise in this situation that Jenny's pain and her inability to take steps were lessened as her mother confronted her own pain over leaving her husband and her anticipated pain over leaving her mother.

The rapid remission of symptoms also spoke well of Ray's therapeutic skill and his ability to shift to a new style of therapy for the benefit of a client. He did not have to completely understand the theory to successfully implement the strategies of the method. The success that Ray experienced with Jenny and her family prompted him to ask for further supervision in cases where he could apply strategic family therapy. Jenny's case began a professional relationship between us that moved in five years from that of supervisor and supervisee to that of friend and colleague.

DISCUSSION

As the supervisor in the case, when I was thinking about what interventions would help relieve Jenny's painful symptoms, I looked for elements in Jenny's social context that if changed would make her symptoms unnecessary. The strategic problem-solver assumes that at the point a child presents a symptom the family unit (i.e., the social situation) has become immobilized in regard to a larger problem than is presented through the child. The child's problem is a metaphor for the larger problem, and it has a protective or helpful function in the interactions of the family in that it serves as a diversion.

Once the larger social-situation problem is tentatively identified—in this case the deathbed promise that prevented Jenny's mother and father from being together to solve their marital problems—the therapist can design interventions that will solve the larger problem, eliminating the cause of the child's problem. The interventions are presented to the family in the form of directives with the rationale that they will solve the child's problem. In this case, Jenny's grandmother was asked to release Jenny's mother from the deathbed promise she had made because Jenny, Ray believed, was worried and upset about her parents' separation and her mother could not rejoin her father because of the promise.

The directive that asked the parents to make a 3-month plan for their lives was also presented with the rationale of helping Jenny. If her doubts and uncertainties about the future were relieved, she could concentrate her mental and physical energy on healing. Having Jenny's mother ask her sister to accept primary responsibility for their mother's care would give Jenny's mother peace of mind and allow her to focus her mental and physical energy on restoring her marriage.

The strategic approach to family therapy makes use of a planned problem-solving strategy for each case. Although some standard strategies are commonly used for solving problem situations, the strategic therapist strives to design interventions based on the particular social situation that seems to be the source of the presenting problem. Rather than attempt to change the individual, the therapist designs a plan to change the conditions, interactions, or relationships that exist in the individual's surrounding environment.

REFERENCES

Haley, J. (1980). *Leaving Home*. New York: McGraw-Hill.

Madanes, C. (1981). *Strategic Family Therapy*. San Francisco: Jossey-Bass.

Biographical Statements

Barbara Peeks, MS, a family therapist and school consultant, teaches systemic problem solving to school professionals and agency workers on the national workshop circuit. She has been a public school teacher, elementary and secondary school counselor, agency worker, and private practitioner, and is a member of the National Board of Certified Counselors (NBCC). She has published several articles on strategic family planning and serves on the editorial boards of Elementary School Guidance and Counseling, Journal of Mental Health Counseling, *and* Arizona Counseling Journal. *She is an occasional book reviewer for* Journal of Counseling and Development *and edits the children and teens column in* The Advocate.

Ray L. Levy, PhD, was born and raised in Richmond, Virginia. He received his bachelor of arts degree from Harvard University in 1979. He then attended Virginia Commonwealth University where he received both his master's and doctoral degrees in clinical psychology. He completed his internship at the Dallas Child Guidance Clinic. Dr. Levy is currently in private practice in Dallas where he works in a strategic-systemic style and specializes in treating children and adolescents.

Ringo: Scars of Violence

Vimala Pillari

Vimala Pillari attempts to intervene with a 12-year-old minority youngster named Larry who has been horribly disfigured both physically and emotionally. While the diagnosis of Larry's violent behavior as "Conduct Disorder" (DSM-III-R *312.00) is accurate, it is also an understatement.*

Pillari brings us a case from early in her career. She brings love and consistency to the chaotic existence of her institutionalized client. Larry responds with impressive behavioral gains. A dramatic encounter between Larry and his estranged mother Sadie illustrates both the tenacity and hurtfulness of a relationship that has been scarred by catastrophic violence.

Twelve-year-old Larry was referred to me for acting-out behaviors while I was a part-time therapist in a publicly funded residential treatment center for emotionally disturbed children. Larry, born into a lower socioeconomic black family, was the youngest of six siblings. Sadie, Larry's mother, had not finished high school. She worked off and on as a maid. Larry's oldest sister was married and lived close to her mother's house. Three of his brothers were living away from home. One of them had been hospitalized for three weeks for "mental problems." One teenaged sister continued to live at home with her mother. Allen, Larry's father, was serving a life prison sentence. Larry had not seen his father since he was 6 years old.

Larry had lived in this residential treatment center for the past three years. He had been expelled from school because of uncontrolled violent behavior. The courts placed him in the center because his behavior had culminated in an incident in which he was found choking a classmate until the victim literally turned blue in the face. To make matters worse, Larry joked about his violent acts and did not understand the seriousness of hurting others.

Sadie had dropped him off three years before as if he were going to a boarding school. She did not tell him that the facility was a residential center for children with serious behavioral disorders. All of my attempts to get in touch with her had proved futile.

CONCEPTUALIZATION

Based on the *DSM-III-R* diagnostic framework, Larry was labeled as having a conduct disorder. This was a common diagnosis for children in our setting who typically displayed acting-out behaviors which made it difficult for them to live at home.

The approaches I used to work with Larry varied from cognitive-behavioral to psychodynamic. Psychodynamic and family systems theory influenced my assessment and planning for Larry. Essentially, I used my relationship with Larry to provide a corrective emotional experience. I set limits in order to promote constructive, acceptable behavior.

PROCESS

By the time I had joined the staff, Larry had been in residence for three years. The first day I met Larry was memorable. I had just enough time to admire the beautiful view of the river through the window in my new office before the peace was shattered by repeated shouts of, "So you are my new counselor." By the time I looked up from a record I was reading, he had slammed the door and was gone. But he was back in a few minutes banging on my door, barging in and out, and repeating with exaggerated sarcasm, "So you are my new counselor." Larry did this a number of times, to my great embarrassment, for I was aware of the presence of other social workers who could not help but overhear this unpleasant commotion.

When he barged in for the fifth time, I demanded, attempting to be reality oriented, that he not bang on my door and said that if he had anything to say he should walk in politely and talk to me directly. To my horror, he doubled over and burst into loud screeching laughter: "You're crazee . . . crazee . . . and you are not supposed to get angry at me. We are crazy kids and you are supposed to be kind and understanding towards us always." With this interesting and somewhat insightful commentary he was, thankfully, gone. My face felt hot as I self-consciously thought of the impression made on my senior colleagues. Of course, in time, I found out that every worker had occasional uproar to contend with in this setting.

Half an hour later, in walked Larry. This time he made his declaration in an amused and triumphant manner: "So you are my new counselor!" I was alert as he moved closer to my desk. Except for a slit through which he could see, Larry's face was covered with the hood of his coat. I asked his name and he responded. I requested that I be allowed to see his face. He hesitated and I persuaded. Finally, he unzipped his hood slowly, revealing his forehead, his brown eyes, and his nose. Then, in a flash he unzipped the hood, and I got a glimpse of his mouth before he zipped it back. What a sight! There was a large scar around his lips, apparently the result of a burn. His lower lip was double the size of the upper. Ignoring my attempts to start a conversation, Larry moved to the window. Seeing that it was closed, he asked if he could open it. It was a winter morning and cold outside.

VP: Please don't.
Larry: Why not?
VP: It's cold outside.
Larry: You cannot open the window because those are the rules. (He spoke in a mocking tone of voice and pointed to a notice stapled on the wall.)

I explained that I had not had a chance to read the material. He laughed raucously and ran out, faithfully slamming the door and screaming, "You are crazee!"

Though I was supposed to see Larry only twice a week, he was back in my office the next day. He mockingly greeted me, "Hello, counselor," and slammed the door. I was frustrated. How was I to deal with this youngster who made me feel so uncomfortable? Again, Larry started his running in and out of my office routine. Then he ran up and put his face almost against mine and asked if he could have the ashtray on my table. I put my hand on the ashtray and told him that he could not have it. Sensing an opportunity, I added that I did not like his slamming my door and running in and out of my office.

I thought I was "structuring" Larry. However, he commented nonchalantly, "You are not supposed to get angry with us. We are crazy, so counselors cannot get angry with us."

It seemed high time to correct this unfortunate interpretation of the rules that was governing our relationship: "Of course, you are not crazy and I'm not going to treat you as if you were," I heard myself saying. "If I'm angry, I will tell you all about it. Counselors get angry, too."

Larry ran to the door and yelled, "Crazee counselor, crazee . . . crazee . . .," and disappeared.

Suddenly, there was a commotion in the corridor and I heard a woman scream my name. I ran out and found the new secretary, pale and shaking all over, holding her throat. Larry had tried to choke her. She was frightened. Larry looked at her and laughed and said, "I was only playing with her." For the first time, I noticed that for a child who was only 12 years of age he was very muscular.

After this incident, new rules were made for Larry's visits. Whenever Larry came to the treatment building, he had to ring for me at the door and I had to go and fetch him. Far from being disturbed by the new procedure, Larry seemed delighted with the special attention.

After the first few sessions, during which Larry (and I) learned that he could not push me around, we got down to therapy. One day I brought up the subject of his previous counselor, a black man who had had to leave his job abruptly because his mother was dying in another state. Larry spoke sadly, saying that he missed the other counselor. He said that he did not like counselors because they came and left so fast. Larry's statement was true enough and I realized that he was suffering from many losses. I attempted to talk about his mother, but he was not ready to discuss her.

I discovered that Larry had some strengths. First of all, he was quite bright and enjoyed reading. He was also musical. We talked about his interest in music. He liked playing the guitar, and he told me that one day he would like to join the band that his brother Joseph had started.

Larry was creative. He would draw pictures and tell stories. He had quite a sense of humor and loved to laugh and joke. However, his jokes were hurtful and targeted at specific people. Still, humor was a means of communication between us. I would bring the newspaper comics and we read them together. This helped both of us to relax.

I constantly drilled Larry on acceptable social behavior, presenting it as normal growing-up behavior. As Larry got comfortable with me, he stopped covering his mouth.

The kids in his cottage called him "Ringo" and sometimes taunted him by singing, "Ring around the lips." One Monday Larry came to my office with tears in his eyes. He said that he hated the boys because they were always making jokes about his lips. I asked him what had happened to give him such a scar around his lips. So, with pain and even amusement, Larry told me what had happened.

When he was perhaps 5 or 6 years of age, his parents, who were always fighting, were having an especially violent argument. Larry was scared but also thirsty. He wanted milk from the carton that his mother had placed near the stove (which was on). Perhaps, at some level, he thought that his request for milk would stop the fighting. Sadie told him not to touch the milk. He would have his milk with supper. However, Allen, taunting his wife, instructed his son to get the milk immediately and drink it. Although his father was rarely home, Larry was afraid of his bad temper. He had been beaten by both parents, but he was more afraid of his father's beatings. Larry decided he had better obey his father. So he picked up the milk carton. Sadie, in a rage, pushed Larry's face into the hot stove. It was several days before Larry received medical attention. The doctors said that nothing could be done to remove the massive scarred tissue around his lips.

Simplistically, Larry saw the scar as the cause of all his problems. He did not blame his parents. I would learn later that Larry was considered the ugly duckling in his family even prior to the scarification. It seems likely that Larry was the least favored child because his heavy features and dark complexion set him apart from his siblings. He described his mother as being beautiful.

Larry asked me if his lips could be "cured." I told him that the original medical report didn't hold out much hope. I also knew that it was unlikely that there would be funds to pay for such "elective" surgery. Nevertheless, I managed to get together sufficient support to take Larry to see a plastic surgeon. Unfortunately, the plastic surgeon did not think anything could be done. Larry was disappointed but grateful that I had taken him to the doctor.

Although I was aware that another catastrophic family incident had been responsible for the father's life imprisonment, I kept wondering about the right time to probe this subject. The opportunity presented itself as we discussed the prison system and why people go to jail. At first, as was his pattern, Larry laughed about his father being in prison, but he was soon caught up in the terrifying and anxious moments that he related to me.

As frequently happened, his father and mother were fighting, although Larry could not remember why. This time his father was drunk. Allen started to beat Sadie. Larry was scared and ran to his maternal grandmother, who was living with them at the time, and hid behind her. Allen became more violent and would not stop beating Sadie, so the grandmother intervened. Cursing and yelling, she came to her daughter's rescue and started to fight Allen. Allen picked up a butcher knife and stabbed his mother-in-law repeatedly until she fell to the kitchen floor. Larry recalled that the floor became red with blood. Petrified, Larry stood in the corner of the room. He remembered crying and his father yelling at him, and he vaguely recalled his father being taken away by the police. His grandmother died. He twitched his nose and said that he still remembered the putrid odors that lingered in the room for a long time. Larry was lost when his grandmother died because she was the only person who would stand by him.

The murder happened when Larry was 6 years of age, and that was the last time he saw his father. For a long time Larry could not sleep at night. At home he was afraid that his mother might kill him, just as his father had killed his grandmother. He had not spoken of this to anyone until now.

School was a relief in the sense that he could act out without fear of being murdered! When Larry was 9 years old, he started getting into serious trouble at school. What he called fun was seen by others as aggressive and abusive. He beat younger kids, sometimes to the point that the other child was bloody. Larry commented that he was only playing.

A number of such incidents paved the road to this institution, where Larry arrived at age 10. He was under the impression that any kind of behavior was acceptable here because crazy kids were expected to be unpredictable.

In therapy, I highlighted Larry's strong points: verbal skills, good academic performance in school, ability to play the guitar, and successful attempts to control his behavior. In response to my caring, encouragement, and consistent limit setting, Larry's behavior began to improve markedly!

There were positive observations from staff and other children. What an ego boost for Larry! He would talk to me again and again about how his cottage parents kept telling him that he was turning out to be a fine young man. I was pleased with his progress, but I wondered where we could go from here? What were Larry's prospects as an adult?

I had been aware for a long time that music was Larry's first love, so we talked about guitar lessons and his desire to join his brother's band. I made arrangements for him to save the pocket money he earned through odd jobs at the center for guitar lessons. The agency that administered the center contributed as well. Larry took to his guitar lessons enthusiastically. Meanwhile I tried to get in touch with his oldest brother, Joseph. I hoped that Joseph would be good role model, and I helped Larry start what would be a sporadic correspondence with his brother.

While the relationship between brothers was being reinforced by telephone calls and letter writing, Larry's behavior continued to improve. After his quarterly assessment by the consulting psychiatrist, I got a telephone call. The psychiatrist was pleasantly surprised at Larry's self-controlled behavior and the manner in which he interacted. I felt very good about that call!

Larry brought up his intense desire to see his mother, Sadie, whom he had not seen in the three years since she had dropped him at the "boarding school." My attempts to get her to visit were fruitless. She would promise to come but would not keep her word. This soft-spoken woman was very elusive about her commitment to her son. I encouraged Larry to write but, of course, Sadie did not reply. He interpreted this lack of response as rejection. He would ask me, "Does my mother really hate me?"

At times, I sat by myself in my office after Larry left, trying to understand his mother's behavior. I had to admit to considerable anger for this woman I had never met. Larry told me that he loved his mother, adding defensively that whatever a mother does to a child is all right because she was responsible for his birth. I had heard this type of logic from other abused kids.

I became almost obsessed with setting up a meeting with Sadie. Thus began a lengthy correspondence with her which included phone calls and letter writing. When I finally got in touch with her, she declined my invitation to visit the treatment center. Fast as lightening, I asked if we could visit her at home. Perhaps caught off guard, Sadie agreed.

Larry and I took the train and then the subway to visit her. Larry was chatty, recalling happy memories of home, mostly things he did with his grandmother and sisters. He said very little about his relationship with his parents.

Sadie lived in an old, run-down brick home. She was an attractive black woman with startlingly large brown eyes. My heart sank as I realized that Larry truly had not inherited her good looks. As we walked into the house, Sadie started talking to me. There were no words of affection or hugs for Larry. She matter-of-factly asked Larry how he was doing in school.

The youngest daughter, Melanie, who was about three years older than Larry and obviously pregnant, lived at home. Although it was a school day, Melanie was at home. Melanie was engaged in various household chores, and there was ongoing arguing between mother and daughter about how these should be done. Melanie made no attempt to interact with her brother. Larry drifted to another side of the house to see his old bedroom. He loitered as he came back to the family room, obviously uncomfortable.

Later, Sadie invited me into the kitchen. Calling out to Larry, she offered us milk to drink. Larry did not want any and I declined as well. Sadie took a swig straight from the milk carton and replaced it in the refrigerator. She did this a number of times, bringing to mind an empty container trying desperately and vainly to fill itself.

I asked about her other children. She seemed particularly proud of her oldest son Joseph, the musician. I interrupted to say that Larry had been corresponding with Joseph. I added that he was learning to play the guitar and would eventually like to join his brother's band. Sadie looked at Larry, rolled her eyes upward and sighed, as if to say, "I can't imagine a loser like Larry playing in Joseph's band." Could her disregard for Larry be based on something so superficial as looks?

Trying to be constructive, I asked Sadie if she had any plans for Larry's future, particularly after he returned home. Now I saw pain and anger written all over her face. In an anguished voice she told me that trouble began in her marriage only after Larry's birth. She saw Larry as an "evil" child, though he could not help it "because he was born that way." She told me that Larry looked and acted "ugly" from birth. I told Sadie about Larry's behavioral improvements at the center. She was silent.

As we were leaving, Sadie put her head out the window and yelled to Larry that he could come and live with her when he had a job.

Larry and I walked briskly to the train station. I was in no mood to discuss the visit. My thoughts about Sadie were not pleasant, and, of course, I didn't want to share them with Larry. I was worried that Larry would act out right there on the train. I wondered if I had done the right thing in taking Larry to visit his mother. Was it useful and important for Larry to know where he stood with his mother? Sadie would never accept him unless, perhaps, he brought money. Was rejection ever helpful to children?

Larry clung to Sadie's parting words. She must love him if she wanted him to come home after he found a job.

In spite of this miserable meeting, I hoped that more communication would follow. I invited Sadie to parent education meetings, promising her round-trip train fare, but she declined.

Following the home visit, as I expected and feared, Larry started to act out in the residential cottage as well as in school. His behavior deteriorated. Thus I was aware that, at some level, Larry was conscious of Sadie's rejection. Larry got into trouble in school and did everything possible in a negative way to get my attention. He threw temper tantrums with teachers and his cottage parents and got into fistfights with other boys. I waited out the storm and stuck by him. It took two full months for Larry to get back the discipline and self-control he had achieved prior to the home visit.

In our staff meetings, we discussed what could be done for Larry when he became a young adult. Eventually, we made plans to send Larry, when he was older, to a group home for independent living if he was not able to go home. I diligently worked at sustaining the relationship between Larry and his older brother Joseph. I encouraged Larry to call Joseph and invite him to come for a visit. Joseph did come and, thankfully, the interaction was positive. Joseph encouraged Larry in his schoolwork and musical aspirations. I believe that this visit was one of the best gifts Larry had ever received!

There were other issues that were unresolved. One included my inability to do anything about his relationship with his father whom he had not seen since he was about 6 years old. The absence of his father was one of the biggest gaps in Larry's life. His father would be ready for parole in another five years. The fact that his relationship with his mother did not progress was another serious issue. I tried to work on this with Larry by pointing out that all people have frailties, including his mother, who had her own set of problems to face and did not seem ready for a relationship with Larry. He continued to defend his mother's behavior. A number of sessions were spent helping Larry understand and accept the fact that he could not reestablish a relationship with Sadie until she was ready.

OUTCOME AND DISCUSSION

My final sessions with Larry were painful for me. I could not change Larry's role in the family as the most disliked child. I could not provide the love he had missed. I could not repair his scarred face.

I resigned from the treatment center to pursue my doctorate in social work. Larry was passed on to another counselor. Later, I was only able to find out that he eventually "left" the agency. The social service system has a short memory; there are too many needy people standing in line.

My skin has grown thicker with experience. I wanted to share this case from a point in time when I may have overinvested in my clients. Certainly, I was deeply touched by the personality of this particular child.

Biographical Statement

Vimala Pillari, DSW, is a professor in the school of social work at Norfolk State University. She also maintains a private practice in Norfolk, Virginia. Dr. Pillari has written extensively and some of her recent books are Pathways to Family Myths: Human Behavior in the School Environment, Scapegoating in Families, *and* Direct Social Work Practice: Theory and Skills.

Healing a Family's Wounds

Linda Provus-McElroy

*Samantha, a 6-year-old victim of sexual abuse by her half brother, is the focus of this case study. The case is diagnosed as Adjustment Disorder with Mixed Emotional Features (*DSM-III-R *309.28). Over the course of 22 sessions, Samantha's understandable emotional neediness is transformed to feelings of acceptance and being in control. The primary treatment is unstructured, psychoanalytically oriented play therapy. However, family systems therapy is essential to keep all family members invested and insure the client's progress. Psycho-educational "biology lessons" also help foster the successful outcome.*

The disclosure of 6-year-old Samantha's sexual abuse 10 days earlier had left her parents in a state of emotional shock. Anticipating that such an emotional crisis would need immediate attention, I arranged to see Mr. and Ms. A. alone for the first session and to see Samantha a few days later.

Several observations I made in the first meeting foreshadowed future treatment issues. Upon entering, Mr. and Ms. A. sat on opposite sides of the room and showed no sign of affection or closeness. Had the disclosure of their daughter's abuse strained their relationship, or were there other factors contributing to their distance?

I asked the A.'s to tell me about their life prior to the disclosure. John A., a tall man in his late 40s, stated he was an engineer at a nearby industrial corporation. Despite the severity of his dark business suit, he made eye contact and smiled slightly when I tried to offer reassurance or support. He seemed realistically concerned, pragmatic, and problem oriented. His manner implied, "Just tell me what needs to be done, and I'll do it." Lisa A., by contrast, appeared taut and ready to break down. In her mid-30s, she too was impeccably, almost severely, dressed. She began by saying that for Samantha's first five years she had given up a lucrative position in order to be at home full-time, but she grew increasingly restless. After much thought, she decided two months ago to return to work as an executive for a local consulting firm. As she spoke, she gazed at the floor. Her eyes had a hurt and frightened look, with perhaps a layer of anger beneath. I sensed guilt and self-blame in her tone as well as her words, but decided to pursue less sensitive areas first.

I learned that Samantha's abuser was her half brother Craig, a 15-year-old high school freshman with a history of poor grades and behavior problems (e.g., truancy, fighting, talking back to teachers). However, Craig had never displayed serious psychopathology, substance abuse, or any indication of a sexual problem. From the A.s' description, he sounded like an immature teenager of average or low-average intelligence with a weak ego and poor impulse control.

Also in the family was Samantha's half sister Cathy, now a freshman at a college 200 miles away. She spent school vacations alternately at her mother's home in a distant state and with her father, and occasionally came to his house for weekends. Cathy A. had no history of behavioral or psychological problems.

Mr. A. explained he had divorced his first wife 12 years ago while living in a western state and received primary custody of his two children, then ages 3 and 6, due to his wife's history of depression and psychiatric hospitalization. He had subsequently accepted a job transfer to Florida where two years later he met his current wife. They had dated for two years prior to marriage and had been married for two years prior to Samantha's birth. Their daughter was a planned child; her father was 41 and her mother 30 at the time of her birth.

As our discussion gradually focused on recent events, the following facts emerged: Ten days earlier the A.'s had informed Samantha that they were to be going on a brief business trip together and that, as usual, Samantha would stay at home in the care of her half brother. "If you go," Samantha said, "Craig will make me touch his penis." Despite their shock, the A.'s responded with impressive urgency; the trip was cancelled, the police were called, and the next day a child psychiatrist was consulted. Following his questioning by the police and child welfare agency, Craig was flown to his mother's home where he was to receive psychiatric evaluation and treatment.

At the time of my evaluation, I had few details of the actual abuse other than the fact that Samantha had been coerced into masturbating her brother, and that this had been occurring for at least one year. The specifics of Samantha's victimization would not emerge until much later.

As I closed the first meeting with Mr. and Ms. A., I tried to leave them with some sense of hopefulness during such a painful time. I explained that we would be working as a team, sharing information to help Samantha and the family deal with the abuse and get back on track. In addition, I told them that since their daughter had two loving, supportive parents and since the abuse had been stopped, the prognosis was encouraging. My remark was made to address both spoken concerns ("Will my child be OK?") and unspoken concerns ("Is it my fault?") while at the same time offering a light at the end of a seemingly endless tunnel. The A.'s seemed calmer and less defensive at the end of the hour, and we made plans for Samantha to come in after school later that week.

Meeting 6-year-old Samantha for the first time two days later, I maintained the same diagnostic curiosity toward her that I had toward her parents. How would she be reacting to the abuse? to the disclosure of it? to the subsequent departure of her brother? What specific problem areas might this situation have triggered for her: guilt and self-blame? unresolved anger? difficulties with trust? with body image? Most importantly, how ready would Samantha be to confront these issues in therapy?

I watched her approach my office that day and wondered about the mother-daughter relationship: Lisa A. got out of the car and walked rapidly toward the office door with long strides. Several feet behind her, a small girl with blond pigtails ran to catch up. Ms. A. stopped at the door and took Samantha's hand as they entered together. After a brief introduction I invited Samantha to join me in the playroom. She separated easily from her mother.

During that first hour I was able to begin formulating a psychological profile of Samantha. Her relative comfort and spontaneity with the toys told me she was not an inhibited or overly anxious child. She chatted lightly with me, making eye contact, laughing at small jokes, and generally relating in a warm, friendly manner. She appeared to be, in general, a psychologically healthy first grader. Knowing this, I decided to assess her readiness to discuss the sexual abuse and began by asking about her family. "I have a mom and a dad and a sister . . . and a brother," she answered. I sought further information. "My sister is nice, but my brother is mean—no, I mean . . . he's nice too!" Samantha's remark revealed the emotional ambivalence victimized children often feel toward their abusers.

As Samantha labored over her family drawing, I gently inquired as to why Craig might be "mean." "Well," she answered, her brown eyes glued to the paper in front of her, "sometimes he does bad stuff. . . . Want to see my picture now?"

Samantha's drawing was simple but told me much about her feelings and relationships at home. Five angular figures stood in a line: Samantha, Craig, Cathy, Dad, and Mom. No figure touched another. Of the five, one lacked hands or arms: Mom. After completing the drawing in pencil, Samantha used the color markers and gave herself red lips, brown eyes, and brightly colored clothing, a sign of being different yet special and further evidence of good ego identity.

When our 50 minutes were up, I told Samantha I looked forward to seeing her again. She was reluctant to leave this new relationship. "Oh, please, can't I stay with you?" Back in the waiting room, Lisa A. greeted her daughter with obvious delight and they left hand in hand.

CONCEPTUALIZATION

Samantha's treatment could be conceptualized on several levels. I identified her as having an Adjustment Disorder with Mixed Emotional Features, a nonstigmatizing label which allowed for a wide symptom picture yet also suggested the immediacy and traumatic quality of the abuse. Looking beyond the *DSM-III-R*, however, I felt that a number of specific interpersonal and intrapsychic concerns needed to be addressed.

The sexual abuse itself would be my primary concern. Using unstructured, psychoanalytically oriented play therapy, I planned to let Samantha show me what her fears or worries were regarding her abuse. My relationship with her, and our use of the materials in the playroom, would be the main avenue for offering whatever support, interpretation, or educational information might be helpful. Children as young as Samantha who have had sexual encounters often also need some reassuring "biology lessons" about babies, anatomy, and the like, as well as psychological strengthening, and I expected to make use of several children's books on the topic.

Second, I was concerned that Samantha's relationships with family members seemed to be characterized by unmet emotional needs and inappropriate meeting of sexual needs. From her drawings and verbalizations, I learned that Craig was a source of positive as well as negative interactions. Samantha seemed to relate in a less conflicted way to her sister, Cathy, and her father, while Samantha's relationship with her mother was probably the most complex of all.

In addition to conducting individual dynamic therapy with Samantha, I planned to use a family systems approach for mother-daughter sessions and also for sessions that brought together Samantha and both her parents. These parent-child sessions, however, would be postponed until Samantha and I had a strong alliance, as such sessions can sometimes become confrontational and uncomfortable.

Finally, the visible strain on Lisa and John A. suggested the need for a limited number of parents-only sessions. As with most parents of victimized children, their feelings of guilt, anger, and blame needed to be identified and resolved if they were to help their daughter. Thus my treatment plan for the A.'s would be a collection of "different strokes for different folks," using dynamic, psycho-educational, and family systems interventions.

■ PROCESS

From our first meeting Samantha seemed to feel at home in the playroom and comfortably used its furnishings to express herself. Each week she was free to select whatever toy, game, or materials might match her current mood. More often than not, the projective-type toys requiring emotional input were her choice.

One of Samantha's favorites was a board game in which players select cardboard people and backgrounds to make up stories. Through this game and also through her play with the dollhouse and doll people, I was able to enter the inner world of 6-year-old Samantha. At our second meeting she told two stories of "a mother and her baby girl" as we played the game.

Samantha: There's a baby girl here, she's sick. And her mother doesn't know what's wrong! (pause.) So . . . finally her mother takes her to a doctor, a lady doctor. And the doctor says, "She has the flu!" And then the baby gets better. (She looks up at me with a smile.)

LPM: (smiling) I'm glad the baby gets better.

Samantha silently returned to the game with intense concentration, rolling the dice and keeping track of our points to see who would win. Next turn, she offered a second story.

Samantha: This mother is going away, she's going on a trip in a plane. And here's the father and the sisters and brother on the ground. . . . They feel sad! That's the end.

Samantha's eyes were downcast and she was silent for some time. I chose my words carefully, since our relationship was still new and our alliance untested.

LPM: Maybe you feel a little sad that Mommy goes away . . . and maybe even a little mad that sometimes she can't seem to help you.

Samantha: (raising her eyes slowly to meet mine) Yes . . . a little mad.

My hopes that a positive transference would safely allow for this early interpretation were confirmed as we prepared to end the hour. Telling me not to look, Samantha wrote on a piece of paper, then elaborately folded it and put it in my hand. "This is my phone number," she said. "Just to make sure you have it." I thanked her warmly and told her I looked forward to our meeting next week.

One week later, Samantha picked up from where we had left off: testing the alliance and sharing painful feelings. On entering, she closed the playroom door tightly, hesitated, then opened and closed it again, as if double-checking our privacy.

Samantha: (walking to the wall calendar) I told you when my birthday is. Do you remember?

LPM: I remember that it's in June.

Samantha: (turning to face me, obviously pleased) Yes! It's June 10th! And I'll be 7. . . . (long pause) Do you know what my brother did?

Afraid of losing the moment, I merely shook my head, showing interest with my expression but saying nothing. Slowly Samantha crossed the room and picked up the boy hand puppet. I sat motionless on the floor, watching. She brought the puppet to my ear and whispered in a snarling voice fraught with tension.

Samantha: (as puppet) I'm mad at Samantha! She told!

LPM: (to the puppet, not Samantha) You're wrong! Samantha was *good* to tell!

Samantha: (as puppet) No! I'm really mad at her now!

Seeing me challenge her steadfast self-blame, Samantha was perplexed. She dropped the puppet and ran to the inflatable Donald Duck knockdown toy, punching furiously.

LPM: Now *Samantha* is mad. Who is she mad at?

Samantha: (still punching) I'm mad at Craig!

LPM: You're mad at Craig because *Craig* did something wrong. *He* was bad, not you!

Later that hour we talked about Craig and his "problem of bad touching." I explained that Craig had gone away not to be punished or because he was mad at Samantha, but because he could see a special kind of doctor there who could help him with his problem. This seemed to satisfy Samantha until she posed a difficult question.

Samantha: Well, if Craig needs a problem-doctor, why don't *you* see him? Don't you want him to come here? Then you could play with *him*.

LPM: (Was this a wish or a fear on Samantha's part? Remembering her emotional neediness, I decided it was a fear.) No, Samantha, Craig isn't going to come here. He'll spend time with his special problem-doctor out West, and you'll spend time with me. I like things just the way they are.

Samantha's sigh and relaxed posture reassured me.

By our seventh session, Samantha was freely sharing her fears and frustrations and clearly feeling good about our time together. Gradually, the focus shifted somewhat away from the sexual abuse to her current unhappiness at home. As foreshadowed by her family drawing, Samantha showed that she felt hurt and abandoned by her mother. Since Ms. A. had begun full-time employment some months prior to the disclosure but, unknowingly, during the time the abuse was occurring, these two themes of hurt and loss seemed to have become intertwined in Samantha's experience. We chatted about her family as we played the story game together.

Samantha: I hardly ever get to see my mom, you know. She's gone when I get up for breakfast. My dad gets me up. . . . I like coming here. Can I come every day?

LPM: You think then maybe you wouldn't miss your mom so much?

Samantha: (rolling the dice) Mm-hm. . . . Here's a story. This is a little girl and these are her parents. The little girl runs away because her parents are mean! Her *brother* made a mess, but they made *her* clean up! They blamed her for what happened!

LPM: Gee, that wasn't fair. Then what happened?

Samantha: (pausing, as if struggling to reach a final judgement) Then . . . then her big sister came in and told the parents where she was! So the parents went and got her, and everybody was OK!

LPM: The sister was *good* to tell. She told the truth and things were OK. I'm glad.

Between our 9th and 10th session, an unexpected blow disrupted our work: Samantha was suddenly subpoenaed to testify before the state attorney. With no forewarning she was asked to recount endless specifics about the events of her abuse. I learned of this through a phone call from a distraught Lisa A. Needing to vent her feelings of helplessness and outrage, she lashed out at me with a barrage of questions: Why had Samantha needed yet another interrogation? How could such repeated inquiries be helpful? Was any of this truly helping her daughter? How would I know for sure when progress was being made?

I let Ms. A. express her distress without comment. While some of her concerns had a basis in reality (i.e., the thoughtlessness of repeatedly questioning child victims), I also felt she was projecting her own feelings of guilt and self-doubt. Had she, in response to this retraumatizing of her only child, become painfully aware of the emotional distance between them? The time had come for our first mother-daughter session. I told Ms. A. I would mention the meeting to Samantha when I saw her the next day, and plans were made for the three of us to meet the following week.

On the appointed day, I watched Samantha impatiently pull her mother into the waiting room, then run ahead into the playroom, looking over her shoulder expectantly to make sure Mom was close behind. Despite her intense positive transference relationship with me, Mom was still the person whose attention and affection were irreplaceable. Samantha had selected a projective question-and-answer game for the three of us, and the play began with Samantha reading her question aloud.

Samantha: "What makes you really angry?" Hmm . . . I'd say not being able to see my Mom, 'cause she has to work! *That* makes me angry.

Lisa A.: (pausing, as if wanting to say the right thing) You know Samantha, that's a good answer, because you told me just how you felt. . . . I like it when you do that!

Samantha: OK, Mom. Now it's *your* question: "What makes *you* really angry?"

Lisa A.: (after nervously glancing toward me) Well . . . well, I think what makes *me* really angry is thinking about what Craig did to you. That was wrong, and it makes me mad!

There was a brief moment when Lisa and Samantha locked eyes, as if each was truly hearing the other for the first time. Then Samantha threw her arms around her mother with abandon, almost knocking both of them over. I could see tears in Ms. A.'s eyes.

Samantha: Oh, Mommy, I love you. And, you know what? What Craig did makes *me* mad too! Even madder than you going to work!

After that 12th therapy hour, the first to include a parent, my individual hours with Samantha were alternated with child-parent sessions or, occasionally, meetings with Mr. and Ms. A. alone. Samantha was better able to acknowledge the abuse and to articulate her needs for support, affection, protection, and the like. New issues arose, such as whether or not to plan a trip West to visit Craig (vetoed for a year after discussion by family members) and whether or not to exchange letters with Craig (agreed to, with close supervision by therapist and parents).

Prior to our 19th session, Samantha and her parents received word that because Craig was being charged with felonies at the adult level he would be unable to return to their home at any time in the near or distant future. This news caused a brief setback, as Samantha's defenses collapsed under the remnants of still unresolved guilt. We processed this in a joint session with her mother.

Samantha:	(crying) I knew it! I shouldn't have told! He can never come back and it's my fault.
LPM:	I'm not so sure, Samantha. I wonder if your mom feels the same way.
Lisa A.:	(taking my cue) No, Sam, I'm so *glad* you told! You helped the whole family a lot! And, you know what? I was a little scared thinking of Craig coming back here. I don't really think I was ready for that.
Samantha:	(looking up slowly from tear-filled eyes) You weren't, Mommy? You know, I wasn't either! I got a stomachache whenever I thought about his coming back!
LPM:	So it seems everyone thinks it's not a good idea for Craig to come back here now, right?

Three weeks later, Samantha, her mother, her father, and I had our last family meeting. A termination date had been set for one week hence, after a final session with Samantha and me. In this session, John and Lisa A. focused on providing their daughter with the support, both emotional and concrete, that would prevent the possibility of future abuse. Family rules were enumerated and elaborately written down by Mr. A., with much input from his wife and daughter. These included "Tell someone if you're upset about something," "If someone is scary, you don't have to be with them," and similar statements of protection and reassurance. Photocopies were distributed to all, and everyone seemed to share a satisfying feeling of closure and resolution. In the second half of that hour Samantha sat on her mother's lap as Lisa A. read aloud *Something Happened to Me* (Sweet, 1981), a sensitive narrative about feelings of victimization. The A.'s then left together, arms tightly around each other.

My last session with Samantha was characterized by a healthy sort of impatience. Instead of the needy, somewhat insatiable little girl of six months ago, Samantha now was someone who had worked through those unmet needs and was eager to get on with her life. She chose her favorite game, and proceeded to tell me a story.

Samantha: There's a little girl, and a boy . . . he's bigger than her. Anyway, he does mean stuff . . . he . . . he teases her! He teases her all the time! And so the girl . . . the girl goes right to her mother and says, "Mom, this boy is doing mean stuff to me!" (pause) And then *he* gets in big trouble.
LPM: And the girl?
Samantha: And the girl is safe for ever and ever.

OUTCOME

After working closely with John, Lisa, and Samantha A. for six months, I was comfortable turning the case over to them for continued self-care. As I had explained to Mr. and Ms. A. at the outset, the consequences of sexual abuse can never be completely erased. Instead, the A.'s will remember the abuse and be sensitive to situations of special stress for Samantha, especially those involving feelings of loss, abandonment, and helplessness. Additionally, John and Lisa A. knew that Samantha's adolescence and introduction to sexuality might reawaken the trauma. In any event, I told them they should feel free to call me or return anytime for follow-up. Likewise, Samantha made sure she had my phone number, just as she had given me hers in our first meeting. I felt confident, however, that she would turn first to her parents at any sign of distress, and that they would both be there for her.

DISCUSSION

The A. family was seen for a total of 22 sessions; of these, 16 were individual psychotherapy with Samantha, 4 included Samantha with one or both parents, and 2 involved my meeting alone with John and Lisa A. Clearly, Samantha had been my primary focus.

Her emotional neediness at the start of therapy facilitated a strong maternal transference to me and expedited the uncovering of painful feelings. This psychoanalytically oriented approach gave Samantha a sense of being in control and of being unconditionally accepted, both feelings that were lacking at home. In this situation she responded excellently to treatment.

However, as in all child cases, to keep the child, you have to keep the parents. Addressing the immediate and ongoing needs of Samantha's parents, especially her mother, was also a necessary part of the treatment plan. Despite the early impression I had of Lisa A. being cold or distant, my continued contact with her revealed that, like nearly every parent, under her defensive armor was simply a woman overwhelmed by the demands of parenthood and the feeling that she had failed miserably.

Mr. and Ms. A. were not perfect parents, to be sure, yet their intentions and values were good. By merely strengthening the relationship between parents and child and enhancing the resources already present, I was able to help this family get back on its track of normal, day-to-day living.

REFERENCES

Sweet, P.E. (1981). *Something happened to me.* Racine, WI: Mother Courage Press.

Biographical Statement

Linda Provus-McElroy, PhD, is a licensed mental health counselor and assistant clinical professor in child psychiatry, University of Florida in Gainesville. She is in private practice in the treatment of children, adolescents, and adults, and is the author of articles on child sexual abuse that have appeared in the Journal of Mental Health Counseling *(1989) and* Psychotherapy *(1991).*

The Three-Generation Triangle: A Noh Drama

Dick T. Sampson, Toshiaki Sato, and Kamiko Miyashita

Dick Sampson, while serving as a Fulbright professor at Tohoku University in Japan, became acquainted with Professor Sato, a psychologist, and Mrs. Miyashita, a health visitor in a rural health clinic. This multilingual counseling trio joined forces to work with a 6-year-old girl, Kodomochan, who refused to attend school (Separation Anxiety Disorder, DSM-III-R *309.21).*

The metaphor of a Noh drama is used to structure the case study. This organization is intended to help the reader integrate Kodomochan's school refusal and the cultural and family transactions that support this behavior. Each Noh drama and family therapy experience is unique and given life by the actors. In this case, the family was challenged to rewrite their script, and they successfully did.

Kodomochan Tomo is a 6-year-old Japanese girl who refused to attend school. This case study explores Kodomochan's school refusal and the cultural and family transactions that supported this behavioral pattern. It also describes the structural family counseling interventions that were used to prompt the family's transitions.

The metaphor of Noh drama is used to structure the case study. This organization is intended to allow the reader to integrate the cultural background of rural Japan with the dynamics of the Tomo family.

Noh drama is a traditional Japanese art form. It presents intensified emotions played out through movement, dance, song, and masks, with plot being only a minor element. The background created by the stage, orchestra, and chorus in Noh is analogous to the broader context in which family counseling takes place, which includes the geographical setting, culture, and community. As with family counseling, Noh drama is best understood as a blending of the actors and the background.

Imagine yourself attending a family Noh drama in the Tohoku region of northern Japan. The stage is a large plain checked with rice paddies. The color and mood of the stage change with the seasons. You can sense from the land a rich tradition of labor, determination, commitment, and loyalty. The backdrop for this stage is the serenity of pine-covered hills and mountains which drop abruptly into the paddies where humans toil.

The orchestra for this drama is at the rear of the stage blending in with the simple pines. The orchestra plays the themes of insider-outsider (*uchi-soto*) and the bonds of family and community (*en*).

Particularly relevant to the drama are cultural rules governing relationships within families of origin. These include marriage arrangements, spouse and parent roles, and child rearing practices. The family is a basic element in the rhythm of traditional Japan. Its survival is entrusted to the oldest son or, in cases where there is no oldest son, to the spouse of the highest-ranking female family member. These males and their spouses must take on the responsibility of the family's growth and care both within and between generations.

The institution of marriage was traditionally seen as an intricate part of family support and bonding. It created the tempo of the family. Although the post-War constitution introduced choice into the marriage process, parental consultation is still important whether the marriage is arranged (*miai*) or a love match (*renai*). Traditionally, the perceptions of men and women and their roles within a marriage have been viewed much differently than in Western societies. Marriage matches the strength of the woman to the weakness of the man and vice versa to form an interdependent relationship. In this relationship, the wife assumes the responsibility for the domestic domain (*uchi*) which includes household chores, food preparation, child rearing, intrafamily generational relations, and the children's schooling. The mother is seen as the key motivator. Problems that a child may have at school quickly become the mother's responsibility. Should a solution to the child's problems not be found, the mother often bears the brunt of the blame. The husband, on the other hand, is in charge of the public domain (*soto*) which includes the world of work as well as the broader realm of extrafamilial social relations.

The spousal roles in the family take second place to the parenting roles. This is especially true for the mother. An excellent example of the primary importance of the parent subsystem is the sleeping pattern in many traditional rural Japanese families. In these families the children often sleep in the same room with the parents, frequently between the parents and close to the mother.

For a Japanese mother, child rearing means encouraging the child's close ties to the family, and to her in particular. Since her sense of worth is closely tied to her children, the mother-child relationship is paramount. The Japanese mother must be a role model for her children, developing the positive interpersonal relations on which family and group harmony (*wa*) are built. She also must act as a motivator, encouraging the children to endure hardship and put forth maximum effort in their scholastic lives. Her skill is ideally based on encouragement and dependence rather than on prodding, coercion, or punishment.

In Noh drama the role of the chorus is to add lyrics to rhythms and tunes supplied by the orchestra. In this family drama the chorus represents the historical and community background of a rural Japanese village. The particular town in this case study has a rich, proud history as a castle town. The community developed not only around the Samurai warrior's power but also around the resources of land and the farming skills of the people that have been passed down through the generations. It has developed a strong tradition of fulfilling its own internal needs without being dependent on those outside the community. The dominance of industrialism in Japan, however, is now challenging the internal order of the rural community. The farm economy can no longer act as the sole economic support for the community and its families. Many of the middle-generation men (from their late twenties to mid-forties) are having to venture outside farming occupations and the community to provide for their families. This act may also signal the need to move outside the community to learn new methods of coping with society's changes.

My entry into this family drama occurred quite by accident. As a Fulbright professor in family psychology at Tohoku University, I became acquainted with Professor (*sensei*) Sato, a psychologist in the faculty of general education. Sato sensei explained that he was interested in adding family assessment data to a 10-year longitudinal developmental study he was conducting. I suggested that genograms, or drawings of a family tree, were an excellent beginning assessment tool for studying individual families. Sato seemed excited by the concept. He stated that he and Mrs. (*san*) Miyashita, a health visitor in a rural health clinic, had a good case to use for learning about genograms. The family had been involved in Sato sensei's developmental study since its inception. He also commented that Miyashita san had developed a positive helping relationship with the family. From this modest beginning, Sato sensei proceeded to orchestrate our multilingual counseling triad.

CONCEPTUALIZATION

The plot of the family drama began with Kodomochan's traffic accident at age 6. While riding her bicycle to school, Kodomochan was hit by a car and suffered a severely broken arm. She was rushed to the hospital where she was confined for several weeks of treatment. Approximately six weeks after the accident Kodomochan's mother asked her to return to school. She fearfully balked at this request. After much coaching from her mother she made several sporadic attempts at attending school but only if accompanied into the classroom by her mother. These attempts, to the consternation of her mother, evolved into complete refusal to attend school. Sato sensei reported that Kodomochan's behavior was having an effect on all three generations of the Tomo family (*ie*). Kodomochan's total number of absences for the school year were well above the 50-day criteria used by Japanese clinicians, educators, and researchers as the diagnostic standard for classifying school refusal.

Prior to the first family session the counseling triad came together at the local community health clinic to discuss the goals and strategies for the ensuing family counseling drama. We constructed a plan to assist us in team building, sharing case information, and setting goals for our visit to the Tomo house (*uchi*).

Our meeting began in typical Japanese style with the serving of green tea (*ocha*). Miyashita san then listed the names of the Tomo family members:

Obasan: the paternal grandmother
Ojisan: the paternal grandfather
Otosan: the father
Okasan: the mother
Oneichan: Kodomochan's 9-year-old sister
Kodomochan: the 6-year-old identified client
Ototochan: her 4-year-old brother

Before discussing our counseling goals for the Tomo family, I asked Miyashita san to share her involvement with and perceptions of the family. She shared this story. At the suggestion of the school she had first contacted the mother (Okasan) approximately nine months ago about Kodomochan's school refusal. As a member of the local community and a highly respected health visitor, Miyashita san was accepted into the house (*uchi*) immediately by the relieved mother (Okasan). Okasan expressed extreme frustration over her daughter's school refusal. She reported that when she tried to coach and pressure Kodomochan to return to school, the grandmother (Obasan) would intervene by holding the child and reassuring her she did not have to attend school just yet. This overinvolvement of the grandmother continued anytime her granddaughter exhibited resistant or fearful behavior. Okasan especially resented the nights when Kodomochan would awake from a bad dream and leave her side for the comfort and protection of the grandmother's bed (futon).

The team was drawn to this overinvolvement of Obasan and her grandchild. It seemed quite obvious that a triangle existed between the grandmother (Obasan), the mother (Okasan), and the child (Kodomochan). The triangle included enmeshed boundaries between Obasan and Kodomochan. The mother and grandmother did not seem to have clearly defined roles, and the underlying resentment between them had led to a passive conflict. Kodomochan seemed to use this relationship between Okasan and Obasan to gain power over the mother.

The mother also had expressed frustration over the lack of support she received from her husband (Otosan). As is typical in Japan, Okasan reported that her husband often felt caught between his mother and herself. She viewed this conflict as the cause of his lack of support for her.

Okasan's frustrations were not limited to relationships inside the household but also occurred in her relationships with the school. In an effort to persuade Kodomochan to return to school, Okasan agreed to attend class with her. There she came to the opinion that the teacher was insensitive to her daughter's fear and was extremely hard on her. Okasan had several confrontations with the teacher which finally culminated in the school negotiating a change in teachers.

Okasan told Miyashita san that she often felt very unsupported, alone, and angry. At Miyashita's suggestion, Okasan risked going outside the family to seek personal counseling. This counseling seemed to help her feel better, but it had little effect on the family relations and no effect on her daughter's school refusal pattern.

Based on Miyashita san's observations and the discussion at our planning session, we agreed to a counseling strategy. The family would be asked to construct a genogram while our counseling triad focused on the dynamics of the Tomo family. We decided to challenge the family transactions through a structural approach to family counseling. Our emphasis was on observing and challenging boundaries, alignments, influence, role definitions, and the construction of reality within the family.

■ PROCESS

Act 1: First Counseling Session

Our counseling triad used the health clinic's small car for the trip to the Tomo family home. As we approached the house, the mother (Okasan) appeared at the door and began walking toward the car performing a formal greeting bow. The grandmother (Obasan) came out the house behind Okasan and appeared to be directing the scene. She also bowed in greeting.

The grandfather (Ojisan) was in the doorway bowing his greeting, while the three children peeked through the doorway to see what this strange trio with the foreigner (*gauijin*) looked like. We joined the family drama bowing and saying, "How do you do? Pleased to meet you." (*"Hajimaemashite! Dozo Yoroshiku."*) Greeting in this traditional manner was critical to my acceptance as I crossed cultural lines. It began the joining process that would allow the counseling triad to become a part of the family system.

The family led us into the anteroom of the house. We removed our shoes while continuing our bows. Donning slippers, the group shuffled across the hardwood floors to the sliding shoji screen which opened into the main living room. This was a tatami-matted room with a large low table surrounded by seat cushions. Next to the sliding screen entry was a Western-style couch. The interior wall of the house included a bookcase and a small family shrine.

We removed our slippers as we proceeded into the tatami room. Sato sensei knelt at the far end of the table, opposite the grandfather, in the position that is commensurate with the respect for his position. On his left, with her back to the outer wall, was Miyashita san. I knelt rather uncomfortably on her left and beside the grandfather (Ojisan), who assumed the power place (Katcho) at the head of the table. Opposite myself and to Ojisan's left, and about a meter and a half from the table, was the grandmother (Obasan). The mother (Okasan) assumed her place on the same side of the table to the right of Sato sensei. She arranged her cushion close to the table for access in serving tea and food. The older daughter (Oneichan) perched on the couch while the young son (Ototochan) enjoyed the freedom to move all over the family side of the table. Kodomochan appeared only in the doorway of the house but never entered the living room. The entire family was present except for Otosan, who was at work. Once we were seated, Okasan served tea and cakes. The members of the counseling team were introduced, and small talk began over tea. Tea and social exchange are part of the Japanese joining process which emphasizes interpersonal relationships.

With my Western cultural orientation, I felt some uneasiness about not moving more directly to the task at hand. After about 5 minutes of social conversation I caught the eye of the home visitor and lightly touched the roll of genogram paper. She nodded and shifted her body position, pushing her teacup slightly toward the center of the table. With this move Sato sensei began to explain the task of genogram construction. As he was making his introductions, I rolled the paper out on the table and prepared to construct the genogram.

Miyashita san asked the mother questions about the children's names and ages. Okasan reported having two daughters and a younger son. Sato sensei translated while I drew the children on the genogram beginning with Oneichan, age 9, followed by Kodomochan, age 6, and finally Ototochan, age 4. The date of Kodomochan's accident was also listed and briefly discussed. After all the children were entered, I tested the relationship of the two sisters.

DS: It must be nice to be a big sister and have a little sister to model for.

Oneichan: Being a big sister isn't much fun.

I decided to drop this track. At this point in the counseling it seemed important to accent the idea of the grandparent subsystem to lay the groundwork for defining the grandparents' roles. I shifted the focus to the grandparents to conform with the Japanese emphasis on generational hierarchy. They were asked about the number, names, ages, and birth order of their children. Ojisan, after conferring briefly with his wife, reported they had two older daughters and a younger son. He stated that their firstborn daughter had died of a childhood illness at age 5. Discussing the illness of their child brought tears to the eyes of Ojisan and Obasan. Their pain was quite apparent even after 30 years. I said, "That was an extremely painful time in your lives." The grandparents nodded their agreement while wiping their eyes.

I made an internal note of the similarity between the two generations of children on the genogram. I especially noted the fact that the age of the grandparent's oldest daughter's illness and death corresponded with the age of their granddaughter's (Kodomochan's) traffic accident.

We proceeded to gather and enter the information on Ojisan and Obasan's two other children with emphasis on their son Otosan. Ojisan reported that his son attended high school and technical school in the large city about 30 kilometers from their family (*ie*). He was now employed in a professional position at a local financial institution. I looked at the grandfather and commented, "You must be quite proud of your son. He has worked hard to become educated and has an important professional position. It's nice to have such a dedicated son." The grandfather's chest puffed up as he nodded his agreement. The grandmother's eyes twinkled with pride in her son.

We queried Ojisan about himself and his siblings. He stated that he was the seventh child of nine. As is traditional, his oldest brother was responsible for the family's welfare. Through his arranged marriage to Obasan, Ojisan had acquired the oldest male's role in his wife's family with the commensurate responsibilities.

Ojisan appeared to me to be a hard-working, strong man's man. This perception was later supported by the local health clinic director. He explained that Ojisan had been considered the town's strong man for several years. This included winning several strength contests at local celebrations.

Probing further into Ojisan's history led us to the discovery that he had recently developed a diabetic condition as well as high blood pressure.

DS: (in an effort to further affiliate with Ojisan) You have worked hard tilling the soil and harvesting the rice. When did your heart problems begin?

Ojisan (with a sigh) Six years ago.
DS: It must be difficult to have your life limited and not be able to work in the fields.

The grandfather's eyes softened indicating to me he felt understood.

Next our attention shifted to Obasan. Although she had at times entered the discussion to jog Ojisan's memory, she had remained mostly in the background. Her influence and direction, however, were felt through her confirming glances toward other members. Obasan related that she was the sixth of seven children. Of the seven children four older siblings, including the only two older males, had died early in life through either illness or war. The death of these older siblings left Obasan the heir of the *ie*. She affirmed her husband's adoption of the primary male role in the family through their arranged marriage.

DS: (pointing to her siblings and oldest child on the genogram) There is a lot of pain and loss for you.
Obasan: (with a painful nod) Yes, that is true.
DS: It is difficult to be a mother with a sick child. I'm wondering if your granddaughter's accident doesn't bring back old memories?
Obasan: (thoughtfully shakes her head in agreement)
DS: How nice it is to have a strong man (a hand gesture links grandfather and grandmother together) for support and to help carry out family traditions.

Obasan responded by looking at Ojisan in a caring way affirming their relationship.

Okasan was the last person to place herself at the table, as was customary. In the same vein the counselor called on her last to comment on the genogram. Okasan provided information on her 10-year arranged marriage to Otosan. She then offered information about her father. "He reads a lot and is interested in politics, especially political discussions." In her comments there is an air of pride and frustration. Her demeanor in discussing her father led me to believe he is important in her life.

When asked for information about her mother and siblings, Okasan could supply little. I was surprised by Okasan's depth of knowledge about her husband's family but apparent lack of knowledge about her own family of origin, though it may have reflected her culturally assigned role as caretaker in her husband's family.

Looking at Obasan then back to Okasan, I began to challenge their relationship and role definitions and to build strength with Okasan.

DS: (directly to the mother and obliquely to the grandmother) You are a really successful mother. You've stayed with Kodomochan's problem and not quit. You even risked seeking help outside the family from Miyashita san and a counselor. I think you have demonstrated your skill as a mother.

At this point Miyashita san and I became joined as a team. Even though we spoke different languages, she began to not only support but to add to my comments. There were times when she even made the lead comments. This amazed our counseling triad. By teaming we had overcome the language barrier.

Okasan: (blushing, nodding, and looking down toward her stomach indicating the accessing of feelings) I want clear direction and help with my daughter's problem. I wasn't getting anywhere inside the family.

DS: Mothers are given an important role as problem-solvers in Japan. That is certainly a lot of pressure. (turning to the grandmother) Grandmothers are important supporters for the mothers' efforts. You are lucky to have a daughter-in-law who faces problems head on.

Okasan looked a bit embarrassed but pleased with this recognition. Obasan had a startled look of awareness, almost as if it is the first time she has thought about her daughter-in-law's strengths.

DS: (to the grandmother) There are two separate roles in the family. Mother, who is the problem-solver and caretaker of her children, and grandmother, who acts in the support role for the mother.

Miyashita san supported and expanded on this statement.

Obasan: She does work at being a good mother.

DS: (to Obasan and Ojisan) You are a good team but you have a new role. The grandparents' job is to support the parents. The parents' job is to make the decisions and take care of the children.

Miyashita san continued on along this line, further defining the subsystem roles. She artfully pushed for the grandparents' agreement to these roles while still emphasizing the idea of a team. All the while the mother watched this dialogue intently with some relief.

DS: (adding intensity to the team idea) This family has the caring to be a good team when everyone plays his or her role.

The seeds of subsystems and subsystem roles and functions once sown were left to grow on their own.

DS: (looking at the older daughter and prepared to close the session) You are certainly a big responsible girl to ride a bike to school all alone.

She beamed and gave a big smile.

DS: (to the son) What do you call that robot toy in your hand?

The boy held up the toy as we got up from our kneeling positions on the tatami. His mother responded with the name of the toy.

The mother wore the formal Noh salutation mask. Yet behind this mask I sensed her questioning the value of the counseling session. Was this all just talk? Will anyone change? Will I always be trapped in a triangle?

We left the living room, retrieved our shoes, bowed, and said, "Yoroshiku."

Kyogen Scene: Between Counseling Sessions

Noh drama is structured with a Kyogen scene between acts, which provides a transition. Counseling also requires a transition time between sessions. This break allows the family and counselors to debrief and process the previous session.

On our return to the health center we discussed the first counseling session. The counseling triad agreed that we had

1. recognized the grandmother's fear and pain from sickness and death in her own family and made her feelings explicit for the other family members;
2. challenged the grandmother's overinvolvement with the Kodomochan by linking it to her past pain and fear;
3. added to the mother's family influence by reframing her actions as a demonstration of strength, competency, and caring;
4. challenged the subsystem boundaries between the grandparents and the parents by clearly defining these roles and pointing out how they could operate as a team with clear boundaries; and
5. freed up the family energy toward flexibility by stroking the family's efforts and caring.

We also agreed that a second act which included Kodomochan and Otosan, but excluded the grandparent subsystem, would be useful. This session would be initiated after time was given for the family actors to process the first counseling session.

In my role as counseling consultant I suggested to Sato sensei and Miyashita san that we continue to work toward our training goals by introducing another counseling intervention. I described the use of both family sculpting and family diagrams or portraits. Miyashita san stated that learning to use family diagrams and portraits would be most useful in her work. Our decision to use this technique in the second session was also based on the assumption that it was best suited to the Tomo family.

The portrait revealed the new alignments, boundaries, influence, and flexibility within the Tomo family (*uchi*). The mother gained influence and Kodomochan began to consistently attend school. Obasan assumed a new role supporting Okasan rather than using overinvolvement to pass her fears on to Kodomochan.

The family members, especially the grandfather, seemed amazed that our strange counseling triad understood the relationships within their home (*uchi*). No longer were we seen as total outsiders but we were viewed as a useful addition to the *uchi*. At a second meeting with the family at the health center, Oneichan picked up the beat. Through her enthusiasm the family was mobilized to make the transition to act 2 of the Noh drama a full month after the first act.

Act 2: Second Counseling Session

The family (excluding the grandparents) arrived and was greeted at the front entrance by the counseling triad. The children, led by Oneichan, seemed pleased and excited. The mother (Okasan) had replaced her questioning mask with one of appreciation and willingness. The father (Otosan) appeared unsure and apprehensive.

I was introduced to Otosan. We bowed to each other, then shook hands. I commented to Otosan on what a nice family he had and how proud he must be to have such a competent wife and mother for his children.

The group proceeded to the counseling room where we knelt around the large coffee table in the center of the room. Miyashita san knelt at the far end of the table opposite Okasan. To her right sat Oneichan. Otosan sat to the right of Oneichan closest to the door. Kodomochan sat at the corner of the table between Otosan and Okasan, who was kneeling at the end of the table closest to the door. The young son plopped himself between myself and Sato sensei on the opposite side of the table from Oneichan and Otosan.

Again, as is customary in Japan, the serving of tea preceded our discussion. Sato sensei and I focused on the young son by playing with him. We asked how his robot toy worked. Oneichan, in her sparkling way, shouted the directions across the table while Ototochan demonstrated with the toy.

Miyashita san introduced the idea of a family diagram or portrait by placing a large piece of poster paper on the coffee table with nine different-colored marking pens. She asked the Tomo family to discuss how they saw their family and as a team to draw a picture of the family. Okasan, Otosan, and Oneichan began to hesitantly discuss the family. They decided that each family member should choose a color. The choosing process proceeded slowly and stiffly. Oneichan became impatient. She grabbed all the pens, placed them in the center of the table, and told the family they were going to play a game of scramble for your color pen. She counted to three. All the family members actively grabbed for the color pen of their choice. Oneichan picked up a green pen, Kodomochan exuberantly grabbed a yellow pen, Okasan selected an orange pen, Otosan took the blue, and Ototochan selected black. The family assigned the brown color to Ojisan and red to Obasan.

The selecting of colors seemed to relax the family and opened the door to more discussion, but the idea of drawing a family diagram or portrait as a team seemed alien to the Tomos. After a bit more discussion Oneichan suddenly began to draw the family while everyone watched. She quickly took Otosan's pen. She placed a circle representing him in the center of the paper. She then surrounded him with the other family members connecting each to the father with a straight line.

After a brief moment of contemplation she exclaimed "No! No!" She redrew the family by placing her mother and father in the center of the family. As she drew, family members commented on the placement. They all agreed that this looked more like their family.

At this point in the drama I intervened by suggesting that the Otosan and Okasan should be surrounded by a circle to indicate their togetherness. Oneichan drew a circle around the spouse-parent subsystem. "How about changing the circle to a heart?" I offered. Oneichan had a blank look during the translation. Then with a sudden flash of her eyes she picked up the pens and began to draw while everyone watched in anticipation.

She began by placing the spouse-parent subsystem on the paper surrounded by a heart. The grandparent subsystem was then added and sur-

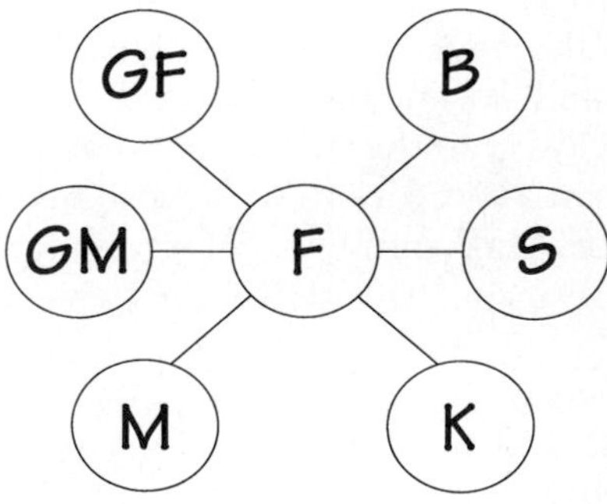

Figure 12–1
First family diagram by Kodomochan's older sister

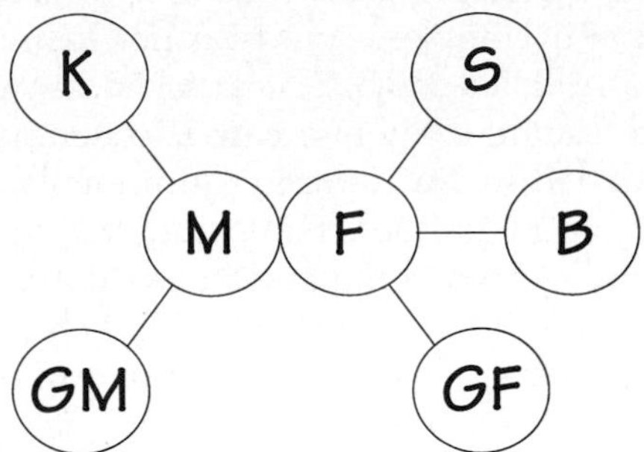

Figure 12–2
Second family diagram by Kodomochan's older sister

rounded by a heart. The grandparents' location closest to the mother may unconsciously affirm the pressure point within the family. The three children were then added in birth order.

We discussed this insightful drawing with the family members briefly. Miyashita san and I used this diagram to explain to the father about the work done during session one defining the parent-spouse and grandparent subsystems. Okasan joined in, sharing with Otosan her view on the need for boundaries between subsystems. Otosan listened in a very quiet and contemplative way and slowly nodded his understanding and approval.

Oneichan, in the true tradition of a Kyogen actor, had used herself to energize the family transition. She was strongly supported in her efforts by both her mother and father. All the family members were now close to the table and intensively involved in the drawing process, including Kodomochan.

I decided to involve Kodomochan by asking her to draw a picture of the family. At this direct request she quickly shrunk behind her mother.

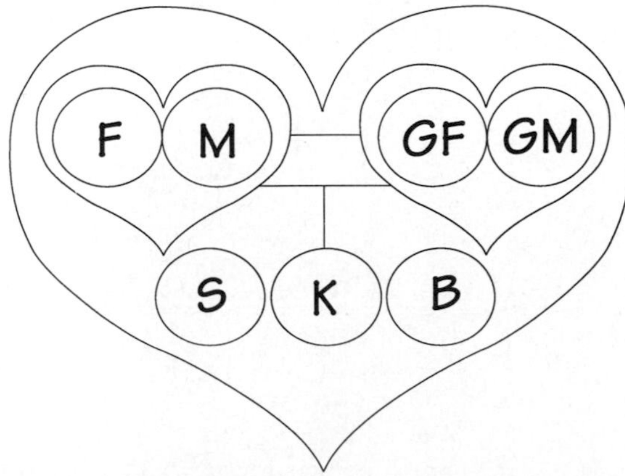

Figure 12–3
Third family diagram by Kodomochan's older sister

Okasan prodded: "Go ahead and draw the family." With this, the daughter touched her mother and withdrew even further behind her. The mother turned to directly confront her daughter and asked her to do the drawing as requested. Kodomochan immediately escaped to her father's side, touched him, and almost crawled in his lap. He gently asked her to draw. She refused as he caringly looked at her. The parent subsystem seems at a loss for what to do. Mother's direct commands and the father's gentle encouragement have both been met with resistance. I looked at the father: "Would you draw on the paper and see if you can get your daughter to join you and draw with you?"

This direction was not clear to the family or the counseling team. The father picked up the message as a command to prod. The mother began to increase her demands rather frantically. Oneichan crouched on the side watching the whole process, as Kodomochan became more resistant in a passively defiant manner tinged with fear. The parents and their child seemed rigidly confused and frustrated.

I considered the alternatives of explaining the directive to the father and to the counseling triad, giving the instruction to the father more clearly, or watching the intensity of the struggle increase. None of these actions seemed appropriate. I decided to refocus on the family drawing, leaving parent-child interaction skills to future sessions.

DS: (turning to the mother) How do you see your role in the family?

Ototochan: (impatient for his turn cried out) It's my turn to draw.

Ototochan drew a picture of the family with the mother in the center surrounded by all the other family members.

Okasan: (with a look of amazement on her face) That's how I feel. I'm caught in the center between everyone. There has been no one to help or support me.

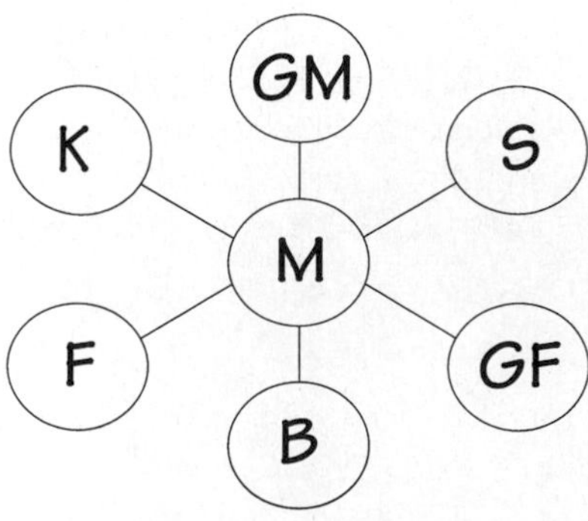

Figure 12–4
Family diagram by Kodomochan's younger brother

She gave a lengthy discourse aimed at her husband about how difficult it was for her to be in the center all of the time. Miyashita san, sensing the need for the spouses to be able to have their own discussion, moved the children into an adjoining area where they drew several pictures. Kodomochan moved to the drawing area freely. She seemed to respond to direction when she was not pressured and given the illusion of choice. She spontaneously joined in the drawing activity. Her drawings demonstrated creativity and strength when she was given freedom to move on her own.

DS: (reframing the pressure for Okasan) Despite your feelings of pressure and frustration, you've been doing a good job of exploring problem-solving options with Miyashita san and your counselor. (Otosan nodded his approval and support) Tell your husband what you want from him to make your job easier.

Okasan: (to Otosan) I want your support, especially with your mother. Sometimes you don't even listen to me.

Okasan then told about the pressures she felt from her mother-in-law. The more she talked the faster her language became. Otosan listened intently and slowly nodded agreement at various points. He had no chance to comment during his wife's steady torrent of words. Okasan seemed more focused on her own words and almost unaware of Otosan's slow, approving responses.

DS: (to Okasan) You've been under a lot of pressure. Has anything changed in the time since we last met?

Okasan: Yes. Obasan is much more supportive now. Otosan could have been more helpful, however. Now the pressure I feel is from Ojisan's constant complaining [about Okasan's new role in the family].

DS: (to Otosan) Tell your wife how you see your family.

Otosan slowly contemplated the question while his wife stared at him impatiently awaiting an answer. Finally she could wait no longer. She took in a breath preparing herself to interrupt her husband. Using my hand, I signaled her to hold her comment. Otosan slowly and deliberately began to respond directly to me. With a hand motion I directed him to respond to his wife.

Otosan: (looking directly at his wife) It has been difficult for you. I do appreciate all you have done. Things do seem to be changing for the better now.

Okasan's eyes softened as she heard Otosan's recognition of her feelings. A definite expression of care for each other showed in their facial expressions.

DS: The two of you obviously care a lot for each other even though life has been difficult this last year.

They both nodded agreement.

I asked the father to draw the family as he sees it now. Slowly he put the knuckle of his right index finger to his lip in a thoughtful gesture.

Okasan looked on impatiently. It was obvious that her pace was much quicker than Otosan's. She began to prompt him on the drawing. I used my hand to again bound her out. Otosan continued his contemplation. Slowly he picked up a pen and, without speaking, drew a diagram of the family.

DS: (to the mother) How does your husband's diagram match with your perception?

Okasan: That's exactly how I see it!

DS: (emphasizing complementarity) Your husband did a nice job of drawing and you were great at giving him time. (Okasan gave an acknowledging glance to her husband.)

DS: Otosan listens to you more than you think. His pace is a lot slower than yours. You may want to slow down so you can listen at his speed.

There was a look of recognition on Okasan's face. Miyashita san supported my observation. Okasan and Miyashita san proceeded to have a short dialogue on the difference in pace between her and her spouse. They also explored ways for Okasan to attend to her husband's pace.

I asked the couple to discuss the family drawing while signaling Okasan to move around the corner of the table close to Otosan. Okasan moved willingly next to her husband into a position where the two were

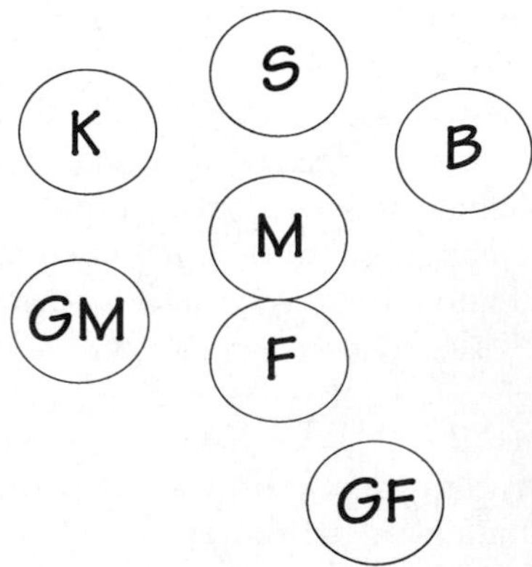

Figure 12–5
Family diagram by Kodomochan's father

touching. The health visitor had a quizzical expression on her face. Expressing emotion through touch in public is not the norm in Japan, especially for married couples.

Otosan and Okasan discussed Otosan's diagram. The conversation centered on the spouse-parent subsystem and the husband's role in supporting his wife. The most dramatic aspects of the discussion were the continued touching, the slower pacing and demonstration of attentive listening by Okasan, and Otosan's overt support of his wife.

DS: (to Miyashita san) I'm so impressed by the caring strength of this couple. Their love for each other really shows through in their listening behavior.

Miyashita san affirmed my comments while I began to arrange the family drawings on the table.

DS: (to the couple) Please work together to arrange your family pictures in order from past to present to how you would like to see the family in the future.

The couple began to share their perceptions of their diagrams. As a team they selected three pictures and arranged them in the order shown in Figure 12.6.

DS: You work well as a caring team. I like the way you support each other.

Miyashita san: (in affirmation) You are a good team, and Otosan is a good support for you when you feel pressure from his parents.

The couple nodded in agreement while Okasan gave a loving look to Otosan.

DS: What would it take to reach your ideal picture of the family?

The couple agreed that the ideal might be difficult to reach since they had little control over Ojisan's behavior. However, they said that the present pattern with themselves together as a supportive team was most important. They agreed this was a workable pattern even if they never reached their ideal.

Otosan: (looking at his wife) It is important for me to be aware of when you are under pressure and to support and protect you.

Okasan beamed at this comment.

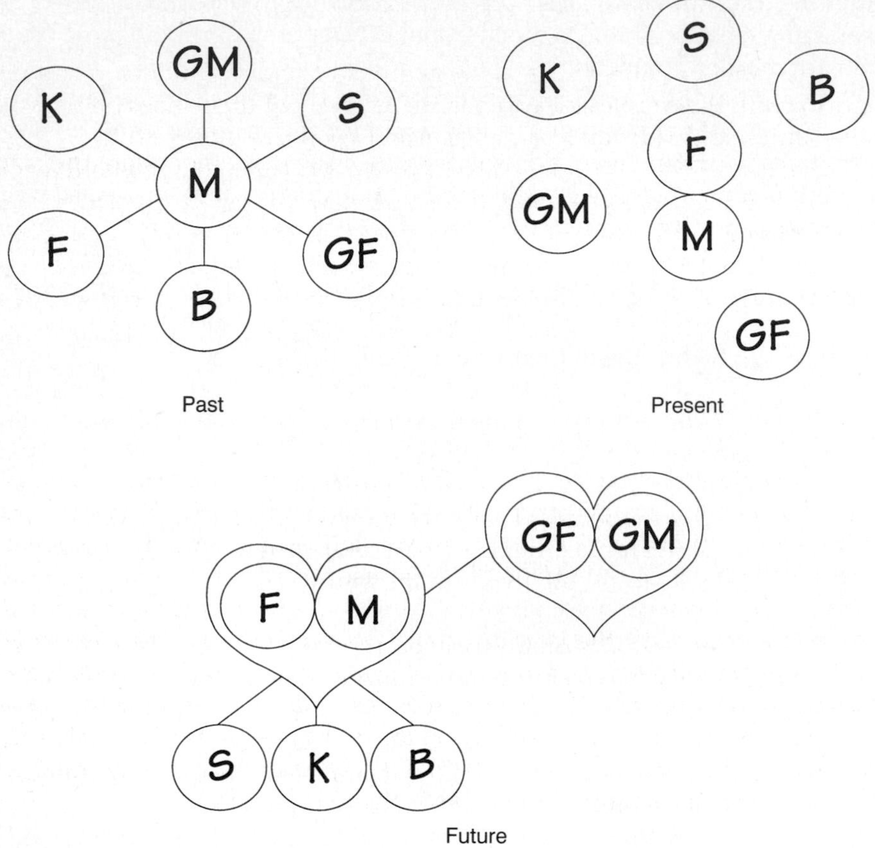

Figure 12–6
Family diagrams arranged by Kodomochan's mother and father from past to present to future

DS: You have a caring, supportive husband especially when you take time to listen and allow him to respond. I'm impressed with the support and care the two of you have demonstrated today. You are good parents and a caring couple.

I moved to get up from the floor cushions. The other members of the counseling session followed, the couple arm in arm. We walked from the counseling room to the hallway where the children had been drawing. The five adults admired the drawings of the children.

DS: You have bright creative children.

Miyashita san joined with the children. She individually reinforced each child for his or her creative work and commented on each picture.

DS: (to the entire family) You certainly have a fine family.

The family members moved together to the anteroom to put their shoes on with the couple still arm in arm. As they put their shoes on they all bowed and said thank you (*domo arigato*) and good-bye (*sayonara*).

Our counseling triad moved to the door and watched the family walk toward their car. The Japanese summer moon was just rising over the rice fields, lighting up the rolling foothills. It silhouetted the family against the tile-roofed houses of the village. The couple strolled together surrounded by their children. They appeared to have mobilized their energy to face their family stresses together.

OUTCOMES

Feedback from the family eight months after the last family counseling session indicated that they had indeed become more flexible. Kodomochan was attending school full-time. She and her siblings remained active together and in support of the family. The spouse relationship was solid and growing. The husband was actively taking a role in the establishment of clear boundaries with the grandparents. Obasan appeared to have been able to separate the fear and pain associated with her own child's death and those of her siblings from the similar feelings aroused by her granddaughter's accident and subsequent school refusal. Ojisan remained cantankerous and protective. However, Okasan, with Otosan's support, was now able to be more flexible in reframing and responding to his barbs.

DISCUSSION

Miyashita san, Sato sensei, and I concluded that this case demonstrated three important elements of cross-cultural family counseling. First, the case clearly brought home the importance of appreciating and understanding the client's cultural background. Second, the power of a multicultural team was demonstrated. Last, the case supported the need for using a consistent family counseling model. This case supported the usefulness and validity of the structural model of family counseling with rural families in Japan.

We believe family counseling must be conducted with consideration and knowledge of the client's culture. While total knowledge may not be required, or even possible, a good knowledge of the joining rules of the client's culture is essential. Once the counselor has appropriately joined the family, he or she must demonstrate empathetic appreciation of the client's culture. This procedure is especially important in Japan where the rules for joining are formal and rigid. The grandfather's comment after the first session that I didn't act like a foreigner points to the family's awareness of the joining process. Once the Tomo family accepted me inside their house, I gained influence and flexibility in the counseling process. As an insider, any minor cultural errors that I made were accepted. Cultural appreciation allows counselors to join families more easily and to effectively select and use appropriate counseling interventions with culturally different families.

Our team gained power and flexibility by being multicultural. Sato sensei commented on the ability of an outsider, once accepted by the family, to challenge the family in ways that would be rejected if used by a person from inside the culture. He specifically cited the direct (Western-style) comments I made to Obasan concerning the strengths of her daughter-in-law. For this intervention to be done by an insider (Japanese), he stated, it would need to be done in a much more indirect manner. The antithesis is also true. Insiders know the key cultural rules. With the Tomo family I consciously followed the cultural lead of Miyashita san and Sato sensei, especially in the joining process.

Finally, despite cross-cultural differences in behavior patterns, we found implementing a single counseling model gave the counseling team a common base for observing, planning, and intervening with families. The structural model espoused by Salvador Minuchin, Charles Fishman, Harry Aponte, and others provided us with this common base. Using this model, we focused on three aspects of the case: the symptom pattern, structural transactions, and family reality.

The overt symptom pattern in this case was school refusal. We challenged this overt pattern to see what covert pattern it might mask. Of course our conclusion was that the covert pattern revealed a lack of a well-defined boundary between the parent and grandparent subsystems, which had led to triangulation.

Several structural patterns or transactions supported this triangulation. Grandmother and granddaughter were overinvolved, mother and grandmother were in conflict, and the mother's feelings were chaotically detoured to the daughter. Establishing a boundary between the grandmother and her granddaughter and unbalancing the power structure between the mother and grandmother increased family flexibility and allowed for change.

The family members' reality, or view of themselves and the world, of course, is a primary consideration in a structural approach. In this case, the grandmother's past experiences with sickness and death seemed to overflow into the family's view of the present situation. Family members seemed to view their present world through a veil of fear. Through our efforts to empathetically reflect the grandmother's feelings, we were able to challenge the family members to recognize and restructure this view. Second, the family seemed to believe that a good mother must prove her competence, and yet there were no criteria for competence. The family's view of the mother's strength and their definition of her competence was challenged throughout the counseling period. As this view changed, the family became more flexible.

To complete our metaphor of the family Noh drama, we point out that no individual Noh drama is exactly like any other. Noh dramas, like family counseling experiences, are written, choreographed, and energized by the actors. The key to our counseling sessions was to challenge the actors and their family system in a manner that freed them to refine or change their drama. Once mobilized, the Tomo family changed the theme of their drama from "The Three-Generation Triangle" to "The Flexible Family: An *Ie* in Transition."

Biographical Statements

Dick T. Sampson, EdD, is a certified family counselor in the State of Washington. He is a professor of applied psychology at Eastern Washington University and was a visiting Fulbright professor at Tohoku University in Sendai, Japan, 1990–91. Dr. Sampson is the author of articles on family counseling and training in family counseling which have appeared in Counselor Education and Supervision *and* Family Strengths.

Toshiaki Sato has been a professor of psychology at Tohoku University in Japan since 1960. For the past 10 years he has been involved with rural Japanese families through a longitudinal developmental research project. He has published numerous articles in Japanese psychological journals.

Kamiko Miyashita is a health visitor and supervisor at the Matsuyama City Health Clinic. She was trained as a nurse. For the past 10 years she has made home visits to local families. Her duties include health care, health information, and family and personal counseling. She is a member of the Miyagi Health Visitor's Association.

13

Off the Walls!

Jose T. Sepulveda, Jr.

This is a case that many school counselors will identify with: a wildly hyperactive 6-year-old child (Attention-Deficit Hyperactivity Disorder, DSM-III-R *314.01), a difficult, frightened parent, frustrated school professionals. Every parent hopes and prays for their child's normal development. Eddy's mother is resistant to a special education placement for her son. She is fearful of the negative stereotypes associated with such a placement. However, in this case, such a placement will enable the school to help Eddy. A young counselor witnesses and describes the struggle between the parent and the school professionals. The authoritative interventions of the school principal and a physician, as well as mounting evidence that a behavior modification program was not sufficient, finally bring about an effective treatment plan.*

This case study takes place over 3 years. The client is a Hispanic male who is now 8 years of age. I met Eddy (Eduardo) Flores during my first year of employment as an elementary school counselor. He was 6 years old and enrolled in a transitional-one class (T-1). The T-1 classroom provides an opportunity for immature children to "catch up" to age-appropriate behavior without being retained in kindergarten. T-1 is also an alternative to special education. Understandably, the school district prefers not to place very young children in special education.

The decision for a T-1 placement was based on the recommendation of Eddy's kindergarten teacher. She felt that he was extremely immature and would benefit from an additional year to catch up to his peers.

As an elementary school counselor, I teach guidance classes at every grade level and visit each classroom once a week. The guidance classes deal with such topics as self-esteem, saying no to drugs, and career exploration. These visits also give me a chance to observe the children's classroom behavior. On one such visit I couldn't help noticing Eddy. He stood out, even in a classroom full of active 6-year-olds. Eddy would instigate trouble by teasing and poking other children. When I confronted him, he would whine and blame others for having "started it." Failing to convince me, he would withdraw, removing himself to a corner where he would lie down on the floor. But the supine position didn't last either. Eddy was not able to stay in one place or devote more than ten minutes of attention to my teaching. This disruptive and inattentive behavior was typical of Eddy during each week's guidance lesson. Ms. Lopez, Eddy's teacher, reported that it was typical of her experience with him as well.

During the third week of school, Eddy's teacher, Ms. Lopez, and his mother, Mrs. Flores, without collaboration, each asked me to see him in individual counseling. Ms. Lopez was concerned about Eddy's oppositional behavior in class. His mother described similar behavior at home.

Eddy is the only child of older parents. Throughout the span of the case, only his mother was involved with me. During a conference with Mrs. Flores, I explained that I was willing to work closely with her and her son. I suggested that we place Eddy on a goal-card contract. I explained that I would need her help in monitoring the contract on the home front and would expect weekly conferences to discuss Eddy's progress. She agreed but explained that her husband would be too busy to participate. Nevertheless, I encouraged her to consult with him about the plan. I was fearful of sabotage if he felt that he was left out.

CONCEPTUALIZATION

The goal-card is a school behavior contract based on a point system—the child earns points for appropriate behavior. In accordance with standard learning theory, the first reward level was set low enough so that Eddy would almost certainly experience immediate success. Mrs. Flores was worried that the major rewards could drain limited family financial resources; Eddy had been pressing for a bicycle. I assured her that the parents, not the child, had final say on the rewards. Mrs. Flores also objected to "bribing" Eddy for good behavior. We agreed that the ultimate objective was to eliminate the reward system once the new behaviors were in effect. I showed Mrs. Flores how we would use a graph to chart Eddy's progress.

Eddy's misbehavior had come to my attention even before I received referrals from the teacher and the parent. My goal was to help the parents and teacher apply behavioral techniques that would shape Eddy's behavior.

Being new both to the counseling profession and the elementary school, I searched my textbooks for ideas. Two that were especially helpful were *Behavioral Assessment of Childhood Disorders* by Mash and Terdal (1984) and *Families: Applications of Social Learning to Family Life* by Patterson (1975). These books gave me the foothold I needed to conceptualize a cogent behavioral plan.

While it is not the school counselor's role to assign a diagnosis, Eddy seemed a good fit for Attention-Deficit Hyperactivity Disorder as described in the *DSM-III-R*.

■ PROCESS

Eddy's initial visit with me was difficult because of his short attention span and his inability to stay on task. He just wasn't able to sit in his seat. High energy! I was lucky to extend the interview to 15 minutes.

JS: Hi, Jito (Spanish for *son*). I'm going to ask some questions, and I don't want you to be afraid to answer. You're not being graded. It might even be fun.

Eddy: OK. I've got a picture I colored in class. Do you want to see it? (He was pacing around the room.)

JS: Sure!

Eddy: I'll get it! (Eddy made a swift move for the door.)

JS: Wait a minute! You can show it to me when I take you back to class. Let's play my question-and-answer game.

Eddy: All right. Shoot! (Much squirming in seat. Some of his distractedness seemed intentional.)

JS: First question. What's your address?

Eddy: I don't have a dress. I'm a boy.

JS: Address. Do you know what that is?

Eddy: Yeah. No. (He crawled under the table.)

JS: Good. If you don't understand, then you shouldn't be afraid to ask. What street do you live on? Do you understand?

Eddy: Yeah. I live in a house with my dog. My dog is my best friend. I love my dog.

Eddy was in constant motion throughout the session, and this was typical of subsequent sessions.

Not long after my initial session, Ms. Lopez told me she wanted to refer Eddy for evaluation for special education. She requested a meeting of our screening committee that was comprised of a reading specialist, math specialist, school administrator, and counselor. The committee met but rejected the teacher's request. The consensus was that a decision to make a special education referral should be deferred until Eddy had more time to adjust to school.

My next meeting was with Eddy and Mrs. Flores. The mother arrived 40 minutes early and we had time to discuss the goal-card contract and the use of the graph. I used an educational approach in which I reviewed procedures for effective discipline. I emphasized the importance of ensuring that behaviors had consequences. I also pushed the idea that Eddy should experience success in the earliest stage. Mrs. Flores said that she and her husband had made a list of possible reinforcers: going hunting with Dad, to the playground, and going to Pistol Pete's Pizza. Mrs. Flores said that Eddy wanted a new bike and a Nintendo but these things were not affordable. She also didn't like the hunting idea, but her husband insisted that it be on the list. I was impressed with her follow-through and told her so.

Eddy arrived out of breath. He said that he had run all the way to my office. When he saw his mother, he became agitated and it took awhile to calm him. We explained the contract, although he was still twitching. Eddy said yes when asked if he understood. He prioritized the reward list with a trip to the playground as first choice, hunting second, and Pistol Pete's last.

Next, Mrs. Flores listed the behaviors she wanted from Eddy at home: take care of (do not destroy) toys, put things away, don't interrupt when others are talking, and stay seated at the dinner table. She said that she wanted Eddy to exhibit these positive behaviors at school as well. Eddy signed the goal-card that specified the consequences for good behavior at home and school. We would be in contact weekly in order to fine-tune the contract.

The results after 12 weeks were mixed. Ms. Lopez reported minimal improvement. Mrs. Flores reported positive changes at home. However, even the graph of his at-home behavior was jagged. The behavior would improve, nosedive, and then rebound. Mrs. Flores was disappointed that the negative behaviors hadn't been eliminated altogether.

At the next weekly conference, the graph depicted Eddy as a model student and son. Something was off. I concluded that Mrs. Flores was taking Eddy's word that he was improving at school or was being overly generous in assigning points. When I shared this view with her, she became defensive.

I became convinced that the contract wasn't working. I suggested that the time had come to phase out the rewards (Eddy had been consistently rewarded with pizza for several months!). Now Eddy would be responsible for his own actions without the support of a schedule of reinforcement.

After withdrawing the rewards, Eddy's behavior was monitored for two weeks. His classroom misbehavior continued, and I persisted in holding individual sessions with Eddy, hoping that he would decide to behave to please me. In March I stopped seeing Eddy. I had grown weary of devoting so much time to him without good results. What's more, there were many other children in the school who also needed my help.

After the sessions stopped, Eddy's behavior must have gotten even worse because Ms. Lopez requested another staff meeting to initiate a referral for special education. Ms. Lopez arranged a conference with Mrs. Flores to explain the referral process. Ms. Lopez came to my office and asked me to assist because she was having a hard time communicating with Mrs. Flores. I joined the conference and found Mrs. Flores in tears and very angry. She said that she resented the school's effort to place her son in special education and wouldn't go along with it. Then she accused us of lying about the T-1 program. She said that the only reason she agreed to the program was because we had promised that it had nothing to do with special education. I tried to acknowledge her fears but I, too, had come to see Eddy as a good candidate for special education. I tried to dispel some of the negative myths about special education—that the label would stick like glue forever, that once in "special ed," you could never get out. In fact, the law requires parental permission for a special education placement and regular reevaluations for a child to remain in special education. She would not be comforted.

At a later date, the school principal tried to smooth things out, but Mrs. Flores was still bitterly uncooperative. Still later, she surprised everyone by asking for a conference to include the principal, Ms. Lopez, and myself. I thought Eddy must be out of control at home, and so she was seeing the urgency of the problem. This was not the case. At the meeting, Mrs. Flores reprimanded each of us for our failure to properly handle this one little boy. She blamed me for failing to change Eddy's behavior. The principal asked Ms. Lopez and me to leave and talked with Mrs. Flores in private. I saw her leave his office, obviously very upset.

Two weeks later, I had a chance encounter with Mrs. Flores in the corridor. She told me that she did not want Eddy in special education because she felt that we would next insist that he be put on medication, and she did not want her son on drugs. It seemed (I hoped) that she wanted to discuss the issue. I explained that we could not put Eddy on medication even if we wanted to. Only the parent and a physician could do that. Further, we couldn't place Eddy in special education without her permission either. With her permission, we could proceed with psychological tests to determine if any of the various special education programs would be helpful. She reminded me of the "promise" that the T-1 class would help Eddy. I replied that my goal was the same as hers: to help her son. I didn't hear from her until the beginning of the next school year.

We began the year with a new principal. He had a strong personality and had a gift for working with people in a nonthreatening manner. Mrs. Flores wasted no time in informing the principal about the plot to place

Eddy in special education. Of course, he came to me to get some background information. Next, the principal made a classroom observation and came away convinced that Eddy should be evaluated for special education.

The principal arranged a conference with Mrs. Flores. To my amazement, I saw her leave the conference in apparently good spirits. Nevertheless, she would not consent to a referral. She did, however, follow through on the principal's suggestion that she bring Eddy's problems to the attention of the family physician. Meanwhile, Eddy was now in first grade. His behavior was unmanageable and he was not learning. I started individual counseling, but it had little or no impact in the classroom.

Then, a breakthrough! The physician told Mrs. Flores that Eddy was hyperactive. Shortly after, she agreed to a special education evaluation. The school psychologist diagnosed Eddy as learning disabled. After experimenting with dietary changes, the physician prescribed Ritalin.

OUTCOME

Eddy qualified for special education. Mrs. Flores and the various school personnel involved agreed to a plan that called for Eddy to leave the classroom for remedial classes in arithmetic and English. His behavior was markedly improved and he made good gains in academics.

DISCUSSION

This case required much effort and energy from many professionals. Dealing with the parent was the hardest part for me. However, I sympathized with her heartfelt fears that her son would be permanently labeled as dumb by virtue of a special education placement and injured by medication. The truth is such fears have been realized in some cases. In Eddy's case, the risks were outweighed by the potential gains.

REFERENCES

Mash, E., & Terdal, L. (1984). *Behavioral assessment of childhood disorders.* New York: Guilford.

Patterson, G. R. (1975). *Families: Applications of social learning to family life.* Champaign, IL: Research Press.

Biographical Statement

Jose T. Sepulveda, Jr., has been working as an elementary school counselor for three years at Mary Hull Elementary School in the Northside Independent School District in San Antonio, Texas. He received his master's degree in counseling from Our Lady of the Lake University in San Antonio.

14

Oh No—Not Again!

Jules Spotts and Jane Brooks

A 7-year-old boy struggles against chaotic life circumstances with the help of two therapists, Jules Spotts and Jane Brooks. Early nurturance by his maternal grandmother allowed Sean to endure the many losses he suffered in his young life. By the age of 11 he had experienced extreme poverty, an alcoholic mother, and the deaths of his grandmother and mother. He had never known his father, who was divorced from his mother during Sean's infancy. He lived with a couple who were acquaintances of his mother in the absence of any other family and was finally adopted by a couple who subsequently separated. Small wonder the therapist who first worked with Sean (Jane Brooks) saw his reactions as consistent with Post-Traumatic Stress Disorder (DSM-III-R 309.89).

Brooks first met Sean when she was a school psychologist working under the supervision of Spotts. Sean's adoption meant relocating, which took him out of the school district in which Brooks worked. Fortunately, Spotts was able to assume the role of primary therapist following the move. Not surprisingly, the main issues of therapy were constancy, predictability, and continuity. The psychotherapeutic approach was augmented with the use of family drawings as a means of building continuity, "feeling stories" designed to help Sean label and express feelings, and structured board games that emphasized following rules and sequencing. Sean's adoptive mother proved to be an able partner in the therapeutic process, and the changes in Sean seem deep and enduring.

I (Jane Brooks) first saw Sean at recess. He was a spindly, wistful boy in a transitional first-grade class. He had been placed there because he was not believed to be developmentally ready for the second grade. He watched as the others played, peering at them with eyes that sought acceptance. Clearly, he was an outsider who did not know how to enter. He played with toys beside his classmates as though he were in nursery school. His only means of joining the group was jumping up and down. Any problem was met with an attempted smile which soon dissolved in tears if the stress continued. He was 7 years old and just beginning elementary school.

Gradually, in counseling I began to know Sean. By the spring of that first school year, it was clear that academic work was difficult for Sean and he was referred to the child study team so that we could learn more about his learning style and psychosocial development. Since those initial school observations, I have been involved with Sean for some five years—first as a consultant, then as an evaluator, later as a therapist, and finally as a family friend. I have been the one constant person in his turbulent existence.

Sean was born in a small rural town several months after his parents divorced. Before their separation, for reasons unknown, the couple traveled extensively in this country. Family photos show Sean's mother as a stylishly dressed young woman. She had, in her youth, a life-style that included riding horses and a private secondary school education. Sean's father was a pilot who received a college degree during or immediately after a career in the army. There was a substantial age difference between the parents with Sean's father being some 20 years older than his mother. Sean was small at birth, received appropriate postnatal medical attention, and developed normally. Health-care records indicate adequate care during infancy. What little evidence there was of Sean's early life seemed to suggest that the family had an upper-middle-class life-style.

Little is known of Sean's daily life before his fourth birthday, at which time he was living with his grandmother and mother in a residence for senior citizens in his mother's hometown. He attended nursery school for a scant few months. This unstable and rather unusual living arrangement resulted from his mother's alcoholism and Sean's need for daily nurturance from a reliable caretaker. His grandmother was best able to fulfill this role. The family's well-furnished apartment had a living room, bathroom, and small kitchen. The grandmother slept on a hospital bed in the living room, while Sean and his mother shared a bed in the bedroom. Children were not permitted in the complex, but an exception had been made for Sean. His grandmother suffered from emphysema, was frequently hospitalized, and eventually died. Sean lost his home and with it the security, consistency, and love which his grandmother had provided.

Immediately thereafter, Sean and his mother moved to a rooming house located between a funeral home and an automobile agency in a neighboring city. They shared bathroom and kitchen facilities with other families. The pair lived in a single room with one bed, a bureau, and a bookcase for toys. Linoleum covered the floor. Food was scarce. Sean describes eating cereal with water when there was no milk, foraging for cans and bottles on the beach and in the trash, and sitting outside playing in the dirt. Their next rooming house residence was near a small shopping mall where Sean was frequently seen playing unsupervised. In a minimally furnished room, Sean and his mother again shared a narrow bed, which he said had "springs that stuck into my back." He was often hungry and, in fact, appeared malnourished when he entered school.

By the time he was 7 years old Sean had experienced the extremes of wealth and poverty. He had observed a parent who could not defer gratification or plan for the future, but had also felt a grandparent's consistent love. He knew little of normal peer interactions or school behaviors. He wanted to learn but had difficulty concentrating. He was easily distracted, yet he wanted to comply and please. Though chronologically 7 years old, his interests and play resembled those of a 5-year-old. His intellectual level fell within the low average range with weaknesses in sequencing, attending, personal knowledge, and immediate rote memory. Emerging strengths existed in abstract reasoning and understanding of social situations. At school, the child study team had added counseling with me and specialized academic services to his regular first-grade program for the coming school year.

■ CONCEPTUALIZATION

Initially, I chose the psychodynamic therapeutic process, believing it to be the best means of trying to compensate, to some degree, for Sean's rootlessness. I wanted to provide him with stability, security, and educational stimuli. Sessions during his first-grade year were concrete and reality based and included teaching basic life skills such as memorizing personal information. Thus, my initial goals were to add more structure and stability to his life and to begin to build his academic self-confidence.

I continued to see Sean regularly in therapy during his second-grade year. Therapeutic goals for that year, which followed his mother's death, were (a) to address his need to mourn and to fully explore his feelings about his biological mother, including guilt about not liking her and his fantasies that he caused her death, and (b) to reinforce as strongly as possible his worthiness and ability to relate to others. In addition, he needed support to become a dynamic part of a new family. At the same time, it was vital for him to gain understanding and eventual control of his internal emotional turmoil.

Once Sean had parents to provide stability, my involvement and school became less important as constants. With continuing and dependable nurturance at home, Sean was more able to focus his energy on learning. The psychodynamic orientation begun in the second year of our therapy would be extended. Key therapeutic issues at this time were Sean's fear of loss and his resulting reluctance to commit. My goals for him were that he become aware of his strengths and begin to trust.

Sean's move to a new school in his adoptive parents' community meant that he would no longer be able to work with me. However, this loss was somewhat mitigated by having a new family and the fact that my supervisor, Dr. Spotts, who was already very familiar with Sean, albeit indirectly, was able to serve as therapist in the new community. His initial therapeutic goal in working with Sean was to help him become aware of, label, and verbalize feelings. In addition, Dr. Spotts hoped that Sean would begin to understand sequence and cause and effect, and do some long-range planning.

PROCESS

Therapy with Dr. Brooks

Sean and I began by telling stories to each other. Sean's chaotic life, his feelings of always being misunderstood, his dissatisfaction with life, his chronic exposure to alcoholism, and his intense need for security all became obvious.

In the spring Sean's mother became ill and died. Sean then lived with acquaintances of his mother, a couple involved with drugs, alcohol, and guns. Sean remained with them during the summer and for two months of the following school year. He then entered the home of his adoptive parents, where he remains. Therapeutic methods, goals, and strategies changed to accommodate his grief and new living arrangements. His stories now were about death, ghosts, and his own demise. His attendance at school and at his therapy sessions became erratic. I did not see Sean during the summer, but a psychological evaluation revealed poor impulse control, lack of trust in adults, anxiety, magical thinking, and denial.

Sean was assigned controlled, structured classes at school which led to improvement in his academic performance. However, from the moment he left school until he returned Sean was in constant motion. He ate voraciously and constantly. His adoptive mother noted that he talked incessantly about trivialities. When he allowed himself to feel his grief, he was inundated with emotion. When his pain became too excruciating, he would vomit and then ask to be held tightly. It was only in the evenings that he could relax for awhile and was able to speak about traumatic events from his past. His intense, somatic reactions continued for several months along with bouts of crying, sleepwalking, and nightmares. Sean's reactions were similar to the symptoms of Post-Traumatic Stress Disorder, not surprisingly, since his needs for stability and security had gone so long unmet. He felt exposed to chronic danger.

As early as December of Sean's first-grade school year, he began to tell stories at our sessions related to happenings at home. He revealed his feelings descriptively without labeling them and continued to intermingle dreams with reality, a confusion that escalated after his mother's death. His fantasies included being devoured by monsters and ghosts: "One kid came in there and he got eaten up by a monster." "The shark got his foot and then all the bones started to float up." He told of how objects came alive and killed him. Concurrently, there were glimpses of reasoning, conceptualizing, and reality testing: "Sometimes bad memories come and hurt us."

When school reopened in the fall after his mother's death, Sean seemed to feel the need to be punished for what he apparently believed was his role in his mother's death. In one of our sessions, he told a story of death and retaliation: "He stabbed the dinosaur and it died. And when he moved his claws he pulled the kid's eyes out and the kid died." Intellectually, he realized that substance abuse was the cause of her death. He said, "Crack is poison." But his feeling of guilt and fear of punishment were deep. Sean sometimes trusted adults and, at other times, was fearful, suspicious, and hypervigilant. His lesson from one story was "not to go near anybody that's going to hurt somebody."

Mutual storytelling was continued in therapy after Sean moved into his adoptive home. He continued to feel unacceptable, even evil, and was haunted by his dreams. He accepted nurturance and love from his new parents but clung to them sometimes as though their love would come to an end. He continued to believe his own death was imminent, and he feared he would be taken away by the authorities. His stories and nightmares were about a bike being taken away, being eaten by a monster, getting killed by the evil in the bookcase, being burned by "red stuff" that oozed from the water fountain, and "running and running and then dying."

Although magical thinking and violence permeated Sean's work, over time his stories began to change. Most importantly, the main character assumed an active role. In one story, "when they fell asleep, the little boy broke the spell and woke everybody up. . . . Then everybody got bats and chased the witch onto a cliff and hit her and she ran off the cliff." In other stories a normal need for nurturance and acceptance was intertwined with lingering concerns about accepting his new family: "And when he saw his grandmother with curly hair, he said it was really his aunt. You can't have a new grandmother. You can't really have a new grandmother."

Then, shortly before school ended, Sean told his first story about himself. "Once upon a time there was a little boy named Sean. On Friday he wanted to go to the grave, and he said goodbye to his mother. After Sean said goodbye, he was happy, and another day he had troubles and talked about them and then they stopped, and then Sean didn't have any more problems, and then he got more problems and more problems—and that's the end." Questioned about these new problems, he said, "I had trouble on my homework. . . . I think I'm never gonna catch up with Mrs. Horowitz's class." During the last session for the year, Sean showed some contrition regarding being "fresh to Daddy."

Therapy with Dr. Spotts

When Sean returned to school in the fall, his adoption was not yet final. Sean began school satisfactorily, but by mid-October the nightmares reappeared. Therapy was reactivated, this time with Dr. Spotts, and Sean began to draw. He drew himself, he drew a train disappearing from view, he drew his feelings about his mom dying, and then he drew the courtroom where he would be legally adopted, as he envisioned it. The day of the adoption finally arrived, and he received the certificate showing his new name which combined the old and the new. He now felt some degree of safety.

Following the adoption, Sean depicted his life in a series of continuous drawings in which he poignantly drew his feelings and struggled to label them. When we reviewed the paintings each week, he denied some feelings. Nevertheless, we persisted in this fashion for many months. Even with his denial, the process seemed to contribute towards his emotional growth. The repeated practice of labeling feelings expressed in his drawings helped Sean stay in touch with his present feelings.

We examined specific emotions, particularly those that were regularly expressed in stories, pictures, and play. In many of Sean's stories, the main character killed someone—a person, a dragon, a witch—and then was killed. It was originally impossible for Sean to say what the character felt. Sean was action oriented; he did not use feeling words or even acknowledge the emotions of his characters. "Feelings into words" became a kind of catchphrase in our sessions. Whether Sean was experiencing frustration at losing a board game or struggling with angry feelings toward a parent, he was encouraged to express his feelings in words. Gradually he began to talk about people's feelings, but he needed continual reminding and encouragement to do so. Any extended discussion of feelings was difficult, despite Sean's expanding ability.

Sean's parents were an important source of information about events in Sean's life, which helped us to address his academic struggles, peer problems, upsets at home, and other significant events in therapy. Three months after my work with Sean began, his parents said they had decided, after much serious marital trouble, to separate. Sean's home was suddenly threatened, and with it the security and continuity which Sean had begun to count on. The therapeutic focus was now expanded to include exploration of Sean's fears about the breakup and his newly learned ability to label his feelings. He was encouraged to examine his feelings about each of his parents as well as their decision to separate.

Board games had proven to be a reliable method for exploring feelings in therapy. The games were also significant vehicles in themselves because they could be used to teach and reinforce turn-taking, reciprocal participation, following directions, operating within an ordered framework, and exercising options with respect to making strategic moves. I hoped that these skills, once mastered, would generalize to Sean's classroom and everyday functioning.

Sean enjoyed the simple card game of War. This basic game allows for continuous reinforcement of order and sequence. At first Sean did not even know the sequential order of the picture cards. Further, War allows for extensive emotional exploration since the game has play-by-play excitement with little planning or skill required.

Sean also participated in the board game Sorry. We changed the rules so that each player was responsible for two colors rather than one. This game calls for planning, evaluation of several alternatives for each move, and a concentrated focus for an extended period of time. Early in therapy this game was not easy for Sean. However, he later came to enjoy the game and often played for an entire session.

Given Sean's chaotic preadoption years, an additional therapeutic task was to provide him with a sense of order and predictability in his life and to help him find his own sense of order and control whenever possible. The above-mentioned games helped to foster a sense of order and predictability. The focus was on increasing and expanding the complexity of the game as well as elaborating and following the rules.

Throughout the game portion of each session—in fact, throughout the full session—Sean was unable to modulate his emotional expressions. As we threw a ball back and forth, Sean often whipped the ball far too quickly and hard (given the limited space in the office), laughed too loudly if I missed a throw, or complained too vehemently if he missed a throw of mine. Such overly intense expressions of emotion and episodes of crying also appeared in daily life, according to Sean's parents. Two basic techniques were used to help Sean with this. Careful pacing of activity allowed Sean to experience a range of intensity and a smooth rhythmic flow of emotions in contrast to his usually spasmodic, irregular, and intense expression of impulses. I did this through very slow speech, thinking out loud when making game moves, and faking throws to model more appropriate ways of teasing or engaging the other player. In general, I modeled a variety of behaviors and kept changing the pace of our activity to illustrate the flexibility that Sean seemed to lack. Nonverbal cues, such as slowly lowering my hand, became a signal to Sean to slow down and regain a measure of control.

■ OUTCOME

Sean progressed emotionally and socially during the two years that he worked with Dr. Brooks. However, in spite of major gains, none of his critical emotional issues were settled when their therapeutic alliance ended. Sean needed more therapy to develop his reasoning, insight, and understanding further. His tensions and anxiety were decreasing, but his self-understanding and play were still well below age level. Too often, Sean could not differentiate, label, or verbalize his feelings. Through mutual storytelling, Sean began to see that a person could make changes in his life and that events did not occur simply because one thought about them. He began to see himself as a change agent in fantasy and in reality. He asked to switch from one classroom to another, and his request was granted. On another occasion he was verbally abusive to his mother and deeply hurt her. He was discovering that his actions had social and emotional repercussions, some positive and others not, and that he was able to control some events rather than being a passive recipient. This understanding resulted in improved peer relationships. Rather than being mystified or devastated by teasing from his peers, Sean began to make the connection between his behavior and the responses he received.

Sean's emotional and social growth continued with Dr. Spotts. Over nine months of psychodynamic therapy, Sean completed mourning and gained enough self-confidence and security to experience and express anger toward his mother and father. However, he still denied many feelings, relived his fears of abandonment, and met new stress by weeping. He almost always covered his emotions with smiles and later broke down. He could not modulate his feelings and was either too exuberant or too sad.

On the other hand, Sean was beginning to lead a normal little boy's life. Magical thinking was taking a back seat. He began to talk directly about his problems, and relationships took on a healthier, more appropriate tone. The therapists hypothesized that Sean had early on developed a basic trust in the world, largely through his relationship with his grandmother. The emotional inaccessibility of his mother and temporary caretakers elicited his defensive armor. With his adoption and the presence of a stable, nurturant home, as well as regular psychotherapy, Sean was able to build healthier ego defenses. Since the threat of loss had abated, Sean could use some of the energy that had been devoted to defending against loss to begin to examine his own behavior. He was less hypervigilant than in the past, able to relax a little, and showed more spontaneity. He was able to understand that his tendency to "overemote" was not working as he had hoped. Rather than attract others, this trait seemed to drive them away. Sean also began to understand that people were not simply "mean," as he had often thought, but rather that his own behavior could influence the treatment he got from others.

Sean was beginning to live an orderly life, to follow the routines of going to school, doing homework, eating, and preparing for bedtime, but an understanding of these cycles eluded him. In spite of working on the continuity and connections in his life (through stories, drawings, and games), the ordering and sequencing of information remained an enigma for Sean. At school he began to comprehend numbers but did not grasp progression and ordering. Whether he had a true learning disability or whether his chaotic life made this concept so difficult remains uncertain.

Sean had begun to invest in emotional relationships with each adoptive parent and in the continuity of their home life. His parents' separation, the attendant uncertainty about their marriage, and the prospect of living in yet another home (the father's residence) were serious threats for Sean. Feelings of rejection and abandonment continued to plague him. All his loved ones or those he wanted to love had abandoned him, either by death or by choice. Loss loomed large for Sean. He was afraid, for example, that the state would remove him from his home, and he would scream out in his sleep, "Don't take me away!" In someone who has lived through so many changes and endured so many losses, a sense of security and self-worth can only be rebuilt gradually. Although Sean had made gains in both areas, controlling his emotions and improving his academic performance will continue to be important goals in the coming years.

Although the future unity of Sean's family remains in doubt, the therapeutic gains Sean has made seem deep and enduring. He appears to possess sufficient ego strength to continue his progress in the face of changes or discontinuities in relationships.

■ DISCUSSION

We carefully formulated an overall, long-term treatment plan for Sean. The key themes in therapy were constancy, predictability, and continuity. Treating Sean at his school made sense initially, and when this was no longer possible because of his change in residence, it was fortunate that therapeutic responsibility could be shifted from Dr. Brooks to Dr. Spotts, who had been serving as supervisor. Sean's fear of rejection and abandonment led Dr. Brooks to continue to see him, albeit irregularly, after her formal work with him had ended.

Sean's adoption into what had the possibility of being a stable, nurturing family was a rare blessing in his young life. With his parents' separation, changes in treatment became necessary. The use of family drawings as part of therapy was an attempt to help Sean create an orderly, sequential understanding of his life. Later in therapy, structured board games were used for this same purpose. These methods were only minimally effective in addressing this problem, so great was the impact of his early fragmented years.

Given Sean's denial of feelings and pervasive underlying anxiety, a primary goal of therapy was to help Sean identify and label feelings through the feeling stories. This technique, augmented with periodic input from his parents about events in their son's life, allowed Sean to begin to practice these skills. Sean's adoptive mother proved to be effective in actively listening to his feelings. Her acceptance enabled Sean to rely less on denial and suppression of feelings. Sean's growing feeling of safety with his mother allowed him to experience and express his feelings *about* her *to* her. This process has been slower with his father, but is under way. Despite the parental separation, Sean has not experienced significant regression, a positive statement about both Sean and his parents.

Biographical Statements

Jane Brooks, EdD, is a school psychologist in a public school system and an adjunct teacher in school psychology at Fairfield University Graduate School of Education. She presented at the 1990 annual convention of the National Association of School Psychologists (NASP) and has had an article accepted by Teaching Exceptional Children. *She is a member of numerous professional associations.*

Jules Spotts, PhD, is a licensed clinical psychologist in private practice in New Canaan, Connecticut and a consultant to the New Canaan Country School. He is the coauthor of the Devereux Behavior Rating Scales for Children and Adolescents and of a book, You Can Say No to Your Teenager *(1991).*

Too Afraid to Talk

Bruce St. Thomas

*Post-Traumatic Stress Disorder (*DSM-III-R *309.89) is a diagnosis that is usually associated with Vietnam veterans or adult victims of crime or natural disaster. Bruce St. Thomas encounters a 7-year-old PTSD client who was devastated after witnessing the tragic death of her younger sister.*

St. Thomas uses art therapy to probe Kathy's complex of blocked feelings, predominantly her sense of loss and survivor's guilt. Through art and play activities her rich imagination becomes a powerful healing force. Extensive use of dialogue enables the reader to get a feel for this child's growth in therapy.

Kathy Peters, age 7, was referred to my practice by her parents. On September 7, 1984, I consulted with Kathy's parents, Paul and Joan Peters. They described the death of their youngest daughter, Kim. Kim was killed at 18 months of age when a car swerved on a major street that Kim, Kathy, and their babysitter were crossing. Kim was in a baby carriage that the babysitter was pushing. Kathy saw the car hit the baby carriage, saw her sister at the hospital, and was frightened that "she wouldn't wake up."

Both parents had observed changes in Kathy's behavior. Kathy was described by Mr. and Mrs. Peters and the school as being bright and mature for her age. Following Kim's death, Kathy regressed by being disobedient and babylike in responding to her parents. She became more distant and refused to talk about her feelings. Affect was markedly constricted. Kathy was fearful of being alone, frightened by the sound of sirens, and extremely nervous about crossing streets.

Her parents were concerned that Kathy had only cried a few times at the hospital and at the funeral. She also refused to discuss the accident, and her sleep was sometimes disturbed. Chiefly, the parents were concerned about Kathy's grieving process. External sources of information, such as school and friends, reported that Kathy was fine. At school no changes in Kathy's behavior had been observed.

High achievement was prominent in firstborn Kathy's early development. Kathy's motor, language, cognitive, and social development were all advanced. She had demonstrated leadership abilities in her peer group and was cooperative at home. She exhibited a high level of autonomy.

By way of background, Kathy's father, Paul, had four younger siblings. As the firstborn son, Paul had assumed a lot of coparenting responsibility because his father was away on business much of the time. Kathy's mother, Joan, was a middle child with an older brother and younger sister. Two years prior to Joan's birth, her parents had lost a female child at birth who had also been named Joan. While Paul felt that he was favored in his family by his mother, Joan had a significant relationship with her father.

CONCEPTUALIZATION

I am trained as a play therapist, and my work draws on three major theoretical sources. My early work in counseling was based on a developmental approach (Erik Erickson, Margaret Mahler). Later, I was deeply influenced by the humanistic teachings of Rollo May and Clark Moustakas; in fact, I received training from Moustakas. I am also influenced by the field of art therapy (Judith Rubin, Edith Kramer).

I bring these three resources—developmental, humanistic, and artistic—to my work with traumatized children. Overall I believe that the structure necessary for conquering fears and anxieties, and for integrating traumatic events, are unconscious and intrinsic to human nature. Furthermore, I believe that human creativity is the primary language for achieving personal insight and healing.

As a child psychotherapist, I knew that Kathy was not yet ready to reveal her inner feelings and thoughts. Kim's death had affected every aspect of her home life and family relationships. Mrs. Peters was hospitalized repeatedly for depression, and Kathy had been moved from one extended family home to another. Kathy found safety in suppressing feelings and thereby doing what she could to avoid any more emotional turmoil.

A therapeutic contract was established whereby Kathy would meet with me weekly to discuss any thoughts or feelings concerning the loss of her sister. I emphasized that anything Kathy shared would be confidential. Kathy would be consulted, and she would have the final say about disclosing any information, if I thought disclosure was necessary for her well-being.

I decided on a *DSM-III-R* diagnosis for Kathy of Post-Traumatic Stress Disorder. All of the classical symptoms were present at the time of referral. Specifically, Kathy showed constricted affect, feelings of detachment from her parents, reactivity to certain environmental stimuli associated with the trauma, sleep disturbance, avoidance of activities that aroused recollection of the trauma, and some guilt about surviving.

Play therapy was chosen as the modality for intervention. Intellectually Kathy was gifted and successful, but emotionally she was highly defensive. The use of nonverbal play materials would be a means for promoting communication about feelings that could not be easily verbalized.

■ PROCESS

Kathy was an attractive, light-brown-haired, blue-eyed girl. She was neatly dressed and frequently smiled. She had good verbal skills and seemed comfortable in adult company.

The playroom was equipped with a hand-puppet theater, string-puppet theater, games, playhouse, sand tray, dolls, marker board, art table (with markers, oil and chalk pastels, paints, clay, crayons, and so on), stuffed animals, kitchen utensils, and a cabinet filled with other play materials.

Three or four sessions were initially devoted to an art therapy interview. I gathered information based on the child's responses to art and play materials, especially the themes of her drawings.

Kathy made an immediate attachment to a large, brown teddy bear. She picked the bear up and held it close while approaching the drawing table. I explained that we would meet for several sessions to draw pictures and to talk about her pictures and herself and her family.

Kathy: I like teddy bears.

BST: You are welcome to hold the teddy bear as long as you like.

I asked Kathy to draw a picture of a whole person. She chose color markers that had various fragrances. After smelling them, she began to draw.

Kathy: I don't draw very good. This one is purple and smells like a grape. This pink one smells like watermelon. This is not a very good skirt. (Kathy colored a sky with the light blue marker and drew bluebirds in the sky.) They don't look right. I drew the birds like a letter *M*. I've done it wrong. This bird almost bumped into the girl. There is a fish factory nearby. I'm going to draw one because these birds are flying around it. This is a small fish factory made out of bricks. This is the ocean, and she is walking home after she went to buy fish. This girl is 7 years old. It's no one I know. She is thinking that the birds might eat her fish, and she is worried that the fish might fall out of the bag.

BST: Kathy, since your first drawing of a person was a girl, could you now draw a picture of a boy? (She quickly starts drawing with the color markers.)

Kathy: He is going to be at his house. His house will be made out of bricks. He lives like in a jail. There is going to be a lot of smoke coming out of the chimney. Me and my mother and father have always wanted to live in a brick house. Pink is my favorite color. Now this big sun smells just like lemons. Mama, why does the sun smell like lemons? He gets to smell the sun every day. His pet bird is the only one in the sky. This boy is 7 years old. He is my boyfriend, Chris. He is thinking that the sun might never smell again, hoping that it will. He is jumping rope and feeling happy. (Kathy continues to draw more bluebirds in the sky.) He just can't be alone and needs more birds because he needs friends so he won't feel sad.

BST: Do the bluebirds help him feel better?

Kathy: Yes, they follow him and make sure that he is safe.

During the second session, I asked Kathy to draw a picture of herself.

Kathy: I have to make my eyes brown, pink mouth, and a black nose. I wish there would be a white marker because it would smell like marshmallows. Pink is my favorite color. It's not yours because it's a girl's color. I'm going to color my dress yellow so I will look like the sun. I'm going to try to make two ponytails. My daddy does my hair sometimes.

BST: Could you draw a picture of yourself and your family with everyone doing something?

Kathy: My daddy is big. My mommy has blonde hair. My daddy has short brown hair and I have long brown hair. My hair color is more like daddy. I look like daddy.

BST: What do you miss about Kim not being with your family?

Kathy: I miss everything about Kim. It is hard to talk about Kim. We don't talk a lot about her. I feel sad about it whenever I think about it.

BST: It is hard for you to remember things about your sister.

Kathy: Yes, I don't like thinking about her. (Kathy completes her family drawing.) We are all going out to eat. My mommy, my daddy, and me are all dressed up. Mommy gets the most upset about Kim. Dad is the strongest because he is still going to work. I'm talking baby talk.

During the third session, Kathy drew a picture of her mother and father's room. She placed herself in her room with a friend. Then she drew her baby sister in her room with what look like toys. Kathy also used the puppets. She played with a squeaking duck who cried out to its mother for her to feed him and take care of him.

Figure 15–1
Kathy's family picture showed her mother and herself as equals. Kathy's deceased sister was not included.

Kathy then returned to the drawing table where she drew a picture of a house and some bluebirds in the sky.

Kathy: Once upon a time there was a little girl who lived in a little house. Four little bluebirds came to visit every day. (I encouraged Kathy to talk about the little girl in the house, and she went on to dramatize the following scene.) The little girl was alone in the house and she kept crying for her mother. The bluebirds kept her happy with their visits to her windowsill. Inside the house the girl screamed that if the mother does not take care of me then I won't take care of her.

In summary, these early interviews with Kathy revealed several specific themes. First, Kathy was feeling the absence of her mother. At this point, in fact, her mother was in and out of a psychiatric care facility. Second, Kathy did not want to discuss her feelings about Kim's death. Yet she did make reference to the difficulty of thinking about it. Third, Kathy was perfectionistic about how she draws. Throughout her drawing activity, she often made critical statements about how she should draw or color better. Such statements indicated the standards she demands of herself. Finally, the bluebirds, as friends to both the boy and the girl, were symbolic of Kathy's need to not feel alone. Her many references to the sun, birds, colors (pink and yellow) were symbolic of her yearning to express her feelings and conflicts. Kathy felt close to her father and yet interpreted his strength as being his ability to continue working. In family portraits Kathy portrayed herself as one of the adults in the family. Her need to not cause more emotional conflict was apparent.

I was surprised that Kathy immediately started drawing images that related to her feelings about Kim's death. In retrospect I can see that because we had outlined the nature of our relationship prior to the interview Kathy was ready to disclose. Her interest in the art materials, along with her ability to create story forms, allowed her to express feelings throughout the therapy process.

The following several sessions involved progressive play therapy interactions that moved back and forth between art, imagery, dramatic play, and verbal interaction.

Kathy's parents reported that she enjoyed her visits with me. At school, her teacher said that Kathy had become attached to her and wanted to hold her hand. Kathy had started talking about memories of Kim but was still unable to cry. She told her parents that she felt guilty about something but won't say what. During the fifth session Kathy completed a drawing of two lakes surrounded by sandy beaches. Kathy filled the entire paper with designs drawn out to the border. She was careful to erase her errors and to color within the lines. Next, Kathy used fluorescent markers to create a drawing she called "Electric Basket." The marks were made quickly and yet were contained within the boundaries of the basket.

Three sessions occurred during which Kathy tried to contain and intellectualize her creative activities. In one session, she made a snowman out of clay. Her approach to this regressive material was restrained. She determined exactly what she would do with the material before she began to use the clay.

During a family therapy session, Kathy's mother made a strong effort to communicate with Kathy. Mrs. Peters talked about her own grief and emphasized that her depression was not Kathy's fault. Kathy's response was inhibited because she felt unsure about her mother's well-being and resentful of her emotional absence.

During the 12th session, Kathy drew another picture of the small house with a windowsill where the bluebirds meet the lonely girl.

Kathy: There is a storm outside and the bluebirds collect on the windowsill. The girl opens the window and the birds fly inside. At first she is frightened. Later she realizes that the bluebirds are talking to her.

BST: What are the bluebirds saying?

Kathy: They tell the girl that the storm and the rain have frightened them. They are sad and scared. The bluebirds cry until the girl cries herself. The bluebirds tell the girl that they will protect her.

BST: How do they protect the girl?

Figure 15–2
These bluebirds were Kathy's friends and protectors. They had magical powers and could foresee danger.

Kathy: They make it safe for her by flying ahead.
BST: So the bluebirds can see danger and protect the girl from going toward dangerous things?
Kathy: Yes, the bluebirds are with her even if she can't see them. They are magic and she can hear them all the time.
BST: So the bluebirds are powerful friends.
Kathy: Yes, and their magic powers now belong to the girl.
BST: How does she know that she has the power?
Kathy: The bluebirds give her a magic feather.

Sessions 13 through 16 were characterized by themes of magical powers of prediction and protection.

In the 17th session Kathy played with the king, queen, prince, and princess puppets. The prince and princess were lost in the dark forest. The king and guard tried to find the lost siblings without success.

Kathy: The princess finally finds her way out of the forest. She is alone and keeps saying to herself that she is very, very strong and knew her way all along. When she makes her way back to the castle, the king is very, very happy. Together, they summon the wizard who finds the lost prince.

Kathy continued the king and queen, prince and princess dramatizations through the next three sessions.

Kathy: The king and queen had a daughter, Sally, and a son, Benjamin. Benjamin and Sally were lost in the woods and the king and queen tried to find them. When it was impossible to find them they called for the bear guide and the wizard to help out.

Kathy then play acted the wizard and the missing daughter. She made it possible for the king to find his daughter.

Kathy: The only way that the children can be found is to go to the wizard who has a magic wand and to put the children dolls onto his wand. After the king goes to the wizard with the children dolls, the wizard says that the children can now be found because through magic. Maps suddenly appear in the dolls telling where the children really are.

Meeting with the parents, I discovered that Kathy was becoming argumentative at home. She angrily fought against time limits concerning dinner and going to bed. Visits to Kim's grave site led to family discussions in which Kathy showed more emotion.

Kathy drew a rainbow in session 21. She titled it "A Rainbow of Raining Hearts." She drew colored hearts falling away from the rainbow design.

Kathy: I want to live at the end of that rainbow. If I lived there, I wouldn't be scared all my life.

Kathy and I discussed her remaining fears about crossing streets, remembering the accident, and seeing Kim at the hospital.

Sessions 22 through 24 saw a regression with more baby talk and scribbling with the markers. She declared that the last time that she was loved was when she was a baby. Kathy invented a new name and a new character for herself, Katie Allan. Katie talked baby talk. Kathy brought her doll and Kim's doll to the next three sessions. In regressive play, she threw the dolls across the room. Then Katie Allan talked with the wizard who placed magic blue powder on the babies so they wouldn't get hurt.

The wizard knew where all the world's lost children were. By session 30, Kathy was talking openly with her parents about the death and was sharing her tears and grief.

In several of the family sessions, I had observed significant marital conflict. In one of these sessions Kathy asked her parents what she would do if they died.

In another session Kathy played out a dramatic story involving a grandmother, Edith, and her granddaughter, both invented characters.

Kathy: Edith has a daughter who telephones for help because robbers are breaking into her house. When Edith goes to check out where the robbers are, no one is at home. The grandmother discovers that her granddaughter is hiding because she is afraid and does not have anyone to protect her. The grandmother asks the girl where her mother is. The granddaughter says that her mother is dead and that she has to kill herself because she doesn't love her mother anymore.

Kathy talked about ways of killing herself. Kathy and I then discussed her guilt and anger about the loss of her mother and her sister.

Kathy's father moved out of the family home, and Kathy was again reunited with her mother who was now being treated on an out-patient basis. Kathy admitted to her mother that every single night she relived the accident.

At school, Kathy was chosen by her teachers as "best student."

Throughout session 32 Kathy's work revealed themes of displacement and survivor's guilt. She drew a picture of a person holding a kite. In the picture Oscar the Grouch is drawn on the kite and says, "Get out of here, scat, go away."

BST:	Kathy, do you sometimes feel like you would like to go away?
Kathy:	Yes, I feel like I should have been killed, not my sister.
BST:	Somehow it would be easier to be dead than to have so many painful feelings about yourself, your sister, and your parents.
Kathy:	Right! I would just like to fly away from here.

Kathy was upset about missing the previous session due to illness. She has become very attached to me and to our process. Kathy went to the window and talked about what it would be like to jump out. More discussion followed about her feelings of guilt and anger that Kim and not herself had been hit by the car.

In sessions 32 through 34 Kathy pretended to be a woman called Tutu. Tutu was concerned about her crying baby and spent a lot of time nurturing her. Kathy played Tutu initially but then switched roles to be the baby. She then asked me to play the role of Tutu.

In the 35th session Kathy drew a doodle of a person with a heart pierced by an arrow. The caption above the person's head said "I'm dying." Kathy talked about parallels between herself and her dead sister.

In session 40 Kathy talked about dealing with her parents' feelings.

Kathy:	I would like to have a place where I could be away from their feelings. I saw a TV program where some penguins said, "Sorry for being alive."
BST:	Have you ever worried about being alive?
Kathy:	I worry about dying every night. Sometimes when I say my prayers, I feel that maybe I won't live until morning. I pretend that I'm the wizard and I can ask the bluebirds for help. (Kathy made a tunnel out of the cushions from my couch. During the next four sessions, she retreated into the magic tunnel.) This is my magic house and when I go inside, you can't see through the walls. When I go through the tunnel, I am killed. I become a magic spirit.

Carrying in art materials, Kathy drew a secret picture in the tunnel. It was of a magical flying tree with wings. One time in the tunnel Kathy regressed and pretended to be a baby. She also became a "magical princess" who had powers to decide what will and what won't happen in her life. Kathy used the flying tree in her magical rituals. The tunnel room became a safe place to regress, as well as a place to be alone. I was told to wait for her safe return.

At times, Kathy involved me directly in her rituals. The flying tree became a talisman, a charm to bring good fortune when she sought answers

Figure 15–3
This flying tree symbolized magical communication between Kathy and Kim.

to hard questions in her dramatizations. I could not help but feel the power of her self-directed use of rituals to repair her own psyche. My role, as facilitator, was to be sensitive to her leadership and to explore the symbols and metaphors that would arise.

During session 46 Kathy gave me a list of questions. She instructed me to ask the questions once she entered the magic tunnel. Some of the questions were about Kim. I asked the questions that she had written, and Kathy answered in a baby's voice as her dead sister.

BST:	Do you like living in heaven?
Kathy:	Yes, and there are angels here to protect me.
BST:	What do you eat?
Kathy:	We don't need food in heaven.
BST:	Do you still love me?
Kathy:	I will always love you. When you look up in the sky and see a bluebird you will know that I remember you.
BST:	What do you need?
Kathy:	I need you to know that I am happy. You should be happy, too.
BST:	Why did you leave?
Kathy:	Because it was time to go.
BST:	Can I see you again?
Kathy:	I will be in your dreams.

This and the preceding sessions involving magic rituals reflected the inner healing that was taking place in Kathy and in her relationships outside of therapy.

In subsequent sessions, Kathy dealt with adjustment to her parents' divorce and her father's remarriage, as well as Kim's death.

OUTCOME

Through art and play, Kathy replayed both the tragedy of her sister's death and the subsequent breakup of her family. Troubling questions were voiced in the drawings, characters, and animals that Kathy used as guides and enactors of the traumatic events. Kathy bonded with me and showed over and over again her need for nurturance. She was not able to integrate concepts of safety and her own well-being until she had answered her own questions about the meaning of the events surrounding Kim's death. I was touched by her willingness, throughout the therapeutic process, to play with the feelings surrounding the trauma.

I continued to see Kathy and her parents throughout the next two years. The portion of the case that I have described speaks specifically to how Kathy resolved her feelings about Kim's death. Playing out an encounter with her sister provided Kathy with a means for diffusing her guilt over not dying herself.

Creating magical images such as the healing bluebirds, magical princess, and flying tree seemed to empower Kathy to speak the unspeakable truth about the traumatic event. I had to patiently follow and support her regressions and her mythical exploration. The patterns in these activities emerged only later.

Enough time has passed that I am willing to comment on long-range outcomes. Kathy made significant gains through the years. Her relationship with both parents improved, and she positively identified with her step-siblings. Her fears about losing her parents, step-siblings, and her own life diminished, and thoughts about suicide did not reoccur.

DISCUSSION

Kathy's giftedness acted both as a strength and weakness in her healing. Her cognitive ability was another defense against awareness of her feelings. Yet, within therapy, her inner explorations were inspired by a mind that wanted to solve questions that could not be rationally answered.

Kathy's story is a classic example of how the unconscious seeks expression through creative materials. Kathy's use of art, drama, and storytelling accelerated the healing process.

This type of therapy requires flexibility, empathy, and humility in the therapist. Kathy was able to trust the therapeutic process when it became clear that I was genuinely interested in her stories and dramatizations. Through my work with Kathy, I have begun to better understand the concept of empathy as it relates to the child's play. I found it necessary to empathize not only with the child's verbalized feelings (animated world) but also with her nonverbal actions.

From the beginning, this case posed significant problems in communication between professionals. Joan was in individual psychiatric treatment, Paul and Joan were in marital therapy, and Kathy was in individual treatment with me. Frequent communication between therapists did not occur. I think that a team approach would have been helpful. I've wondered if a coordinated effort would have enhanced communication between individual family members and, thereby, strengthened family relationships.

Legal problems were another complicating and unpleasant factor. Kathy and Joan sought compensation for personal damages caused by the accident. Each family member's reaction to the accident became evident as the legal case proceeded. I am not an expert in forensic psychology and must admit to feelings of dread when confronted with a subpoena for counseling records and the ordeal of appearing in court.

In summary, Kathy has helped me to respect the individual needs that traumatized children have to play out and to create their own myths as a form of healing. I believe that Kathy's stories have a universality that may be useful to other children's healing.

Biographical Statement

Bruce St. Thomas, EdD, ATR (Art Therapist Registered), is a psychotherapist and art therapist in private practice in South Portland, Maine. He is a clinical member of the American Association for Marriage and Family Therapy. He has taught graduate courses in art therapy and counseling at the University of Southern Maine. Dr. St. Thomas is coauthor of the revision of Developing Understanding of Self and Others (DUSO I, *American Guidance Association) and coauthor and illustrator of a children's book, entitled* The Sandbox. *He is a research member of the Center for Arts in the Basic Curriculum, a national, nonprofit organization dedicated to improving American education.*

Frederika: Wrapped in Layers of Burgundy Wool

Donna Lee Turley

What a unique case! Donna Turley introduces us to her very first severely disturbed child and to her renowned mentor and supervisor, Clark Moustakas. Frederika's behavior suggests to Turley a diagnosis of "autisticlike" (Pervasive Developmental Disorder Not Otherwise Specified, DSM-III-R *299.80). Of course, a diagnosis is not a primary focus in existential play therapy.*

Turley is determined that nothing that is dishonest will contaminate her work with Frederika. The power to heal resides in being fully authentic. Therefore, she devotes herself to a journey of self-understanding and mutual respect.

My professor asked, once again, was I ready to begin? He meant was I ready to meet my first severely emotionally disturbed child. Was I coming to know and trust myself? Had I gained a feeling of where we might go? Perhaps more importantly, was I ready to enter fully into the unpredictable world of another person?

I took an unexpected quick, deep breath and expelled it as a sigh; I must go ahead, ready or not.

Dr. Clark Moustakas, who was to teach me the most dependable things I would learn in school, then handed me some notes, which were all he knew of Frederika. Two months ago she had turned 5 years old. She attended a school for mentally handicapped children.

In a university bookstore a few years earlier, I had found the book *Loneliness* by Clark Moustakas. It caught my eye because I had been making notes for a book about loneliness from the perspective of different young persons. In this book I found page after page of feelings and thoughts I felt were my own; it was one of the most knowing responses I had ever had to a book. At the time I was eligible for a sabbatical leave from Brigham Young University Laboratory School in Provo, Utah. In an adventuresome way not like me, I knew I must study under this man's tutelage. Fortunately, I located him at the Merrill-Palmer Institute in Detroit and was able to obtain a one-year fellowship to study there. My major courses were psychotherapy with both adults and children; at the institute I would be working as a therapist in both areas, under Dr. Moustakas's supervision, while taking course work to understand what existential psychotherapy and humanistic psychology meant.

It was a long drive from my home state of Arizona to Detroit. It was a longer voyage from the small, dependable world I had known to the noise, wonder, and unpredictability of the incredibly varied lives of which I came to be a part. Never again would I look at individual persons from the narrow framework of "normality." Never again would I look at unusualness and have no idea what it meant.

I had completed an MA in counseling and practiced counseling for eight years with students from kindergarten through 12th grade at the university's laboratory school, but I had never known a severely emotionally disturbed child. I wanted to, but was amazed to find myself frightened as well. About 12 months later, I knew why it had seemed so overwhelming. The experience was not easy because it involved all of the known and unknown parts of myself, along with discovering the same in another.

CONCEPTUALIZATION

My mentor, Clark Moustakas, was a student of Virginia Axline and of existential psychotherapy. He had over many years developed humanistic methods of working with children and adults and had written extensively about his methods and philosophy.

The approach to therapy that I came to learn and apply relates to heuristic research, *heuristic* coming from the Greek word *heuriskein*, meaning "to discover" or "to find."

> It refers to a process of internal search through which one discovers the nature and meaning of experience and develops methods and procedures for further investigation and analysis. The self of the researcher is present throughout the process and, while understanding the phenomenon with increasing depth, the researcher also experiences growing self-awareness and self-knowledge. Heuristic processes incorporate creative self-processes and self-discoveries. (Moustakas, 1990, p. 9)

Fortunately, at the time I was involved with such learning, I also had the luxury of time to ponder, meditate, and explore. There were things to read, and persons to engage, particularly Clark Moustakas himself and his other students in the small, intense seminar classes. All of us were engaged in productive self-discovery and understanding. I had never had so clear a vision of the components of healthy relationships.

> Heuristic research involves self-search, self-dialogue, and self-discovery. When I consider an issue, a problem, or question, I enter it fully. . . . I search introspectively, meditatively, and reflectively into its nature and meaning. But when I persist in a disciplined and devoted way I ultimately deepen my knowledge of the phenomenon. In the humanistic process, I am personally involved. (Moustakas, 1990, p. 11)

It was this absolute faith, or knowledge, that Clark Moustakas shared on every occasion (whether in the small classes or in enlightening supervisory sessions) and to which I clung as I embarked on my new adventure as a counselor.

In learning to work with children in existential play therapy, one comes to see one's own being more clearly than through direct study.

> Dialogue with the other and dialogue with oneself requires active listening, reflective listening. This means tuning into the other person's communications or one's own and noticing moment by moment what they mean. (Moustakas, 1990, p. 118)

Moustakas refers to a 1988 article by Barrett-Leonard, regarding the process of personal healing and growth through listening.

> Sensitive, nonjudgmental, empathic listening, which leads to the experience of being deeply understood, helps to open inner channels and serves as a powerful bridge to others. By being clearly and distinctly heard around some acute but unclear concern, we hear or see ourselves more clearly, and often with less

> fear. Inner divisions and boundaries tend to dissolve, doors we may have shut on some of our experience begin to open. We may feel freer, more whole, released from some bondage or drain that has been sapping us. We realize we are not alone at the moment of understanding and are freshly aware of what this is like. If this understanding recurs, our sharing can develop a self-propelling quality. (quoted in Moustakas, 1990, p. 118)

With these touchstones I began my journey with Frederika.

From the notes I had received I learned that Frederika was referred by the director of her school. He had referred other students to the Merrill-Palmer Institute for therapy with Clark Moustakas's students. When I called the director, he indicated that Frederika communicated at an early age but that after about age 2, interactive talking stopped and her only verbalizations were stilted, nonsensical imitations of TV advertising or repetitious chanting or screeching noises. She did sometimes give directions regarding her wants, but they were formalized, empty-sounding, harsh expressions. Because Frederika was now of school age, further diagnosis and treatment were sought.

Initially it was expected that Frederika's mother would provide transportation. Had that been the case, I would have talked with her face to face, at least briefly, from time to time. However, it was more convenient for the school's driver to drop her off and pick her up, so the only communication I had with her mother was infrequent and by telephone.

After receiving the referral, I went to Frederika's school to talk with the principal and the teacher and review the records. I learned that Frederika was not formally considered to have an emotional disturbance until age 4. She had had lifelong constipation problems. Her first sign of withdrawal was at 5 months, at which time she was having regular digital rectal examinations. Comments about her included the following: "Following her struggle in the bathroom, she goes into a closet with her blanket and closes the door. Screaming should be brought under control and eventually eliminated. Frederika has a behavior problem, handling her doll in a loving manner, then in the next moment tearing it apart. Mother agrees management is becoming more of a problem as she becomes older and bigger." The diagnosis was: "Destructive, antisocial, manifestations of retreating and withdrawal, psychotic reaction, symbiotic-type. Able to use her mother to bolster her own adaptive maneuvers. An extremely disturbed youngster. Severe autism."

Autism, as I came to understand, was a more organic, less remediable condition than I found to be true with Frederika in our months of weekly meetings. From later understanding, I would call her condition autisticlike, which I feel is much more accurate. I learned with experience that diagnoses are somewhat dependent upon the background and experience of the diagnostician and therefore not always consistent.

PROCESS

With much trepidation, which was curious to me yet impossible to deny, I called Frederika's mother. Her fear of me was so much greater that it dissolved my anxieties immediately. She said "We been thinking we would get a call. I know it will help her. I can bring her; it won't hurt me. I'll be right there and can bring her right back home. Her Dad is too far gone; they can't do anything except ease him a little. I only have $18 for food and that doesn't go too far. The rest has to go for the rent."

This conversation led to one of the most challenging, stirring experiences I've ever known, partly because Frederika was my first severely disturbed child and partly because Frederika was unique, complex, and exacting—a teacher of self-discipline. She taught me the limits of togetherness, the impenetrability of self-insulation, the price of trust. But she also allowed me moments of openness and oneness that were pure joy.

The girl handed over to my care had tousled, dark hair, a pale face with strong features, and darting, frantic eyes; she was panic in the absolute. Her chaotic words conveyed a specific message.

Frederika: I am not a sick girl! I don't want to be a sick girl. I am a *well* girl! I am a well girl. I don't want to be a . . . I want to be a *well* girl!

Her words rang out as we moved to the corridor where she cowered in coming with me. My compassion further reduced my feelings of unpreparedness. I reached out to her in my heart and wanted to touch her hand and make everything right. The power was not mine.

As we entered the playroom and closed the door, I became aware of the noise she was making. It was a high, shrill noise made by an extreme tightening of the vocal cords. In between the breaths of air there was a rushing out of unexpelled air she had held so tightly forced against her throat. Her sounds made a monotonous, rhythmic chant. She moved far from me and tried to attend to something.

I wanted to use her name and ask if she would like to take her coat off. She had on a burgundy wool coat, all buttons buttoned and the hood over most of her hair. When I came near her and prepared to speak, her sounds grew louder, drowning out any possibility of my being heard. She repeated the hollow sounds in an even cadence, interrupted at times with nonword chatter. The further she was from me, the lower the volume of the chatter. Then suddenly she needed to speak.

Frederika: Time shall I go?
DT: Twelve o'clock. Shall I move?
Frederika: Oh, *yes*!

I was to learn that no matter what I would ask or suggest, Frederika would either ignore it or give the same formal, dramatic response, as if speaking an overlearned line from a script. I also learned that most of the time it was simply her way of distancing herself by getting rid of the question. In her frantic glancing she spied a game on the counter.

Frederika: Lego.
DT: Would you like it?
Frederika: Oh, *yes*!

Frederika sat for most of the hour handling Lego pieces and sorting them out, laying aside the unusual ones. She tried putting together the others without successfully connecting the pieces. Throughout the hour, Frederika's shoulders were hunched forward, and her long dark hair shielded her face. She never looked at me or spoke in any ordinary tone. When she looked at the side wall of one-way glass, she seemed very pensive and threatened.

Frederika: It's not television. It is something very dangerous. It is something very dangerous. It is not television. It is something very dangerous.

Gradually the nonwords resumed and she repeated a television commercial for cereal over and over, with phoney enthusiasm. All of her body was unbelievably tense, and if I moved any closer, she immediately jumped up and rushed farther away; I was never within 8 feet of her. I ached for her muscles and felt her rejection, or unwillingness to acknowledge me. Nevertheless, she showed a painful, constant awareness of me.

When it was near the end of the hour, I said we would leave in 5 more minutes. There was no lessening of her nonword chatter. When it was time to go, and I said so, she skirted the furniture to stay far away from me, but she did willingly comply in leaving. Since she did not yet know the exact protocol, she stayed across the hall from me and did not run ahead as she would later do.

As we returned to the waiting room to wait for the driver, Frederika was increasingly agitated. I sat but she stood, tense and anxious. She strode across to the secretary's desk, furiously speaking her nonwords and furtively reaching out to touch some papers. There was a tightening in the secretary, who looked angrily toward me to take care of the problem.

In my inexperience, I hurriedly went to Frederika to remove her while giving my reasons. She immediately freed herself from my hand and walked around the desk. She touched nothing, but frightened and infuriated the secretary even more. The secretary grabbed at her things which further agitated Frederika, who then tried to touch anything she could. Each thing was immediately removed by the angry secretary, who had said not one word. Frederika interrupted her nonword chant: "A piece of paper. One piece of paper." She seemed to be demanding, but her words had a hollow tone that sounded derisive. The secretary tried to return to her work. I suggested we go to the playroom and get a piece of paper. Frederika came along.

We took a large piece of paper from the easel and she held it, doing nothing until we arrived again in the waiting room. Once there, she walked over and stood directly in front of the secretary's desk, where slowly, deliberately, she tore the piece of paper into long strips. She stood looking at the stacks of paper in front of her, and then she handed me the shreds when the driver came.

We had completed our first hour. I returned to straighten the playroom, which had been disturbed very little.

The playroom was very large, with a tile floor. On the right-hand wall was one-way glass, which I could imagine having somewhat of an ominous look as I now saw it through Frederika's eyes. In the right-hand corner, near the front of the room was a very large sandbox, about 9 by 12 feet and probably 2 to 3 feet deep. On the left, as you entered, was a kitchen-type area, with a sink and wall cupboards in which paint and other materials were stored. Beyond the cupboards was a wall of corkboard with a bullseye target for darts. The steel-tipped darts were generally available, except on occasion when a child might be dangerous with them. At the back of the room, on the left, were two toilet stalls. In the center was a large, round, low table with chairs. Further back in the room were two large easels stocked with paper and having trays for paints which were kept on shelves near the sink.

The rules of therapy in the playroom were very open but also quite clear. Things were not to be taken from the playroom. Things could be used in the way the child chose unless it was destructive, in which case verbal limits and expectations were given, and reminders if necessary. The adult was to be involved to the extent that the child wanted companionship. When the therapist was fairly certain about a message being demonstrated in the child's play, she would make a statement expressing the child's feeling. The therapist was not to determine the activity or its direction. In expressing his therapeutic philosophy, Clark Moustakas did not state these rules, but his students learned them by observation or through discussion which they initiated in class or in supervisory sessions. The rules also evolved during therapy sessions by intuitive, careful listening, observing, and searching to determine what would be helpful. Students had to find their own way, and their clients also had to make allowances for any errors as they grew together.

On her second visit Frederika behaved much the same as she had the first time, replaying the parting scene almost exactly. After circling the secretary's desk, Frederika suddenly stopped in front. She spoke abruptly, with a harsh voice. "What's your name, Miss?" There was no response. From that time forward she gave absolutely no attention to the secretary, even through a few long waits.

During this second visit Frederika constantly spoke in her high-pitched nonwords. As we walked down the hall of many doors and corridors, Frederika remembered exactly where we were to go. As we came to the door, she announced, "In Conference," very loudly, though this had not been said the week before. Looking across to another door (to the observation booth), she announced, "No Admittance."

When Frederika came for her third session, she seemed slightly less tense. She went immediately to the sandbox, which she apparently had not considered before. She played there for a long time, holding up a scoopful of sand and watching it gradually sift down into the sandbox.

I asked, as I had wanted to before, whether Frederika would like to take off her coat, as it was bumping things out of place. She responded with a flat, guttural no. I realized I had forced an interaction. She stopped all activity, increased the pressure in her voice, and spent the balance of the hour, and many hours thereafter, with her long burgundy wool coat buttoned under her chin and her leggings on.

At one point in the third session, Frederika spied the stethoscope and shrank from it as if from a rattlesnake.

Frederika: Get it out of here! Get it out of here!
DT: Shall I put it on the shelf?
Frederika: Yes!

Frederika drowned out anything else I could have said with her nonwords. I stayed fairly near to her, trying to give her freedom while maintaining close interest, wishing with my whole being that I had the power to loosen and warm her.

At our fourth session Frederika again sifted the sand but had to hold one hand over her nose because the sand was so dry and dusty. I suggested she might want to sprinkle the sand with water. She seemed not to hear.

Later, she suddenly got up, took the watering can, and filled it at the sink. I was amazed that she knew exactly how to do things and what equipment to use; she obviously had thought through the whole action before undertaking it.

Frederika poured four or five cans of water on the sand, and I began to worry about the amount of water. Finally I suggested it was enough for one day. She continued as though I had said nothing. After one more can, I could no longer resist.

DT: Frederika, this is the last water. The sand is too wet. It won't dry out.
Frederika: (As she finished pouring the can, she spoke.) Get some water!

DT: No, we've already had enough.

Frederika stood and started toward the sink, and I stood and followed to stop her. As I crossed the room, I felt like a giant at her side and must have frightened her. With a quick snatch, she picked up a piece of paper with some printing on it from the lower shelf and sat in a chair at the table with it, turning it over and over. She looked at the paper for 20 minutes. I wondered painfully if I had needed to stop her with the water.

Finally, Frederika moved to the shelves again, touching lightly on many things until our rather unpleasant fourth visit was over. When I said it was time to go, she put her well-looked-over piece of paper in her pocket and started for the door. I was not near her and mistook the paper for the instructions to one of the playroom games. I said, "You will have to leave the paper here." Frederika held her hand in her pocket. I spoke again about leaving it. Finally she threw it into the closet. I said it would be there when she returned. She ignored my comment, refusing to be patronized, and I followed her out the door.

At the fifth session Frederika again played in the sand, using considerable water, until finally I said I thought it was enough. She dropped the can and played in the wet sand, making shapes.

Later, with more experience, I felt unhappy about having stopped her watering of the sand. Other children using the playroom had used so much water that the sand did not dry from week to week. I was concerned that my feelings of propriety had restricted a person who needed so desperately to be accepted and to be allowed freedom.

After the sand play, in the fifth session, Frederika rushed suddenly to the closet to check to see if her paper was still there. I had made sure it was, though I still had not taken time to inspect it. She looked at it and put it in her pocket. At the end of the hour, I returned to it.

DT: Frederika, put the paper in the cupboard, so we can go.

She went into the hall still holding it. I waited in the playroom.

DT: We have to have the piece of paper. It has to stay in the playroom. I can't let you take it.

Frederika took the paper from her pocket and stuffed it up her sleeve. I again told her to take it out of her sleeve, and she handed it to me, angrily.

Frederika: Put it up the sleeve.
DT: No, we have to leave it.

She grabbed the paper out of my hand, threw it back toward the shelves where she had found it, and stomped out the door and up the hall.

This time, on leaving her, I did what I should have done the week before. I looked for the paper, took the time to read it, and found it not to be a set of game instructions but simply an advertisement for children's games. I wondered about my own need to draw limits. I waited all week to take up the subject.

At the sixth session Frederika went immediately to the sand and played a long time. When I could wait no longer, I got the piece of paper from the shelf and sat near her.

DT: Frederika, that little piece of paper, the one you wanted—you can have it. I found out that I don't need it after all. It can be yours.

For the first time, Frederika looked up at me. Her gaze continued for a few moments before she took the paper and stuffed it into her pocket.

I puzzled for weeks to understand why, but I knew something magical happened at that moment. Frederika seemed more at ease with me from that time forward. It felt as if we were now on the same team. I felt it was important to her for me to acknowledge that I had been wrong, and also for her to know that I wanted her to have the thing she wanted so much. The paper was probably inconsequential, but the drama of checking the limits, finding limits, responding to those limits, finally accepting them, and in the end finding them removed was probably quite significant, if also confusing to her. It was not good therapy practice, yet the outcome was positive.

At the seventh session I saw Frederika's first happiness. On that day she discovered cold cereal which had been left on the closet shelf, placed there by another therapist for her hungry client. It had not been there in previous sessions. Frederika left the sandbox, glanced about the room, took a brush, and began painting at the easel. She began printing words. She, who only recently had begun school, wrote "conference," "information," and other words, which she quickly painted over in black. Then she wrote, "Quisp and Quake." The phrase had no meaning to me. She took the picture down and placed it on the table. She walked to the closet and took out the cereal package. To my amazement, the cereal was Quisp and on the box were comics of Quisp and Quake.

It almost seemed a coincidence to me that she had written these words before going to the closet. It seemed impossible that she could have done more than glance around the room before going to the sand. I was at a loss to explain how she knew about the cereal, and particularly the name of it. When I said, "That's what you were writing!" she gave no response. The boy for whom the cereal was purchased also attended Frederika's school. In my bafflement I wondered if somehow he had communicated to Frederika about it. I could not decide which improbable explanation to settle on.

Frederika wanted to eat some cereal. There was no milk, so having cereal was postponed until the next week. For some weeks after that she had a ritual of getting out the bowl and spoon, pouring her own cereal, opening her milk carton, and eating the special cereal. She always ended by looking in the box to see if it contained a small packet of comics.

On the first day Frederika ate cereal, she wanted to take the box home with her. It was almost empty, and she wanted the outside comics. She went into the hall, box in hand.

Frederika: Come on, let's go.
DT: We have to leave the cereal in the playroom.
Frederika: Come *on*!
DT: Bring the cereal back so we can go.

Frederika came inside, then went back into the hall. After looking up and down, she came stealthily back to the door, dramatically stretched her head inside, and spoke in a conspiratorial tone.

Frederika: C'mon, the coast is clear!

I was secretly entertained, but simply waited inside the room. She finally came in and gave me the box. I put it on the shelf and accompanied her down the hall.

I found Frederika's playfulness both enchanting and disarming. I might have enjoyed joining her in fantasy. However, I felt absolute responsibility to conduct myself in a way that I hoped would be helpful to her in sorting out her feelings. I sensed that she must have separateness, firmness, consistency, and no opportunity to manipulate, along with the unusual freedom of choice possible in the playroom.

Some of the learning was frustrating, some was painful or uncomfortable, but all of it was energizing, sometimes exhilarating. After each session with Frederika, I would write what I thought she was conveying to me. I searched to try to grasp the meaning of her ways, the antecedents of her self-insulation. I marveled at her ability to create boundaries through which another could not pass, despite her evident vulnerability. I repeatedly had to examine my own tendency to control, to make decisions about the ways we should travel, to be sure I was guiding without manipulating her, or trying to.

I knew from my studies that if I were able to accurately identify Frederika's feelings and state them simply, it would be liberating for her. It seemed as if many months went by in which I could not come to this truth, and that was a new experience for me. I learned that a severely disturbed child, as a result of untold pain, achieves some self-determination and self-insulating power that overrides the usual need to please in children.

At Frederika's next session, while playing in the sandbox, she was able to hear the sounds of struggle and crying from the child who should have been in the next playroom but was resisting in the hallway. She had arrived with the boy, whom she knew at school. Hearing him disturbed her very much. She seemed afraid that he could enter our room. In her fear she communicated more directly than usual with me. She looked at me frantically.

Frederika: Don't let them come.
DT: This is *our* playroom, Frederika. They have another room. They don't come here.
Frederika: Don't, don't. I am a *well* girl.

When the crying increased and sounded closer, she jumped out of the sand, came running to me, and threw herself on me while I was quickly trying to open my arms to her. She seemed so awkward in the position that resulted yet frantically in need of assurance and safety. I told her softly that everything would be all right, that the other teacher would not let them come into our room.

Suddenly she recovered herself and went back to the sand. After a few minutes, I tried to initiate further conversation to help her feel at ease: "Did the driver bring the boy when he brought you?" This question seemed to agitate her. She gave me a frightened glance and began her rapid nonwords. But she stayed at her play. During several later sessions we again heard the crying, but she never again sought reassurance, and it did not appear to upset her.

During our sessions at this time and later, the sounds she made were less constant and the tension in her vocal cords relaxed somewhat. Her usual response of "Oh, *yes*!" in a stage voice continued as an automatic response to almost any comment that seemed to request response.

After the third month Frederika became able to use the restroom within the playroom, and this seemed to add to her security. Gradually I also relaxed and thought about limits a great deal before imposing them.

I always warned Frederika five minutes before ending time, and though she continued to play until it was time to leave, she did not resist when it was time to go. She did, however, test limits with me in other ways. She participated more and more in the playroom and obviously enjoyed the many rituals she established, but she never asked to stay beyond 12 o'clock.

When Frederika began exploring the games on the shelf, she had the ability to read the instructions. She might look at a comic, saying nonwords as if reading, and then say a phrase or two. At times she would say an entire sentence in words. I could see that she could read anything she might encounter. At this time she had been moved to a more advanced class at school. The principal indicated that she was very proud of the move. I sat near the sandbox one day wanting to communicate: "They told me you were moved to a new class at school." She gave no response. It felt to me as if she preferred keeping her world separate.

One day as I sat with her, as she chattered her nonwords, I suddenly realized that she was saying sensible things but with a particular distortion.

At times the distortion was less and I was able to understand what she was saying. Gradually she would say a few recognizable words along with her nonwords. I realized with curiosity and amazement that she had been talking all the time when she seemed to be saying nonwords! How I wished I might have known what she was saying during some of our earlier sessions.

The usual extent of our conversation was that I would make a statement as to what I thought she was showing me, and she would give a standard, "Oh, *yes*!" in her rushed, stage voice; or she would make a demand in an impatient tone, and I would respond with a small comment. She might say, "I want cereal." I would say, "We have milk. Here it is." She would get the bowl and a box of cereal. Our interactions were this simple for months.

One of the expectations that is firmly established in the philosophy of existential child therapy, as I was learning, is that one does not give material things to clients, such as buy them a soda from the pop machine near the stairway, bring them something they would wish to keep, or allow them to take things they wanted from the room. The cereal was a special exception. It had been purchased for another child who was hungry enough to be preoccupied with food and was eating paper and crayons. Since Frederika came to the playroom after that child, and had spied it, it seemed right to allow her to have it. And it seemed to give her a freedom she needed.

Another expectation is that a therapist should never transport a child, even if it means missing a therapy session. This seemed surprising at first. Then I realized how difficult it would be to impose a different set of rules and boundaries outside the playroom without taking an authoritarian stance. This was particularly true with a child who might use poor judgment in traffic.

As I became steeped in existential, humanistic philosophy and more at ease with the pattern of what I was doing as a psychotherapist in child therapy, it was easy to understand the necessity of not giving things to a client. For the child to begin to expect or extort material gifts from the therapist would obscure the true gift that was being offered: time, a caring person, a place where there were unusual freedoms, togetherness.

Frederika's artwork, pieces of which I kept, told the story of her progress. For months she would generally use only black paint and paint the entire surface. If she did paint with colors or write some words, she carefully covered them with black, even asking me to lift the clips on the easel so she could paint under them as well. In the spring it was very satisfying to see her leave black for colors. Toward summer she would paint large colored balls and delighted in filling up page after page, though she never seemed concerned about keeping any of the pages or taking care of them once painted. During the last few months of therapy she used no black paint at all.

After some months, during one of our sessions, Frederika sat in the sand and played briefly with water, then played carefully and for a long time with the xylophone, then started looking into the cupboards. It seemed she now rushed to fill the time as completely as possible. She took out the clay for the first time, but did not seem to know how to use it. She sat at the table looking at the container. Without looking up, she proceeded in a much more normal tone.

Frederika:	What's your name?
DT:	My name is Donna.
Frederika:	(looking up at me) Donna, make me a clown. (She handed me the clay.)
DT:	Do you want me to make a clown out of this?
Frederika:	Yes. (normal tone)
DT:	Do *you* want to make the clown or do you want me to make it?

Her silence told me it was not necessary to talk further. I tried to work with the clay, but it was impossibly hard.

DT:	I'll see if I can find some better clay, some that is softer.

While I explored in the cupboard, she seemed to take an interest in the xylophone. I found better clay, and she glanced up and saw the new package.

Frederika:	Brown.
DT:	Is brown all right?
Frederika:	Yes.

I spent some time working with the clay trying to soften it. She seemed engrossed elsewhere in the room. I decided to try to make the clown pictured on the box. I made a crude, simple clown. When I was ready to give it a face, Frederika came and sat next to me. She began making tiny round pieces, which she then placed for eyes. It was difficult to know if I should continue. I made large ears, while she made a nose and mouth, then buttons, many buttons. I made a cone-shaped hat, as pictured on the box, and she made a pom-pom to put on top.

Despite the rules of the playroom, I felt so pleased about the new togetherness that I wished to celebrate it somehow.

DT:	Would you like to have the clown?
Frederika:	Oh, *yes*!
DT:	(I immediately recognized her guarded stage voice.) Frederika, you can have him if you like. (She did not respond.)
DT:	I will find a box to put him in.

Frederika got out new bottles of poster paint, rather than the ones she usually used, and the brushes. She began painting a clown. She had problems with the paint running down the clown, onto her coat and dress and the table and the floor, but she was very excited and did not mind. She always came the next week with her coat clean. When I reminded that there were five more minutes, she discontinued painting and wanted to cut the comics from the cereal box. She first tried to use small scissors, but it was an awkward job. She handed me the box, impatiently: "Cut it. Cut it." I took the scissors and proceeded to cut out the comics. I felt we were together in a new way. We had spoken, and she had not needed to immediately isolate herself.

When it was time to go she looked at the clown, but made no move to take it.

DT: Should we leave the clown on the shelf until next week?
Frederika: Yes.

She seemed sincerely delighted. She quickly stuffed the cardboard comics into her coat pocket and we left. I saw the comics as a consumable item, something that would be discarded when the cereal was gone. That was the basis for my making an exception to the rule of not allowing a child to take things from the playroom. Possibly I should have discussed this with Frederika.

When we got to the top of the stairs and saw the driver, Frederika suddenly turned to me.

Frederika: I'll see you next week.
DT: I will be here. Goodbye, Frederika.

When Frederika returned the week after making the clown, she seemed to have forgotten it. She played in the sand, painted at the easel briefly, washed her hands and played in the water a moment, played a tune on the xylophone that was now becoming familiar, and then got down new bottles of paint and the brushes and asked for paper. I got some out of the closet. She carefully painted colored balls on three pieces of large paper. Next, she laid them out on the table, one at a time.

Frederika then proceeded to climb up on the cupboard. It was difficult because there was nothing to hold onto and her coat was bulky. When she had finally succeeded, she reached her hand up high over the shelf, took down the box with the clown in it, held it carefully, and then jumped to the floor. It seemed to me that she had not glanced toward that place and would not have known exactly where I left the clown, and yet she knew. I was learning that she made quick, almost unnoticed, glances and checked out everything in the room. The clown was taken down again once or twice in other sessions. Then Frederika seemed to forget about it and enjoy other things in her short hour.

The paintings spoke more than she could say. She was beginning to trust. I was afraid something might cause her to close herself up again, and then it would be even more difficult to regain entrance. We were dancing a very complicated dance.

After the first time of saying "I'll see you next week" as a farewell, it became a ritual ending to our sessions. One time in midspring, when a two-week vacation was coming up, I mentioned to her for several weeks ahead that she would not be coming during those two weeks. She did not give any response to this information. At the last session before vacation I told her she would come again in two weeks and I would be here and be happy to see her. When we walked up the stairs that day, I stopped for a moment and she did also, to make a final agreement.

Frederika:	I'll see you . . .
DT:	It will be two weeks before I will see you again.
Frederika:	When will I come?
DT:	It will be two weeks. It is a vacation. You will come the week after. It will be April 12.
Frederika:	I will come on April 12. I'll see you.
DT:	Goodbye, Frederika, I'll see you soon.

On one visit, after Frederika had briefly done all the things she enjoyed, she asked for crayons, using my name, which she was doing more and more. I gave her a new box and some paper. She colored for a long time, not making anything distinguishable but putting pretty colors together and not covering them over. I sat nearby watching, occasionally making a small comment about how much I liked colors and how she seemed to enjoy coloring. She received my statements with silence. After I gave her the five minute reminder, she took a few crayons and put them into her sock.

DT:	You will have to leave the crayons in the playroom. They are here to use. You can use them when you come again.
Frederika:	No, I will take them.
DT:	No, you must leave them in the playroom. They will be here when you come again.
Frederika:	I will take them home.
DT:	No, you cannot take them. Put them on the table. It is time to go.
Frederika:	(shouting) Stop! Stop!

She began screaming as if I were hurting her, which greatly surprised me. I restated the rules. She hurried to the door, waiting for me to come. I remained on the stool.

Frederika:	Come on, my driver's here.
DT:	You leave the crayons on the table, and we will go.

She looked at me. Then she angrily took the crayons from her sock and handed them to me.

Frederika:	Put them up my sleeve.
DT:	No, I will leave them on the table.

She again began screaming. I tried to talk softly to her, laid down the crayons, and rose to leave. She was still crying, but more quietly, as we opened the hall door and started toward the stairs. She walked very resolutely, shutting me out. I followed. She stomped up the stairs with no farewell.

For the next three sessions, the parting scene was almost an exact duplicate of this one. Finally Frederika felt she had found a creative solution. She took a crayon and broke it in two, threw one half down and kept the other.

DT:	Put it on the table, so we can go.
Frederika:	I did! I did!
DT:	No, you still have a piece in your sock. Put it on the table so we can go.
Frederika:	I am going to take it.
DT:	You must leave it here. You can use the crayons next time.

She then broke the crayon in increasingly smaller pieces, but I held firm, stating that they must be left in the playroom. She was extremely exasperated with me.

Then Frederika, who still had a small piece of crayon, decided to end the dispute. She went into the hall, and I followed her. She walked rapidly to the stairs, then waited for me to catch up. As I walked, I questioned my own judgment. Somehow the rules of the playroom seemed terribly important. I am not sure why. I wished I could have conferred for a moment with Dr. Moustakas. As we went up the stairs, Frederika was more friendly than usual to me.

DT:	Frederika, I am not happy.
Frederika:	Yes, you are happy. You *are* happy!
DT:	No, I am not happy because you still have a piece of crayon. It was supposed to be left in the playroom.
Frederika:	(screaming) I am going to take it.
DT:	Then I am not happy. I don't want you to do that.
Frederika:	(stopping midflight) I want it. I want to take it.

I decided to say no more. Frederika paused a moment, looking up the stairs to where she was to meet her driver; he was waiting. Suddenly she reached down into her sock, turned, and ran back down the stairs. She ran all the way to the playroom. I followed and arrived in the hallway in time to see her throw the crayon into the room. When she returned, I tried to thank her. She would have nothing to do with me, and hurried up the stairs.

That week I called Frederika's mother while Frederika was in school. During the conversation I asked if Frederika had crayons at home. She said,

"Frederika has many broken crayons, a whole can of them." She noted that Frederika seemed happier and was beginning to talk at home.

The crayon saga continued for a few weeks, with Frederika replaying the same drama over and over. I felt we were no longer working productively on this issue. When Frederika returned to the playroom, I wanted to settle the matter. She began playing in the sand. I came near and sat on a low chair: "Frederika, we have had lots of problems about the crayons." I received no response; she appeared not to hear. I said, "I don't want to have any more problems with the crayons. If we have more problems, there won't be any crayons in the playroom when you come." With that she looked up, not toward me but into the distance. I saw that her face was very troubled. I felt sad as I watched her. She took a long time, then stood up, letting sand fall over the floor. She finally spoke: "All *right*!"

That was the end of the crayon incidents. Strangely, I felt a sadness. It was not a victory. I was puzzled about the high value I gave to that piece of crayon. I was still learning.

When I had my next supervisory session, I related the incident to Clark Moustakas. When I was through, he simply said, "I wonder why it was so important to you?" I had been thinking that the limit I felt I had to impose might not be valid. However, Dr. Moustakas was suggesting that I had some purpose in clinging to this limit, even if I could not then identify it. Possibly he was right. From the moment of resignation, Frederika became more free with me. I always had to wonder, at what price? It seemed that she needed something hard to come up against, and to discover that she could neither forge nor manipulate her way through it. Somehow, by firmly establishing a limit, whether or not it was valid, I had helped Frederika feel safe. It was an important time for both of us, yet a confusing one.

After the final crayon incident, Frederika seemed to spend more time using poster paints. She never showed any interest in taking a picture with her, nor did she look for them when she returned. What was important was the process. I said little about the muted, colored balls she painted. She did not want an evaluation.

On one occasion, when she seemed particularly at peace, she asked me to look at a game with her, touched the dolls and puppets briefly, for the first time, and then painted until it was time to go. At the end of the hallway she generally struggled with the heavy door at the bottom of the stairs until I caught up to help. This day, she got to the door, and clutching her coat front tightly in her two hands, she squealed wildly and jumped up and down. It was a totally happy response. When the door was opened, she went up the stairs with enthusiasm and closed our visit the usual way.

Frederika:	I'll see you next week.
DT:	Goodbye, Frederika.

Later that spring, when her tight screeching had almost been forgotten, Frederika played with things only briefly so she would have time for everything. She had long since stopped wanting to take time for cereal. On one occasion she climbed again onto the cupboard counter, reached up high, and took down a box that I had forgotten. It held our little clown, our first joint project. She sat it on the table, looked at it briefly, then went to the xylophone. She did not sit long, but kept twirling around the room and running from place to place. Several times she passed near where I was sitting. She was making happy, choppy, humming noises. I wanted to stay out of her way because she was lost in activity. As she passed, I could not resist making a comment: "Frederika, you are just so happy today that you have to skip around the room." Frederika laughed, thrust herself on me for a moment, then went to the easel and resumed the picture she had worked on earlier. Finally she responded, "Aaaaaaa-huh!" Frederika skipped down the hall that day, possibly using a newly acquired skill. As we started up the steps, she was laughing. When she got to the top, she remembered and turned to see me.

Frederika: I'll see you next week, Donna.
DT: Goodbye, Frederika.

I had never seen Frederika without her burgundy coat and hood throughout the school year, so I decided to rearrange my plans and stay through summer session. In the summer she came one day in a long-sleeved cotton dress. She seemed very tentative and shy, but she played with her favorite things. I believe I missed the burgundy wraps more than she did. It was the first time I had seen her full head of dark hair.

During our last few weeks together it seemed to me that Frederika and I used each other's names more frequently. We never played a game together, but she allowed me to hold her equipment while she played in the sand; in fact, she demanded that I hold it just right. She did not look to me as she painted, but somehow I felt she knew that I had saved some of those paintings.

When the time of our last parting came—I had reminded her of its coming for several weeks ahead—it was as natural, though more poignant, as any day leading up to it. When Frederika started to say, "I'll see you next . . .," she caught herself and stopped. She turned around for a moment two stairs ahead of me, threw her arms around me, then turned to go on. Before she reached the top of the stairs, she shouted, oblivious to the secretary, "Goodbye, Donna," and again, with a wave, even more loudly, "Goodbye, Donna!"

Frederika's therapy was about herself; I was simply her support person at one time and place. As I returned to clean up the playroom and saw strewn sand, dripped paints, and things out of the cupboards from use, it was as easy as it always had been. Actually, it was my privilege.

■ OUTCOME

It is my belief that these precious moments we spent together were a turning point for Frederika, and I know they were for me. Though I have not had the opportunity to follow up in later years, I saw her take steps to open herself up and begin to trust. A bright, creative force, she captivated me each hour we were together from the first to the last. She had a uniqueness I will never know again.

Frederika, in one year, progressed from a state of diagnosed autism to become a child who had a capacity for happiness and self-expression, a degree of interaction with a trusted adult, and a more normal school placement where she began to be successful. When I left her, she continued to attend a school for "mentally handicapped children." She was a person for whom there was hope of normalcy, giftedness, and satisfying relationships.

There was a long road ahead for Frederika at the time I had to leave, but it appeared that she had left behind the tense, unreachable, frightened lonely self who had begun our weekly sessions. At the Merrill-Palmer Institute Frederika and I were both born into a new way of being which I hope has stayed with her and blessed her as it has me. A year later, I had the privilege of coming to Detroit for a conference, and by happy coincidence I happened to be there on Frederika's therapy day at the Institute. I did not see Frederika in person, though I would have loved to. Instead, I watched her interaction with her new therapist. Frederika was now even more inventive and engaging. She chattered on and on about how washing machines were televisions, how the stove was really the refrigerator. Somehow I could see the connections. I could imagine an old front-loading washing machine, with the clothes inside turning, looking like a snowy television screen.

Fortunately, an unwavering, marvelously gifted teacher and support person was available to me during this experience. My work with Frederika under Clark Moustakas's supervision launched an inexperienced, anxious adult on a path that has included years of work with intricate and complicated children. That path has also offered the sobering experience of becoming the support person for inexperienced but gifted therapists. Frederika and Clark Moustakas have always remained the reference point.

The gift to the therapist was possibly more wonderful than that to the child. The learning that needed to take place was vast, the experience confusing, painful, and exhilarating. Two people were forever changed through being with each other. Though I cannot know Frederika's present life, I am certain that she has a great capacity for living. Since the day that she grasped her heavy, stuffy burgundy coat in joy as she jumped up and down, I have never doubted the potential for merging freedom and attachment in my future relationships. Realizing this truth in my relationship with Frederika has helped me to balance my future relationships with other clients. As two lives join, even for a brief time, a unique creation emerges which takes both persons closer to a full realization of the self and the other.

DISCUSSION

When my work requires me to place autisticlike children into special educational programs, I have often tried to imagine Frederika's response to those settings. I believe that Frederika's healing was assisted by allowing her to be in a situation where freedom and independence are valued and guaranteed, as far as is possible with a disturbed child, and where manipulation is non-productive. I have observed teachers who use a behavioristic approach as they work to shape more normal behaviors and have seen growth in that direction. However, I have not been convinced that those results would be lasting without providing a behavioral structure. I felt that Frederika's growth would be sustained unless unforeseen trauma occurred.

I suppose Frederika might have progressed farther and more quickly had I been more consistent and secure. I cannot be certain. Nevertheless, Frederika had developed very dysfunctional patterns over a long time and they were worsening, and in one year's time she showed significant growth. Long-term therapy, of course, would be essential for Frederika to consolidate and extend the gains she had made, and many therapists lack this luxury.

I also realize that many therapists believe that working with a child separately from the family is not the most productive approach. In my view, as Frederika changed and grew, her total family constellation changed and improved, and progress became self-perpetuating because all persons involved wished for a healthier, happier, more productive relationship. Before working with Clark Moustakas, I would have felt it inappropriate to work with Frederika without seeing her parents (or mother) at least on a semiregular basis. But the proof of the individualized approach in this case is its remarkable success. I have since confirmed similar results with other children and families using humanistic psychotherapy.

If I had the chance to go back and work with "my first child" again, I must say that I probably would change nothing. We did what we were ready to do at all times. The relationship between us was fiercely direct and became comfortably secure.

If I had taken a more directive approach, I believe Frederika would have wasted her energies resisting instead of discovering the challenge of using them to create, to express her own way of being, and finally to find pleasure. In response to a humanistic, existential approach, Frederika's disturbance gradually fell away, and a positive, inner-directed, and fascinating person emerged.

If I were speaking to a beginning therapist, I would say, you must be ready to reach inside yourself and examine every fiber, you must be willing to experiment and to trust, and you must have the capacity to give your total respect to another. You will come to know there is an explanation for every characteristic a client has, but it is likely that you will never know that explanation. Knowing the explanation doesn't matter; that it exists is enough.

You must learn not to control and be aware of manipulation in any degree. You must search yourself deeply and carefully to recognize and then remove all traces of superiority and authoritarianism.

You must search to find in yourself the things that need reexamining, and you must find someone you can trust to help you openly examine them. There will be tears of frustration and self-doubt but also tears of pure joy if you learn the lessons that lie within yourself. These cannot be acquired easily or from the outside. All that you will ever have to give lies within, is already the core and substance of yourself. And if you do not feel and know and then gladly give those gifts, then you will not be helpful to a lost child, or any other needing person.

You must become able to set aside your own feelings and needs and enter fully into the world of another. As you become temporarily a part of that person's reality, you must bring with you all of your knowledge and intuition about healthy interpersonal relationships. This involves long periods of selfless concern.

You must grow to be strong enough to require that certain limits be observed, while not undervaluing the other person's preferences and needs. And you must, after being totally present and sincerely caring for the other, be able to return to your own reality just as fully, without becoming preoccupied with the client's ongoing needs.

You must be an extremely careful, diligent observer and have faith in your own sense of the level of disturbance and need in the client, so you can respond and follow through appropriately, naturally, without stress or doubt.

You will find that no person is fully broken, but some are so wrapped in pain that the healthy parts are no longer visible. To unravel the truth, to discover the real person, the healthy being, takes incredible patience and faith, sometimes more than you feel you have. But if you persist, and are able to keep your defenses in check, you will learn that even mistakes can have a productive effect. *You* are a part of the therapy equation, and by being all that you are, all that you can be, you contribute directly to the successful outcome of therapy and growth in the client.

I may never know why a tiny piece of crayon became so important to me, but I feel that Frederika forgave me that idiosyncrasy. She did not understand it, but she forgave it. By exploring together the limit I had set she benefited and we became better friends. In such instances I can believe what I cannot explain. Clark Moustakas is right. There is a guide and a light within which leads one and which can partially illuminate the path for another. In a therapeutic relationship I have to trust the existential self, to ponder what it means, why it is, how can it best be expressed. Dr. Moustakas did not tell me these things, but I learned them from him.

Through the years I have become only further confirmed in the truth and dependability of existential and humanistic theory and process. My first successful experience with this approach has been extended and enhanced by further learning at Arizona State University and elsewhere. Ever since I have taken the bright illumination of this learning with me into many confusing, dark corridors, and I have been overjoyed again and again at the miraculous blending of freedom and togetherness that is possible in relationships both in therapy and outside of it.

REFERENCES

Barrett-Leonard, G. T. (1988). Listening. *Person-Centered Review, 3*(4), 410–425.

Moustakas, C. (1961). *Loneliness*. Englewood Cliffs, NJ: Prentice-Hall.

Moustakas, C. (1990). *Heuristic Research: Design, Methodology and Applications*. Newbury Pk., CA: Sage Publications.

Biographical Statement

Donna Lee Turley, PhD, is a certified psychologist with 22 years of experience in Redwood City, California. She specializes in the identification and treatment of severely emotionally disturbed children as well as those with learning problems and physical handicaps. Dr. Turley taught child development at Arizona State University and was a counselor for nine years at the laboratory school of Brigham Young University, after teaching for two years at Snowflake High School in Arizona and for three years at Dixie Junior College in southern Utah. She is the author of Mosaic of My Self *(1968), a compilation of pieces intimately describing human experience, which were collected during her postgraduate studies in psychotherapy at the Merrill-Palmer Institute in Detroit, Michigan. She obtained her master's degree at Brigham Young University, and her PhD in counseling psychology is from Arizona State University.*

Index